13 Things Mentally Strong **Couples** Don't Do

13

Things

Mentally

Strong

Couples

Don't Do

FIX WHAT'S
BROKEN,
DEVELOP
HEALTHIER
PATTERNS,
AND GROW
STRONGER
TOGETHER

AMY MORIN

wm

WILLIAM MORROW
An Imprint of HarperCollins*Publishers*

The names and identifying details of the individuals discussed in this book have been changed to protect their privacy.

HarperCollins books may be purchased for educational, business, or sales promotional use. For information, please email the Special Markets Department at SPsales@harpercollins.com.

FIRST EDITION

Designed by Diahann Sturge

Library of Congress Cataloging-in-Publication Data has been applied for.

ISBN 978-0-06-332357-5

23 24 25 26 27 LBC 5 4 3 2 1

To all those who believe we have the power to be stronger when we're working together

CONTENTS

INTRODUCTION

When I was thirteen, my best friend, Emily, paid a palm reader to tell her fortune at the county fair. The palm reader predicted Emily was going to marry twice—the first time would be just to upset her parents, and the second time would be real love.

After the reading, Emily and I laughed hysterically. We didn't believe a word of what he said, but of course, I then wanted my palm read too. After viewing the lines on my hand for a minute, the palm reader said I was going to find true love and have a very happy life with the first person I married. Although I didn't believe in fortune tellers, I secretly hoped he was right. My parents had been happily married since they were eighteen and nineteen—and I wanted a long-lasting love like they had.

As we walked away from the palm reader's booth, as a joke, I said to Emily, "Let me read your palm." I grabbed her hand and said, "Your first husband is going to be named Linc . . . Linc Framingham." And we laughed some more at the idea of Emily getting married to someone just to anger her parents.

I didn't think about the palm reader again until I was in college, when the girl who lived across the hall in my dorm room invited me to hang out with her and a friend she was meeting up with later that day. Her friend's name was Lincoln.

I immediately called Emily and said, "I think I'm meeting your husband tonight!" We reminisced about that palm reading and laughed some more. I said, "I don't think his last name is Framingham but he's the only Linc I've ever heard of, so maybe I *can* read palms after all."

But it turns out, I can't read palms. She didn't end up marrying Lincoln. I did.

From the moment we met, I was struck by how different he was—from me, and also from anyone else I'd ever met.

I was shy and avoided embarrassment at all costs. He was the life of the party and lived for good stories—especially the embarrassing ones.

I was the type of person who ended vacations two days early so I could get home in time to unpack, unwind, and get ready for work on Monday. He was the kind of person who vacationed until the last second, which meant he often stepped off the red-eye flight on Monday morning and went straight to the office.

While I was capable of making polite conversation with strangers, he could turn a stranger into a friend in the blink of an eye. Whether we were at a wedding or a retirement party, he made friends everywhere we went.

We were only twenty-one when we got married. But, that meant I got to have him by my side for some huge milestones: I graduated from graduate school, we bought a house, and I landed my first big job as a therapist. We became foster parents too—something I'd always wanted to do.

Not all milestones were good ones, though. My mom passed away unexpectedly when I was twenty-three. I was close to her and losing her was difficult, but I was grateful I had Lincoln there to help me work through my grief.

Life with Lincoln was amazing. And I was optimistic about the future I thought we were going to have together.

But life had other plans for us.

Just five years into our marriage, and exactly three years to the day that my mother died, Lincoln passed away. He had a heart attack at the age of twenty-six. In an instant, the great life I knew ended.

I plummeted into a dark hole of grief for several years. During a time when all my friends were getting married and talking about kids, I was a widow. And I missed Lincoln more than I could explain.

Every once in a while, people would ask me if I was going to date again. Sometimes they'd say things like, "Oh, you're young. You'll get remarried." But I had no intentions of dating—and certainly no intentions of marriage.

I had squeezed a lot of life into my five years with Lincoln, and I was grateful for that. I didn't think I would ever fall in love again. It just didn't seem right.

That was, until I met Steve. We had been friends for a while, but our friendship eventually turned to romance.

I wasn't sure how another relationship could work. I frequently gave Steve warnings like, "I spend holidays with Lincoln's family." But he was good with that. And he didn't bat an eyelash when I said, "Oh, and by the way, Lincoln's family and I go on weird adventures for his birthday every year."

He wasn't deterred by the fact that I was a foster parent either. In fact, he eventually decided to go through the process and become a foster parent too, so we could foster together.

Steve was very different from me as well. He'd done lots of cool things—like he knew how to sail, how to fly a plane, and how to build just about anything. But he never bragged about it. There was a quiet confidence about him that assured other people they could talk to him, and he gave everyone his undivided attention.

For the first time, I could picture myself getting remarried and having a different kind of life—different from the one I had once imagined, but still an incredible life.

We decided to get married, but I didn't want a traditional wedding. While I knew my friends and family would be thrilled I was getting married—and they all loved Steve—there was no denying the fact that the only reason I was getting remarried was because Lincoln was gone. And I didn't want anyone to feel sad on my wedding day.

A drive-through ceremony in Las Vegas with a rented '57 Chevy Bel

Air seemed like the perfect way to launch our new life together. We moved to a house in central Maine and I started working as a therapist in the new town where we were living. But just as we were getting settled, we got the news that Steve's father had been diagnosed with terminal cancer. I couldn't believe it—just as life felt good again, I was about to lose another loved one.

I spent the next couple of days thinking about the unfairness of life. I had spent a decade grieving and I was about to face another big loss. Steve's dad and I had become close. But I knew I couldn't do anything to change the situation—instead, I had to find a way to cope with the pain. I wrote myself a letter about what mentally strong people don't do. It was a list of 13 habits I wanted to avoid so I could work through the heartache—not just distract myself from it. I found that letter helpful so I decided to publish it online in hopes it might help someone else.

To my surprise, that list went viral. The article was read by more than 50 million people. It was a surreal time in my life as we celebrated the success of my article while privately dealing with the loss of Steve's father (who passed away soon after I made my list public).

Within a month, I had a book deal and my first book, *13 Things Mentally Strong People Don't Do,* became an international bestseller that's been translated into more than forty languages. That led to a series of books (this is the sixth) that have sold more than a million copies across the globe.

Steve supported my career shift every step of the way and once I began writing more books, we moved onto a sailboat in the Florida Keys. Steve had dreamed of living on a boat since he was a kid, so we decided to give it a shot. At first, we thought it might just be a six-month adventure, but that was seven years ago, and we have no plans to move again anytime soon.

If that palm reader had told me what my life would be like all those years ago, I would never have believed him. Not only were his predictions about my life wrong, but my predictions were also wrong. Everything is different from how I imagined it, and for so many reasons. But I've learned so much about love and life. I may not have the once-in-a-lifetime love that I dreamed about, but instead, I'm fortunate I found love twice. My personal experiences—from getting married, to being widowed, then getting remarried—have taught me a lot about the power and complexities of relationships.

THE FIRST TIME I ever saw a couple in my therapy office, I remember thinking, "I don't want to do couples therapy." It didn't seem like either individual was there to create positive change—they just wanted my validation that the other person was wrong. As soon as the appointment was over, I walked straight to my boss's office and said, "I feel more like a referee than a therapist. I don't think I should be assigned couples."

He smiled and said, "Don't worry. Most couples who walk through our doors aren't looking for help. They're looking for permission to get divorced. But before they do, they want a therapist to let them know that it's OK to go their separate ways."

As a newly minted therapist, that was news to me. He was right, though—some couples seemed intent on divorce and merely wanted to check "tried therapy" off the list so they could feel confident they'd "tried everything" before signing their divorce papers.

But that wasn't always the case. I saw plenty of couples who just wanted some reassurance that they were on the right track, or they wanted to address a few minor issues before they became major problems.

Despite my initial reluctance to do couples counseling, I quickly realized that almost everyone who walked into my therapy office was going to want to address their relationships in one way or another even when they were there for individual treatment.

In fact, no matter the reason people first enter my therapy office—

depression, anxiety, or something else—relationships almost inevitably become a regular topic of discussion.

Some people want help healing from a broken relationship. Other people want to know how to support their partners or want their partners to learn how to support them. And many people struggle with specific relationship problems, like infidelity or ongoing feelings of loneliness. Sometimes the relationship issue is a side effect of another problem. At other times, relationship problems are the reason for a decline in mental health.

In many cases, getting a partner involved in therapy can make treatment go better. Someone's depression might improve if their partner learns how to be supportive. Or someone's anxiety might get better when their partner supports their efforts to take medication or to get a gym membership. And sometimes, one of the best ways to decrease someone's mental health symptoms is by improving the quality of their relationship with their partner.

When relationships improve, so does each individual's well-being. And when each individual's well-being improves, so does their relationship.

In the twenty-plus years I've been a therapist, I've seen therapy become more widely accepted and more readily available. The stigma around couples counseling has also diminished. Going to couples therapy no longer seems to mean a couple has extreme problems or that they're on the brink of divorce. Instead, more people are looking to proactively improve their relationships.

That's why I wanted to write this book for couples. My other books focus on what individuals can do to build mental strength. But, if you are fortunate enough to have a partner in life, the two of you have the power to build strength as a team. And you can accomplish incredible things together.

Here's what I believe:

1. **Not everyone should stay together.** I don't think everyone should insist on staying together at all costs. Some differences can't be solved or some things shouldn't be compromised. I also don't believe in staying together for the kids. As a therapist, I see what happens to kids who grow up in homes where their parents fight a lot or where their parents don't love each other.

2. **You have the power to change your relationship.** Even if your partner has no desire to address problems or learn about building mental strength, changing your behavior can shift the relationship dynamics. Relationships are like a dance. When you change your steps, your partner will change theirs. You'll see many of the clients I worked with to heal their relationship came to therapy on their own, not as a couple.

3. **You may need professional help.** You might be able to make a lot of progress on your own. But if you get stuck, talking to a therapist might be the key to moving forward. Sometimes individual therapy is needed—you or your partner might need to work through past trauma or address a mental health problem. At other times, couples therapy could be the key to a better relationship. And if your partner won't go to couples therapy, go by yourself.

How to Use This Book

You don't necessarily have to read this book in order. You might skip ahead to the chapter you think you need the most. It'll still make sense. But I encourage you to eventually read each chapter—you might find something is more of a problem for you than you think, or you might discover you're doing better in some areas than you give yourself credit for.

If you picked up this book, you are probably in one of three scenarios:

1. **I want to read this book and my partner has no desire to hear about it.** Don't insist your partner answer questions from the chapter and don't point out their shortcomings based on what you're reading. Instead, work on changing yourself (something we'll cover throughout the book), and you might see that the changes you make help you, your partner, and your relationship.

2. **My partner requested I read this book.** Maybe you aren't really into reading relationship books, or you don't think you have any of the issues raised in the book. Good for you for picking the book up anyway. If you've already read this far, your eagerness to be a team player speaks volumes. I appreciate your willingness to keep reading—you might find you can make some changes that will inspire confidence in your partner so that you won't need to read any more relationship books down the road. And if you don't think your relationship has any problems, that doesn't mean there aren't any. If your partner thinks there are issues, there are things that can be addressed regardless of whether you agree.

3. **My partner and I are both reading this book.** If you and your partner are tackling this book together, that's great. The two of you may learn and grow with each chapter as you discover more about yourselves, one another, and your relationship. Keep in mind you might not agree on a lot of things—and that's OK. Hopefully, this book will be an opportunity to safely discuss your disagreements.

Who This Book Isn't For

If you're in a relationship that isn't safe, this book isn't for you.

The truth is, no matter how much inner strength you build, an unsafe environment will hold you back from being your best. And I don't want you to blame yourself if you aren't able to create change.

Aside from that, asking your partner tough questions isn't a good idea if you're not in a safe relationship.

If you're in a relationship that is emotionally or physically abusive, there are resources available. From hotlines to local domestic violence programs, please reach out to an appropriate source.

Working Through the Book

As you read each chapter, you might recognize some of the unhealthy habits that play a role in your relationship. You'll then develop one of these four conclusions:

- **I struggle with this**: If you struggle with a bad habit, look at it as an opportunity to change. The book provides exercises that can help you grow stronger so you can stop doing the things that likely hurt you and your relationship.
- **My partner struggles with this**: If your partner struggles with something and they're open to change, you can support their efforts. If they disagree with you that they have a particular problem, don't give up. You can make changes in your behavior that can inspire change. I'll show you how.
- **My partner thinks I struggle with this**: Your partner might see things differently than you do. If they think you have a problem, be open to change. Remember, even if you don't think you have a problem, there's a problem if your partner thinks there is one.
- **We both struggle with this**: If you both struggle with the same problem, you can work on it together. Avoid the tendency to declare which one of you is the biggest offender—instead get proactive about creating positive change.

In each chapter, you'll find quizzes, exercises, and conversation starters. If you're reading this book on your own, you can answer the questions yourself to see what areas you struggle in and to identify strategies that can help. You might also recognize some shortcomings your partner has, but there's no need to announce what you've discovered if they aren't interested in the book or building mental strength. Saying things like "I'm reading a book written by a therapist who says you aren't supposed to do that!" won't help your relationship—nor will it inspire your partner to change. Instead, work on creating change for yourself and that can improve the relationship even if your partner isn't on board.

You'll also find interviews with some of my favorite relationship experts. At the end of each chapter, they weigh in on what their research has uncovered or how they treat specific issues in their therapy offices. Their perspectives may give you more insight into how you want to address your relationship.

Mental Strength and Relationships

My other books are focused on building mental strength for yourself. Learning skills to manage your thoughts, feelings, and behavior can help you become the best version of yourself.

Growing mentally stronger can help you become a better partner. Your growth can also bring out the best in your partner and improve your relationship. As a therapist, I've seen many couples challenge one another, support each other, and inspire each other as they take steps to grow stronger and become better.

I conducted an independent survey that I named "Couples by the Numbers" to gain some insight into the struggles couples across the United States are experiencing in today's world. I wanted to see if the relationship issues I had seen as a therapist in Maine during the past decade and the relationship issues I'm seeing in South Florida today are the same problems other couples are experiencing across the country.

I hired an independent research company in February 2023 that surveyed 1,032 married people in the United States. Four hundred ninety-three respondents were men and 539 were women. They were spread out fairly evenly across the regions of the United States and they ranged in age from 18 to over 60 but the bulk of the respondents were in the middle. Thirty-seven percent of the individuals who took part were between the ages of 30 and 44 and 31 percent were between 45 and 60. Their incomes varied from below $10,000 to over $200,000, but 18 percent earned between $50,000 and $74,999, and another 18 percent earned between $75,000 and $99,999. I asked a total of 16 questions, including how often people engaged in each of the 13 unhealthy habits that can hold couples back from growing stronger together.

I also asked about mental strength and the desire to strengthen their relationship. Here's what I discovered:

- 74 percent of people said their relationship would get better if they worked on building mental strength.
- 74 percent of people said their relationship would likely get better if their partner worked on building mental strength.
- 86 percent of people want to strengthen their relationship with their partner.

I was excited to see that so many people believed they had the power to improve their relationships by building mental strength. And an equal number of people wanted their partners to grow stronger. That's incredible—because not only do you have the power to build mental strength, but you also have the power to help your partner grow stronger too.

I'm thrilled that so many people want to strengthen their relationship. I'm guessing that if you're reading this book right now, you're one of those people. The good news is, you've come to the right place. This book is filled with strategies that can help you grow stronger, help you support your partner in growing stronger (even if they aren't on board quite yet), and help you strengthen your relationship.

Why the Focus Is on What Not to Do

Just like in my other books, I keep the focus of this one on what *not* to do. Plenty of couples have great habits—but those habits won't be effective if they continue to engage in behavior that tears them apart.

There's a lot of advice out there about all the things you should be doing to create a healthy relationship. And while weekly date nights and using one another's "love language" might be good for your relationship, nothing will work as long as you are engaging in counterproductive bad habits.

I've had many couples walk into my therapy office saying things like, "We do all the things we're supposed to do. We hold hands, eat dinner as a family, and share household responsibilities. Why is our relationship falling apart?" Well, the answer is that they're engaging in a counterproductive bad habit or two that holds them back.

Your weekly date isn't going to do your relationship much good if you're disrespectful to one another while you're on that date or if you neglect your partnership the rest of the week. And your family dinners might be nice, but if you refuse to set healthy boundaries, those meals aren't going to save your relationship.

This book is all about how to eliminate the common but unhealthy habits that will undermine your mental strength—both from an individual standpoint as well as a relationship standpoint. Eliminating them from your life can help you and your partner become the strongest and best versions of yourselves.

So, in this book, I share what not to do. Then, you can work smarter, not just harder, because the good habits you already employ will be much more effective. Keep in mind that progress isn't always linear, and it's not as if people either do or do not have bad habits. If we're honest, we all engage in these unhelpful patterns sometimes. But as you grow stronger and become better, you'll find it's easier to avoid these habits and turn to habits that can strengthen your relationship.

CHAPTER 1

They Don't Ignore Their Problems

47 percent of people don't bring up problems with their partner because they fear they'll make things worse.
—Couples by the Numbers Survey

Angela arrived at her first appointment an hour early. The receptionist feared she'd gotten the appointment time wrong. I overheard her say, "Oh no, your appointment with Amy isn't until eleven."

But Angela said, "I know. I just wanted to make sure I got here in plenty of time. I brought a book to read in the waiting room."

When I went to the waiting room to greet my ten o'clock appointment, I saw a woman I later learned was Angela, trying to converse with people waiting for their therapists. By the time I went to retrieve her for her appointment, she was reading her book and I got the impression she hadn't been successful striking up conversation with anyone. When I called her name, she smiled and jumped out of her seat, looking eager to get started. As soon as she stepped into my office she said, "I think I have empty nest syndrome." She acknowledged that she'd arrived early for her appointment because she felt lonely and just wanted to be around people.

After being a stay-at-home parent for the past twenty-five years for her three sons, Angela wasn't sure what to do with herself now that they had all moved out. She said, "I did my job well and that means I raised them to be independent young men who can do things on their own. I don't want to be the kind of parent who pesters." Her older sons had jobs and her youngest son was in college. She felt like no one needed her anymore and she could no longer ignore her relationship problems.

She'd been married to her husband, Carl, for over thirty years. "His job was to earn the money and my job was to manage the home," she said. "We ran our lives like two separate businesses." Now, he still had a job and she felt like she lacked a sense of purpose.

"We just don't have much in common outside of the kids," she said. They had spent the last two decades attending their sons' sporting events and after-school activities, but they never did anything that didn't involve their sons.

When I asked Angela what she wanted to gain from therapy, she said, "I want an emotional connection with Carl. I wouldn't be experiencing empty nest syndrome if he and I had a better relationship." When I asked if Carl shared her concerns, she said, "I have no idea. We've never talked about this." She explained that he wasn't the type to hold deep, serious conversations. And she thought if she sat down and told him he felt distant, he might roll his eyes and minimize the situation.

She said, "If I told him we were going to go on date nights, he'd probably think I was being corny or that I'd just read that suggestion in some women's magazine." She was confident Carl would never want to attend couples therapy with her.

She said, "I want to enjoy this next phase of my life. The best way to do that is probably to start putting my energy into making the best marriage I can."

Angela had felt lonely for decades, but in the past, her kids distracted her from her pain. She had some friends and extended family but felt a close connection with Carl was missing. She didn't want to bring it up because Carl might think she was being "dramatic"—something he occasionally accused her of. She also tried to convince herself that their marriage was good enough. They didn't fight. They'd raised great kids. And they were financially secure. But as time passed, she said she and Carl seemed to connect less often, and now she was ready to tackle their emotional distance head-on.

I've worked with many people who ignored a problem in their relationship. Sometimes, one individual looked the other way despite an obvious problem affecting their partner. At other times, there was a single traumatic event that was never discussed. Other couples, like Angela and Carl, can't pinpoint a single issue or moment in time but instead, they ignored something that was building a little more each day.

I'll share what happened with Angela and Carl a little later in the chapter. But before we get to that, think about the problems you or your partner might ignore in your relationship.

Quiz

Read over the following statements and think about how many of them describe your relationship.

- ❑ We rarely discuss big issues in our relationship.
- ❑ We argue over small things, but don't discuss the underlying problem.
- ❑ We talk to people outside of the relationship about our problems but not to one another.
- ❑ Our problems are evident to our friends and family, but we don't discuss them with one another.
- ❑ We'd rather look the other way than acknowledge what's happening between us.
- ❑ We don't work together to address our individual problems with one another (like a health problem).

❑ We share some individual bad habits and we never talk about them (like we both eat unhealthily or we're both bad with money).

❑ We're more likely to address a problem in a roundabout way—like leaving a bill on the table for one another to see without talking about it.

❑ We make it one person's responsibility to address specific difficulties (like the finances or day care issues), so we don't have to talk about problems.

Starting Point

Some problems are sudden—like when your partner unexpectedly gets laid off from work. But other issues evolve slowly, and it's challenging to find the "right" moment to address the issue. This was the situation with Angela and Carl.

Angela had tried to convince herself that they were doing the right thing by making the boys' activities the focal point of their lives. She said, "I knew the kids would only be home for a short period in our lives so it never occurred to me that Carl and I should go to dinner by ourselves sometimes or go anywhere without them." But on the nights when the boys were at friends' homes, she said she and Carl barely had anything to talk about and they often retreated to separate rooms in the house. She said, "Deep down, I knew that was a bad sign but I didn't want to do anything about it."

I've seen plenty of couples dance around their problems, skirt the real issues, and ignore the crisis before it reaches a boiling point and the problem can't be ignored any longer. That's when things implode.

Everyone has problems. That's life. When you enter into a relationship, you share problems. Even your individual issues impact one another.

Your work-related stress will affect your partner and your partner's student loans will impact you.

There will be some problems that are yours to solve, and your partner doesn't necessarily bear any responsibility—other than to offer emotional support. If you have an issue at work, you wouldn't expect your partner to call your coworker on your behalf to solve the problem.

Other problems have a clearer shared sense of responsibility. Unresolved differences in parenting styles or a home that has gone into foreclosure is a shared problem. But that doesn't mean anyone will discuss the problem. I've seen some people attempt to handle a shared situation on their own—where one partner tries to save everything. And I've seen other couples devise separate plans to fix the same problem.

In general, you don't want to ignore problems. But there's a balance to be made. You don't need to bring up every minor issue all the time. If you hold a sit-down meeting because your partner left their socks in the middle of the floor, you won't have the energy to tackle bigger problems. You should address hurt feelings, problems that are likely to grow bigger, and those that will take a toll on the relationship if ignored.

Here are some examples of common problems couples ignore:

- Being in debt or struggling to pay bills
- Disagreements about parenting issues
- In-law issues
- Disliking the other person's friends
- Sexual problems
- Division of labor issues
- Mental health issues
- Not spending enough quality time together
- One partner working long hours

Spend a minute thinking about the following questions:

○ Do I avoid addressing problems with my partner?
○ Does my partner avoid addressing problems with me?
○ Do we both ignore problems?

Why We Ignore Our Problems

For years, Angela didn't want to admit that she and Carl had a problem. There were times when she worried that they didn't have much in common and she wondered what life would be like when the boys moved out. But she pushed those nagging concerns away by promising herself there was plenty of time to figure those things out later.

> If you avoid difficult conversations, you'll have a difficult relationship. The good news is, by acknowledging the situation now (even if it's just to yourself), you can develop a plan for addressing problems moving forward.

But now that "later" had finally arrived, and she was faced with the problem head-on, she felt uncomfortable suddenly pointing out that she and Carl had grown apart. She feared the conversation would potentially make things worse.

Perhaps you can relate to Angela's situation. Maybe you avoided addressing problems with your partner because it just leads to arguments. Or maybe, when you bring up issues, your partner dismisses your concerns and you regret bringing them up.

You might also have found yourself on the other end of this. Perhaps your partner ruminates on problems or insists on rehashing things you can't solve. And the last thing you want to do is keep revisiting problems from the past or perseverate on potential issues that haven't even happened yet.

Ignoring problems makes sense in the short-term. You can keep the peace and status quo for one more day if you don't bring them up.

Addressing a problem is risky. Your partner might get upset. They might refuse to address the problem—even after it's brought to light. And there's always the chance things won't get better.

It's common for both partners to experience the same individual problem—like both individuals might have a substance abuse problem. They may avoid expressing concern for one another because bringing the problem to light will mean they'll likely have to address their issues. The idea is, "If I say you have a problem, you're going to point out my problem and I don't want to hear that."

Before you start thinking about how to address some of your problems, take a few minutes to think about why you've ignored them in the past or are ignoring a problem right now. Do any of these statements sound true?

- ○ Our problems crept up on us so slowly that we didn't ever have a moment when we needed to address them.
- ○ Our problems can't be solved.
- ○ Discussing a problem leads to a massive blowout.
- ○ We'd rather keep the peace than stir up issues.
- ○ My partner refuses to talk.
- ○ Our problems are vague (like we just don't have fun together) and aren't something we can quickly pinpoint.
- ○ I don't want to make things worse.
- ○ We aren't good problem solvers.
- ○ I am afraid my partner won't want to address the problem and then I'll feel rejected.
- ○ I don't want to bring it to my partner's attention because they might not know the problem exists.
- ○ I don't have the energy to deal with it.

○ I'd rather just solve a problem on my own than get my partner involved.

○ I don't dare to bring up the issue.

Spend a few minutes thinking about why you avoid addressing problems. When you understand your reasoning more clearly, it's easier to move forward and create change.

Mental Strength Exercises

Angela knew she wanted to address the problem, but didn't want to directly say, "Hey, we have a huge problem here."

So I worked with her to find ways she could tackle the problem without announcing her concern. She thought saying, "We don't spend quality time together" was too direct. She didn't want Carl to feel like she was blaming him and didn't want him to get defensive. So rather than focus on the problem, she encouraged a solution. She started suggesting they spend time together doing various activities.

Carl wasn't much of a planner—Angela knew if she asked him to plan something fun for them, she'd end up sitting home all weekend watching sports, which meant they wouldn't talk. So she took charge and bought tickets to a play. The only other play they'd ever been to together was their son's seventh-grade school play. When Angela initially told Carl about the plan, he wasn't overly excited, but she suggested they go to his favorite restaurant before the play and he agreed. They ended up having more fun than they thought they would.

Bolstered by the first outing's success, Angela asked Carl if he would be interested in a weekend getaway to the mountains, and he said yes. She took charge of the planning and asked for his input on various activities. He expressed interest in hiking and taking a bike tour, to her delight.

During their weekend getaway, Angela made a point to say how much she enjoyed their time together. She said, "I love that we are doing things together, just the two of us." And Carl agreed.

At Angela's first therapy session after their weekend away, she said, "I discovered that I love hiking. And when Carl and I hike, it seems easier to talk. Carl started talking about things, like how much he missed having the kids home and sometimes wonders if he was a good enough father. He's never really talked to me about that stuff before."

So we developed a plan for how she could continue to grow her relationship with Carl. She said, "I want to keep finding fun things for us to explore and do together. My hope is, if we keep having fun together, we'll naturally grow closer without ever having to discuss the distance that's come between us." Angela was determined to focus on the solution and together, they could work on their relationship. After a few months of therapy, Angela said, "I don't think of myself as a lonely empty-nester anymore. Instead, I think of myself as someone who has more time to do fun things with her husband."

Like Angela, you may be able to address a problem without ever directly talking about it. But that's not always possible. Some issues need to be tackled with a conversation.

Define the Problem

Before you can address the problem, define what the problem actually is. For example, you might say the problem is that your partner is a slob. But your partner might say the problem is that you're a "neat freak." Pointing fingers at the other person won't solve anything.

The real problem might be that you have differing views about how clean the house should be. Or it might be that you disagree about who should do the cleaning. Until you identify the problem, you aren't likely to arrive at a solution—at least not one you can agree on.

After all, if you think your partner is too messy, your solution might be that they should clean more. But if they believe the problem is that you're too obsessive about having a clean house, they might think the solution is for you to relax a bit.

Disagreements often aren't about the problem—they're about a symptom of a much bigger problem. Here are some examples of when the problem on the surface is actually a symptom of an underlying issue:

- Frequent arguments about money might not be a financial conflict. Instead, you might have different priorities.
- While you might argue about your partner's irresponsibility, the real problem might be that they have a substance use issue.
- Your arguments about your partner going out with friends might be a sign that you feel like your partner doesn't spend enough quality time with you.

Of course, these are just some examples. There are many other potential underlying problems you might be experiencing.

Sometimes, the underlying problem might be one person's issues—like an untreated mental health condition—but it affects the relationship. At other times the underlying problem might be a relationship issue—like distrust stemming from a past betrayal.

But it's important to consider whether the problem you argue about is really the problem or if it's simply the symptom of a much bigger issue you haven't addressed yet.

In the case of Angela, she came into my office saying the problem was that she was struggling with being an "empty nester." And while her children moving out did exacerbate her loneliness, that wasn't really the problem. The problem was that she and Carl hadn't spent quality time together emotionally connecting over the years. Now that she didn't have children at home to distract her, their lack of emotional intimacy felt amplified.

Before diving into trying to fix the problem, spend a little time reflecting on the real problem. Ask yourself whether the issue you're concerned about is the problem or just a symptom of an underlying issue. Think about how your partner might define the problem from their perspective as well. You don't need to talk to your partner about it right now; instead, try to make sense of it to yourself first.

Differentiate Between Problems That Can Be Solved and Problems That Can't

You don't need to address every problem in your relationship. Research shows addressing every single issue might make things worse.

A 2019 study published in *Family Process* found that the happiest couples tend to only address problems that can be solved. Researchers found the couples with the most relationship satisfaction rarely argued about problems that were more difficult (or impossible) to resolve.

The researchers hypothesized that happier couples focused on building one another's confidence in resolving issues that could be solved, like disagreements over the division of labor. And they were less likely to bring up issues that couldn't be easily resolved, like differences in religious beliefs.

Addressing problems in a healthy way doesn't mean you'll always agree on the solution. But it does mean you'll separate the problems that can be solved from the ones that can't.

Not all problems have a solution. If your partner smoked for twenty years and developed lung disease, saying, "I told you that was bad for you!" isn't addressing the problem. They can't change the past. The problem you need to tackle now is how you can support their efforts to care for their health moving forward.

Talking longer about a problem that can't be resolved won't help you find a solution. If you want three kids and your partner wants one, begging them to change their mind won't help. Talking about it every night over dinner also won't resolve your differences. And while you might be tempted to say, "Let's compromise and have two kids," meeting in the middle might mean neither of you is happy with the result.

Addressing your disagreement over how many children you will have might not be about coming to a firm agreement. Instead, you might work on solving the issues that you think could crop up if you don't have the number of children you want.

Relationships get better when you get better at answering this question: Do I need to solve the problem, or do I need to solve how I feel about the problem?

Too often, we focus on the wrong thing. We work hard to minimize our stress rather than fix the problem that's creating our stress. Or we try to tackle a problem that isn't within our ability to solve.

If you and your partner have different values, you aren't going to convince one another to change—and you shouldn't. Don't try to talk your partner into valuing something they don't value. That's not to say they won't ever change but if they do change, it's unlikely a lecture from you will have inspired that change. (In Chapter 6, you'll learn more about how to support change in a healthy way.)

> Relationships get better when you get better at answering this question: Do I need to solve the problem, or do I need to solve how I feel about the problem?

Identify and accept the things within your relationship that aren't going to change. Then, work on how you respond to those things.

For example, if your partner developed a serious health condition that limited their ability to do something you loved to do—like climb mountains—you probably wouldn't try to convince them to keep climbing mountains. You'd accept they can't do it any longer and then you'd decide what you are going to do—climb alone, find someone else to climb with, or give up mountain climbing altogether.

But too often, we fight against the problems that aren't solvable—or aren't our job to solve. And everyone is left feeling frustrated in the end.

That doesn't mean you shouldn't address problems that you can't solve. It just means you should handle them differently. Talk with your partner about how you feel, rather than how things need to change. Or you might work on navigating your distress together, rather than tackling the issue alone.

Create a Plan to Tackle the Problem

You know your partner and your situation better than anyone. So it's up to you to decide if you need a sit-down conversation to address the problem or whether you want to take the approach Angela did—and work on a solution without necessarily announcing how you see the problem.

You can address solvable problems with a conversation or a series of discussions. Asking, "How can we work together to develop a plan we're both comfortable with?" is a question that can help you start solving the problem together. It can work for issues related to money, parenting, household responsibilities, and boundaries with extended family.

As you saw with Angela, however, you don't always have to talk about a problem to address it. You might decide to change your behavior—which can address the problem without your ever saying a single word about it.

Angela, for example, wanted to be in a relationship with someone who spent time with her doing fun things. So she got the ball rolling and made it happen. Then, during their quality time together, conversations about their relationship and feelings naturally unfolded.

Keep in mind that just because a problem isn't your fault, doesn't mean it isn't your responsibility. Sometimes, the best solutions involve both partners working together even if it's an individual problem.

One such issue involves medication. When one partner requires medication—whether it's for bipolar disorder or high blood pressure—getting both individuals involved can increase compliance. In therapy, I often work with couples on how they might do this. Sometimes, this means one partner gets a glass of water and hands the pills to the person who takes the medicine at breakfast every day. The chances that a person will comply with their medication routine increases dramatically when their partner gets involved in a loving way. By sharing the responsibility, the person taking the medication is less likely to forget or find excuses for why they should skip a dose.

Your effort doesn't have to be 50/50. One person might put in more effort or take more responsibility. The joy of being partners is that you can work together. Keep your plan flexible though as you'll have weeks when you can do more or times when you need to step back. Revisit your plan and re-evaluate it as necessary to see what changes you want.

Who's Motivated?

Take a minute to consider who thinks there's a problem and who is motivated to create change. Then decide how to approach your situation best.

1. You want to stop ignoring problems.

You may need to work up your courage to tackle a problem you've ignored for a long time—or a problem you know will likely lead to heartache or conflict.

One of the best ways to build courage is by writing a list of reasons why you should address the problem. And on the back of that piece of paper, list the reasons why you shouldn't ignore it any longer.

Here's an example of how someone's list might look if they were thinking about addressing some financial problems.

Why I should address it:	Why I shouldn't ignore it:
We will feel more secure when we are out of debt	Our debt will keep growing bigger
If we talk about it we can develop a plan	I'll continue to feel resentful
When we work together, we can pay off our bills faster	We will get more calls from debt collectors

Looking over that logical list of reasons might help you push through the anxiety you have about finally addressing a problem.

If you're tempted to keep ignoring the problem for "one more day," write a list of reasons why you should address it today. That might bolster your courage and give you the motivation you need to tackle the issue.

2. You want your partner to stop ignoring problems.

If you've tried to address a problem but your partner doesn't respond well, change your approach. Use "I statements" and keep things as positive as possible.

Instead of saying, "You never spend time with me," try saying, "I'd love for us to spend more time together." You'll get a lot further when you don't place blame on the other person.

You'll get even further when you accept some responsibility for your role in the problem. Say something like, "I know I haven't been around much on the weekends," or "I know I get tired early in the evenings." You might even accept responsibility for how you've handled the problem by saying, "I know I nag you a lot about your drinking. I'm going to work on changing that."

Stick to the facts and your feelings. Say, "I feel overwhelmed lately. I look at our bills and see that we're falling behind. I want to work on a plan to address it." Remember, your partner can't argue about how you feel. They're your feelings.

3. Your partner thinks you should stop ignoring problems.

If your partner says you have a problem, you don't have to agree on the problem to tackle a solution together. Your partner might think you're overly critical. You, on the other hand, might think your partner is excessively sensitive, but you can still agree to stop teasing your partner if they don't like it.

If your partner comes to you with a problem, thank them for bringing up the issue, regardless of how you feel about it. This is tough because your first response might be to become defensive or argue about it. But if you respond negatively, you'll discourage them from talking about their concerns in the future. So while it's hard to say, "Thanks for bringing that to my attention," saying it sincerely can go a long way toward opening the door to a respectful conversation.

Validate your partner's feelings even if you disagree. If your partner says you hurt their feelings, acknowledge their pain—don't say they're being sensitive or dramatic.

4. You both want to stop ignoring problems.

There may be times when you both know there's a problem but you've chosen to look the other way. For example, if you haven't had sex in a decade, both of you are aware even if it's never been discussed. Or maybe you've both been irritable since your brother-in-law moved in so he could "get back on his feet," but you haven't talked to each other about it yet.

It's going to take courage to address the elephant in the room. But don't wait for your partner to bring it up first. Instead, sit down and invite them to share how they're feeling. Listening is one of the best places to start.

How Addressing Your Problems Helps You Grow Stronger

Angela may have been able to continue to have an OK relationship with Carl if she ignored the fact that she felt distant from him. She said she and Carl rarely argued and as a couple, they didn't have a ton of stress in their lives. She probably could have found plenty of activities that didn't involve Carl to occupy her time.

But she was lonely. She said, "It's one thing to feel lonely when you're all alone. But somehow, it feels even worse to feel lonely when your husband is sitting in the same room." She said she spent her days cleaning the house and doing errands alone. When Carl came home from work, they stared at their phones during dinner and watched separate TV shows in the evening.

If she addressed the fact that she felt distant from Carl head-on, there was a good chance she could turn an OK marriage into a great one. And if she improved her relationship with Carl, she could resolve her loneliness. At her last therapy session, Angela said, "Part of me is angry at myself for not addressing things sooner. But, I'm also grateful that I didn't wait any longer. From here on out, I'm confident I can address problems sooner."

Sometimes, it takes more energy to dance around a problem than it does to just address it. Once you address the problem, you have more energy left over for you and your relationship. That's better for you and your relationship.

Addressing your problems can make you stronger as an individual too. I can't tell you how many people in my therapy office have told me how relieved they felt when they tackled a relationship problem they'd ignored. Some of them had spent years walking on eggshells or pretending they didn't care about something deeply troubling, only to find the solution was simpler than they'd imagined.

Troubleshooting and Common Traps

Waiting for the Perfect Time to Address a Problem

Timing matters. Starting a major conversation ten minutes before your partner heads out the door on a business trip isn't a good idea.

If you both have busy schedules, planning a time to talk to your partner about your concerns can be helpful. Saying something in advance like, "I want to talk, and here's when I want to do it, and here's what I want to talk about," can help you both prepare for a productive conversation. Or you might sit down after work one evening and just dive in.

Don't convince yourself you should wait until the perfect time, though. It doesn't exist. When people tell themselves the timing needs to be "just right," their anxiety builds. Then at some point—often during the worst time possible—their anxiety spills over and they blurt out the problem either during a disagreement about something else or while they're about to head to a family gathering.

Bringing Up the Same Problem Over and Over

Sometimes people think they're addressing a problem when they keep bringing it up repeatedly.

But rehashing your frustrations, lecturing, nagging, and repeating yourself can damage the relationship and usually doesn't fix the problem.

Ask yourself, "Am I dwelling on the problem or working on a solution?" If you find yourself bringing the same issue up, ask yourself why. Are you dissatisfied with your partner's response? Do more obstacles need to be addressed? Are you feeling stuck about what steps you can take to create change?

In some cases, you may need to work on healing an emotional wound that hasn't been addressed yet. If your partner betrayed you two years ago, talking about it repeatedly now won't necessarily help. You may need something you're not getting before you can feel better—like an apology, an acknowledgment, or a behavior change. Try telling your partner what you need (if you know what that need is). If you're struggling to let something go, it may be a sign that you could benefit from talking to a professional.

Using the Silent Treatment

The silent treatment is a form of manipulation that can become emotionally abusive. It's sometimes used to avoid a problem or punish a partner for bringing up a subject the other partner doesn't want to discuss.

When someone gives you the silent treatment, it activates the part of the brain that registers pain, meaning it can be both emotionally and physically painful. It can damage your well-being and your relationship.

If a conversation becomes emotionally charged, taking a break and saying you'll revisit it later is OK. But the silent treatment involves avoiding a problem altogether and trying to punish the other person in the process.

If your partner gives you the silent treatment, don't try to trick them into talking to you and don't make promises that you'll change or fix things. Instead, consider talking to a professional to get some help. If your partner won't talk to a therapist (or is likely to punish you for encouraging them to go), get help for yourself.

Conversation Starters

Here are some questions you can consider on your own. If your partner is open to talking about mental strength and welcomes your questions, use these conversation starters to learn more about their thoughts. Even if you disagree with their answers, don't argue. Just listen and you could learn a lot about yourself, your partner, and your relationship. If they're interested in your answers, share those too but ask them to respectfully listen as well.

- What's a problem we've worked well to address?
- What's an example of a time when you were glad I addressed a problem that affected our relationship?
- What's an example of a time when you were glad you addressed a problem that affected our relationship?
- How did you find the courage to address it?
- What's something I do that helps you address our problems so we don't ignore them?
- What's a problem that we tackled together that you're glad we addressed?

Interview with Ruth Cohn

While couples might ignore many different problems, sexual problems are especially ignored. That's why I contacted Ruth Cohn, a marriage and family therapist who specializes in trauma and neglect and sexual issues. She's written two books, *Working with the Developmental Trauma of Childhood Neglect* and *Coming Home to Passion*. She's a wealth of information about how our childhoods can impact how we view sex and why so many couples ignore sexual problems.

Based on the couples that you see in your therapy office, do you find that most of them either talk about sex or they don't?

Mostly they don't, and my big beef with the world is nobody talks to people about sex. Psychiatrists don't tell people the sexual side effects of their medications. Cancer doctors don't tell people what's going to happen to their sexuality when they have cancer treatment. Nobody talks about it, including people who have been in couples therapy numerous times before. They tell me, "Nobody ever talked to us about sex," so they think they're not supposed to, or they think they're supposed to know already or that it's natural, so you're supposed to know what to do or that everybody wants the same thing. They learn it from porn, they learn it from locker rooms. There's no good information. Here's my big beef: we're surrounded by titillation, there's no information. Sex education in schools now is minimal.

What are the most common sexual problems couples are ignoring?

The big problem I see is no sex. It's astonishing how many people have not had sex with their partner in years; I'm not kidding, not two years, but five years, ten years. These are not older people. These are young people. The sex stopped. They didn't know what to do about it. They were ashamed. They were blaming each other. They were blaming themselves. They were blaming trauma, you name it.

Then what often happens, they hit fifty, and they start realizing how much of their life has passed and that they could lose function. They may already have started losing function, and they get really freaked out about not having sex. So then either they want to leave their spouse or they want to jump-start the sexual relationship.

Why do you think it is so difficult for people to talk to their partner about sex?

Because first of all, they think they're supposed to know. They think, "Oh, it's natural. You're supposed to know." There's no information anywhere that tells people, "Everyone is different."

Some people like a light touch. Some people like a rough touch. Some people like to get dressed up. There's no pathology in it as long as there's consent, but people don't know about different-ness, so they think everyone's the same. They don't know how to talk about sex or they're ashamed, or they think there's something wrong with themselves. There's awkwardness and there's taboo, and there's religion, and there's culture, and there's fear and trauma.

How about the mismatch in sex drive? How do you work with couples when one has a higher sex drive than the other?

Well, first of all, I tell them that that is the norm, that it's not atypical for couples to have mismatched sex drives. In fact, I think it's evolutionarily designed that high-drive people match up with low-drive people because if all the low-drive people got together, we wouldn't have any preservation of the species, so it's about empathy. A lot of it is work where if I care about you, what does it cost me to be available and to open up and to be turned on and let you know what makes me feel good, even if I don't have an orgasm every time you do?

Some people have a much greater drive than the other, and so they have to develop an empathic understanding of where each other's at and learn things to do that will work for both of them. It's about give-and-take in any relationship, which is what it's all about in a relationship anyway.

What would you say to people who say, "Talking about sex with a therapist isn't going to help. Why should we talk about it?"

For people who think, "It's no point talking to you," well, the door's open, you don't need to talk to me. But I think as soon as people start talking about things and have the experience of being understood, they feel different. They probably never had the experience of feeling understood, feeling like, "Wow, somebody really gets me," because that's a game changer; feeling understood, especially by someone that they care about, is life-changing. So many people have never had that.

So if there's a couple who's reading this book and they've ignored sexual issues for a long time, how do you suggest that they find the courage to bring it up?

Well, if it's not bothering them, there's no reason to bring it up. If they haven't had sex in a long time, and it doesn't bother either one of them, it's no problem unless they want to have a family. But if it's bothering one of them, then it tends to come up, or they might be afraid to bring it up because it brings a lot of conflict. But they will because it hurts, or they're angry or they're scared, or they want to leave or something like that.

So, make it safe enough to talk about things, even if they are afraid. "You'll leave me if I talk about this": we have to see if we can create safety and see, is that true? Is she or he or they going to leave you if you talk about it, because you might be surprised to find out that maybe they won't?

I want to encourage people—especially parents—to learn the language to talk about sex respectfully. Say the words, say vagina, say penis, say masturbate, say orgasm, instead of beating around the bush as if there's something wrong with using the language. If we create comfort talking about sex, maybe more people will talk about sex in a respectful, healthy, consensual, open way where it becomes a part of life that isn't bad or wrong or something that people perpetrate on each other, but a good thing. So, every chance I get, I try and teach people to talk about sex in a way that's healthy, joyful, respectful, and natural.

CHAPTER 2

They Don't Keep Secrets

Forty percent of people suspect their partner keeps secrets.
—Couples by the Numbers Survey

Autumn called my office asking for the next available appointment. She said, "My husband is a liar and a cheater, and he needs to figure out what's wrong with him. Or maybe we need to figure out what's wrong with me for sticking with him. Either way, we'll both be there so you can figure out who needs the help." About a week later, Autumn and David arrived for an appointment together.

As soon as I called their names in the waiting room, Autumn leaped up and marched to my office on a clear mission. David lagged, but on the walk down the hall he smiled politely and said, "This is a nice place you have here." As soon as I closed the door to the office, Autumn said, "David usually pays the bills, but last month, I pulled up the credit card bill and noticed several charges to OnlyFans. I looked over the old bills and saw that David has been doing this for months. I'm upset my husband was paying to see nude photos of other women, but when I learned he was subscribing to his college girlfriend's account, I felt especially betrayed."

In response, David quietly said, "I didn't think it was a big deal. If I did, I obviously would have tried to cover my tracks better and not use a credit card that Autumn had access to."

That enraged Autumn, who said, "So your only regret is that you got caught? Obviously, you knew this would upset me. Otherwise you would have told me. Instead, you went sneaking around and lying about it!"

David tried to laugh it off. "I thought you might be a little annoyed, but I had no idea you'd freak out. A lot of married men go to strip clubs and view pornography. It's not like I was cheating." That turned their civil conversation into an argument where they began talking over one another.

Arguing about whether David's behavior met the technical definition of cheating wasn't going to be helpful, so I interrupted them before the conversation deteriorated further. I had a clear picture of what was going on. Autumn felt like David had just committed the ultimate betrayal and David thought he could minimize her feelings and make things better by convincing her that his behavior wasn't a big deal.

We established some simple ground rules for the therapy office. There would be no yelling, attacking, name-calling, and interrupting. If they couldn't listen to each other and have a respectful conversation, therapy wouldn't work.

Once they agreed on rules, we discussed what they hoped to gain from therapy. Autumn said she wanted to make sure David wouldn't do something like this again. And David said he wanted to get Autumn's trust back.

Autumn agreed that she wanted to be able to trust him again but she said, "It makes me wonder what else you are hiding. For all I know this isn't even the worst of it."

"I don't want you to feel that way," he replied. "I want to fix things."

With that, they agreed to start couples counseling to address Autumn's feelings of betrayal and rebuild trust so they could have a healthier marriage moving forward.

We'll return to Autumn and David later in the chapter. But even if you can't relate to the secret David kept from Autumn, there's a good chance you may have wrestled with a secret at one time or another.

Quiz

Whether you've got a few secrets you don't ever want your partner to know, or you worry that your partner is hiding a secret or two from you, secrets affect every relationship. Take a minute to read over the following statements and see how many of them sound true.

- ❑ I hide things from my partner because I don't want them to get upset.
- ❑ There are things I don't share with my partner because I am ashamed of myself or feel embarrassed.
- ❑ I suspect my partner keeps secrets from me.
- ❑ We lie to each other because we don't trust each other.
- ❑ I do things behind my partner's back because they wouldn't understand or appreciate my behavior.
- ❑ I keep secrets because my partner would blow little things out of proportion.
- ❑ I snoop or spy on my partner because I think they keep secrets.
- ❑ My partner and I disagree over what to share with one another.
- ❑ I want to protect them from the truth.

If any of those statements sound true, don't worry. You're not alone in struggling with issues of secrecy in relationships. Secrets are something that can be addressed.

Starting Point

While David initially agreed to attend therapy with Autumn, he hoped the whole thing would blow over soon. During our first few sessions, he sometimes accepted responsibility while at other times he tried minimizing and justifying his actions. He said things like, "Well, I only subscribed to my ex's account because I was curious to know what she was up to these days," and "I actually forgot I had subscribed. I rarely looked at those pages anyway."

Until he was honest about what he'd done, Autumn couldn't begin healing. They couldn't work on trust unless he took full responsibility for his behavior.

If you've ever harbored a secret, you know how stressful it can be. You might go to great lengths to keep the secret hidden from your partner because you fear the consequences of that secret coming to light.

When a secret finally gets revealed (as they often do), you might feel pressure to lie. It may be your last-ditch effort to try and avoid the consequences you're about to face. That cycle of secrecy and dishonesty can be tough to break.

What's easy, though, is justifying your secret to yourself. You might tell yourself that not being honest about how much you paid for those concert tickets is harmless. Or you might tell yourself that your conversation with your ex wasn't a big deal so there's no need to mention it to your partner and cause them to get upset.

Of course, you don't need to tell your partner everything. It's healthy to have privacy, even in a committed, long-term relationship. You might keep your password to social media private. Hopefully, you have private conversations with friends and family members that don't always include your partner.

But secrecy is different than privacy. Secrecy is about not sharing something with your partner—or outright lying—because you know they'd be upset by the information. It's motivated by fear and shame. Privacy involves keeping something to yourself that would not benefit nor hurt your partner.

With that in mind, think about these questions:

○ Do you keep secrets from your partner?
○ Do you know (or strongly suspect) that your partner keeps secrets?
○ Do you both keep secrets from each other?

Most people have secrets. In fact, researchers estimate the average adult keeps thirteen secrets. Not all those secrets are kept from partners—as we might keep secrets from our friends, colleagues, and extended family too. But holding on to those secrets can take a toll on your well-being. Whether you keep secrets or suspect your partner does, you can take steps to develop a more forthcoming and honest relationship.

Why We Keep Secrets

Like many people, David kept a secret because he didn't want to "get in trouble." He knew there would be consequences if Autumn found out what he was doing. He also knew if his secret came to light, he'd have to change his behavior. And he didn't want to change his behavior.

Take a few minutes and think about why you keep secrets from your partner. Remember, we all have some secrets at different points in our lives. Understanding why you withhold information can help you move forward productively.

I'm trying to protect myself:

○ I don't want my partner to think less of me.

○ I would feel embarrassed if my partner knew what I did.

○ I am ashamed of my behavior.

○ I want to continue my behavior and if my partner knew what I was doing, I'd have to stop.

I'm trying to protect my partner:

○ My partner gets unreasonably upset.

○ My partner would jump to conclusions that aren't true.

○ My partner's feelings would be hurt.

I'm trying to protect our relationship:

○ I know my behavior would damage the relationship.

○ My partner would overreact to it.

○ My partner would be mad at me.

○ My partner would be hurt to know what I've done.

○ My partner would want me to stop doing something I don't want to give up.

○ My relationship would likely end.

○ My partner would be mad at me for not saying something sooner.

You might try to convince yourself that your efforts to keep something hidden are altruistic—you're protecting your partner from unnecessary hurt. But, in reality, you're likely also protecting yourself.

Mental Strength Exercises

David had broken Autumn's trust. It caused her to question whether she was desirable enough and whether he was still attracted to her. She was also concerned that he might still have feelings for his ex and that he may have been in contact with her on the phone or even in-person. Although David denied these things, she wasn't sure she believed him.

Autumn wasn't comfortable with David viewing nude images of other women, but she especially didn't want him viewing pictures of his ex. She thought the only way she could trust him going forward would be if he gave her the passwords to his laptop and phone and allowed her to look at his online activities whenever she asked.

David wasn't thrilled with this idea at first. But Autumn said, "I know myself and I know that I'm going to doubt you sometimes. I don't want to go snooping and spying on you. I want us both to be honest with each other so we can rebuild the trust we lost." With that, David agreed that he would give his passwords to Autumn.

We reviewed David's decision to subscribe to his ex's explicit content. He offered a variety of reasons why he did it—including that he was starting to feel older and looking at an ex reminded him of college. But he assured Autumn that he was deeply in love with her and did not have feelings for his ex.

It took months for Autumn to start to feel like she could trust David again—and there were times when she asked to check his electronics. David agreed to let her look at his phone and laptop because he knew he needed to show Autumn that his behavior aligned with his words.

They also talked about their expectations regarding secrets. Autumn made it clear that if David were to look at sexually explicit content again, she wanted him to tell her. They also discussed her expectations about what he should do if an ex ever texted him or what her expectations were if someone sent him sexually explicit content.

By the time they ended therapy, Autumn felt more confident about their relationship. She said, "We'd never really discussed our expectations about secrets before. I feel better now that we've laid out the rules."

You can prevent some secrets from happening if you talk about your expectations ahead of time and create a safe environment for both of you to share. You can also learn to reveal secrets you've been holding on to in a healthy way and find strategies to heal if you discover your partner has been keeping secrets from you.

Examine Your Relationship

While secrets can damage relationships, there's also evidence that damaged relationships harbor secrets. Your need to keep secrets might indicate your relationship is unhealthy. Some research indicates secrets may be a symptom of an overall bigger relationship problem.

A 2023 study published in *Personal Relationships* found that the reason people keep secrets in the first place is most likely because they're in a disloyal, distrustful, unhealthy relationship.

This isn't always the case. I've seen plenty of individuals who wrestled with a secret for a long time before telling their partner, not because they were in a terrible relationship, but because they were in a good relationship that they didn't want to ruin.

But this is something to keep in mind. If you're in a rocky relationship already, you may be harboring secrets because you know your partner won't be supportive or it will just lead to more arguments.

Zoom out a little and consider the overall health of your relationship. Are the secrets you keep a problem or might they be a symptom of a bigger problem? If they're merely a symptom, take steps to work on the relationship. Whether that means you practice new skills from this book or you meet with a therapist, improving the overall health of your relationship might help you become more honest with one another.

Talk About Your Privacy Expectations

It would be ideal if everyone had upfront conversations about their expectations early on in relationships. Discussions about what you'd expect your partner to do if a coworker expressed attraction to them or if an ex sent a sexy text message may help solve some problems before they start.

But most couples don't ever have such conversations. And those conversations can be a little trickier later in the relationship.

That doesn't mean you shouldn't still have those conversations. Of course, you can't plan for every possible scenario, but you can talk about what you'd feel comfortable with and what you wouldn't.

Make this subject an ongoing conversation. After all, many couples got together long before social media was invented. They couldn't have possibly planned for all the complications social media would bring regarding privacy and secrecy.

There's not always a "right" choice when it comes to the things you should keep private. You and your partner make the rules about what you feel comfortable with.

Here's a sample list of what a couple might agree on should be kept private as well as secrets they wouldn't want one another to keep:

Private:
- Your email
- Your social media accounts and passwords
- What you spend a certain amount of your money on (like $100 a month)
- Conversations with friends and family that don't involve your partner
- Things other people ask you to keep private that don't involve your partner (like a friend says they're having some marital trouble and they ask you not to tell anyone)

What we should discuss:
- A coworker or someone who flirts with us
- An ex who reaches out
- If you reach out to an ex

It seems simple enough on the surface. But there will always be some complicated areas. For example, let's say you think your spouse's cousin is attractive. Should you reveal that? One person might say yes because keeping that information to yourself constitutes a secret. Another person might say you should never reveal anything like that if you don't plan to act on it because who you are attracted to is private.

You might find that you're comfortable hearing your partner tell you about a celebrity they find attractive. Watching a famous person in a movie might not seem like a threat to your relationship. But you might decide it's uncomfortable to hear if your partner finds someone you both know in real life attractive.

But it's up to you to decide what you are comfortable with. Having open conversations ahead of time can help you both establish more precise boundaries.

You and your partner can decide what you're comfortable sharing about your romantic history too—and what they're comfortable knowing. Sometimes people think they want information and later regret finding out.

It's also a personal choice about what to share regarding your childhood or any past trauma you've endured. You might need some time to work through some issues on your own before telling your partner or you might decide that you are going to keep some things private.

Address Your Existing Secrets

Avoid keeping secrets in the first place if you can. But, what do you do when you've been holding on to a secret for a long time? Should you come clean about something you did a decade ago?

Many therapists will say there's no use revealing something that will only hurt your partner if it's a long-since-buried secret. After twenty years of marriage, saying, "Hey, I actually kissed someone else when we were dating," might not heal the relationship.

But most secrets damage the relationship—especially if they've happened recently or are ongoing.

Bringing up something you've been trying to cover up can be hard, though. How do you suddenly say, "Hey, honey, you know how you think I've been going to the gym after work every day? I've actually been going to the bar with my friends for months."

It's tough to come clean about something small. But coming clean about something big is even more challenging. Telling your partner you've been having an emotional affair or that you lied about something takes courage. Confessing a sexual affair or admitting you have a secret addiction might seem too risky.

But actor and TV host Terry Crews says acknowledging his secrets is what helped him break free from shame. When I interviewed him on my podcast, he said he had a pornography addiction that interfered with his ability to function. He was opting out of everyday activities to stay isolated with his computer, and his wife had no idea what was happening. He felt shame and pressure to keep a huge portion of his life hidden from everyone.

He finally told his wife that he had the addiction—and that he'd cheated on her. And she left him. Fortunately, Terry decided to get professional help. He checked himself into a rehab center and began working on his addiction.

Over time, he and his wife reunited and healed their relationship. But the more he held on to his secrets, the worse he felt about himself. And the worse he felt, the more he indulged in pornography. Telling the truth was the only way to break that cycle.

If you are holding on to a big secret, think about coming clean. If that seems too hard to do or you're concerned about the toll it could take on your partner, talk to a professional counselor, a pastor, or someone else first to get some support.

If you have a therapist already, be honest with them. There's research that shows about 93 percent of people lie to their therapists. I've had clients tell me they have no idea why they got fired (only to later reveal they got caught drinking at work) or they weren't sure why their partner moved out (only to later say they got caught cheating). It can be tough to be honest about the behaviors we aren't proud of. But telling a therapist first might give you some insight and courage to tell your partner.

Over the years, I've helped people figure out how to reveal many secrets to partners. They range from gambling issues they'd hidden for years to secretly giving their adult children money when they knew their spouse would disagree. Having a little support gave them the courage to take that step so they could figure out how to share the information compassionately even when they knew the news would hurt the other person.

Who's Motivated?

Take a minute to think about who thinks there's a problem and who is motivated to create change. Then, you can decide how to approach your situation best.

1. You want to stop keeping secrets.

One of the reasons you might be keeping a secret is because you don't want to change your behavior. Telling your partner that you're having an emotional affair with a coworker will likely end the affair. And if you aren't ready to end that relationship, you will guard the secret.

Yet, you might find that your internal struggle is about the wrong thing. If you're struggling with a secret, the solution doesn't end with revealing it. It's about changing your behavior.

If you feel uncomfortable talking about a behavior, it's either a sign that you don't want to change or you don't want to upset your partner.

Of course, your answer might be that you want to avoid both. But one of those issues is weighing on you more than the other. Consider that discomfort something you need to confront. You can be courageous enough and respectful enough of your partner to share.

Let's say you spent money on something, and you know your partner won't be impressed. It might be too late to return the thing you bought and revealing it now might seem unnecessary since you can't fix it. And you might use that as an excuse to keep your secret hidden.

Here's a sample script:

"I'd like to talk to you about something. I messed up. I did something that you aren't going to like. And because I didn't want you to be upset, I didn't tell you about it. That was wrong. I shouldn't have kept this as a secret. Here's what I did . . ."

2. You want your partner to stop keeping secrets.

Your response to a secret makes a huge difference in how likely your partner is to share more things with you in the future.

If your partner reveals they forgot to pay a bill—and they didn't tell you because they knew you'd yell and get upset—you might want to look at shifting how you respond. If, out of sheer frustration, you say condescending things like, "Clearly, I need to handle the finances from now on since you can't handle them!" you'll discourage them from sharing a mistake with you next time (and there will always be a next time when it comes to mistakes).

The best response you can give when your partner tells you something that was hard for them to share is, "Thank you for being honest with me." Your mind will likely be screaming, "How could you do this to me?" but that's the last thing you want to come out of your mouth.

Take time to process what you heard. You might need to say, "Thank you for being honest with me. I know that must have been hard. Let me take a little bit of time to think about what you said." End the conversation for now if you are feeling upset.

But that one little shift in how you respond in the minute can make a massive difference to how likely your partner is to be honest with you down the road.

3. Your partner thinks you should stop keeping secrets.

When you're holding on to a secret, you'll try to justify your reasoning. You might tell yourself that it's best for your partner or that your secret isn't harming anyone.

Ask yourself, "Would my partner be upset by this information?"

If the answer is yes, you're holding on to a secret.

Once you uncover that you are keeping a secret, your brain will try to convince you that this secret is the exception to the rule. You'll think that it really is a harmless secret and it really would make things worse to tell.

You might even try to convince yourself that your secret is good for your relationship. People say everything from, "But I'm happier when I'm having an emotional affair and that makes me a better partner," to "I'm just blowing off steam when I go to the casino. It's a good stress reliever."

If your partner accuses you of keeping secrets, get honest with yourself. Sometimes, I see people hiding small things—like not telling their partner they went out for lunch to prevent an argument over money. But if their partner finds the receipt, they now have reason to believe you might be hiding bigger things too and they may resort to snooping, spying, and accusing you of doing something you aren't doing.

If your partner falsely accuses you of being secretive, you may want to get some professional help. Talking to someone might help you decide if they're unrealistically suspicious or if you're doing things that fuel their doubt.

4. You both want to stop keeping secrets.

You likely know couples who keep secrets from one another. Maybe you have a coworker who says, "My daughter and I decided to tell my husband that her prom dress was on clearance. He'd be shocked if he knew how much we really spent!" Or perhaps you have a friend who tells his wife he's going fishing for his friend's weekend-long bachelor party, but they're really planning wild nights out on the town.

People who do that often imply they're being protective of the other person. But, really, they're sending a message that says, "We don't trust each other enough to be honest."

If you tend to keep little secrets from your partner, I suspect your partner does the same thing. This might be because you haven't created a safe environment to have hard conversations.

Have a conversation now about what you can do to support each other in being honest when you make a mistake or do something that is likely to upset one another. Talk about what you need—like "please don't raise your voice or say sarcastic things." And ask what you can do to make things easier for your partner to come clean too.

How Being Open Helps You Grow Stronger

Over several weeks in therapy, David slowly acknowledged that the reason he kept his behavior a secret was because he knew it was wrong. He called his behavior immature and reckless. He put his entire marriage at risk just for a bit of excitement.

He also admitted that deep down, he felt terrible while he was doing it. He knew that by subscribing to his ex's content he was betraying Autumn. But that was hard to admit so he tried to convince himself that it wasn't a big deal so he could ease his guilt.

Once he started to be honest, they were finally able to have some constructive conversations about how to move forward. If Autumn was going to forgive him, she needed the full story. And she needed to establish rules to help David regain trust.

David's response to his mistake was common—he kept a secret and then made excuses to justify his actions. Once the secret came to light, he focused on minimizing the issue, instead of taking responsibility for his behavior.

> **Healthy relationships are built on trust. And it just takes one secret to erode that trust.**

Healthy relationships are built on trust. And it just takes one secret to erode that trust.

Here's why secrets are so damaging:

1. You'll waste a lot of energy keeping your secrets hidden.
2. Secrets take an emotional toll on you.
3. You might have to do things that further damage the relationship to prevent your partner from uncovering a secret.

Imagine someone who is hiding an affair or an addiction. They may spend much of their waking hours not only thinking about the object of their desire—but also how to ensure you don't know what they're thinking about.

They also must invest a lot of time in covering their tracks. Whether they hide text messages or pay for their bar tabs with cash only, they're likely to live in fear of being found out. If they could invest that same energy into working on themselves or working on their relationship, they could see some amazing results. But keeping those secrets means they have little energy left over for anything else.

Companies know secrets damage relationships and they try to capitalize on this. They know that secrets lead to guilt. And guilt leads to buying your partner gifts. A research study found that even when partners keep what they consider to be "harmless secrets," they're still more likely to spend money on their partners out of guilt. They defined a "harmless secret" as anything from a vegetarian eating meat to someone splurging on something their partner would disapprove of. So even a secret you think is harmless can eat away at your conscience.

While on the surface someone might say the secret led to nicer behavior that ultimately benefits the relationship, no one wants to be treated well just because their partner did something wrong.

Doing kind things out of guilt might temporarily relieve your conscience but it doesn't do anything to build trust in the long term. It'll only further erode the relationship if your partner later learns your kindness stemmed from selfishness.

Troubleshooting and Common Traps

Being Overprotective

You might be tempted to keep secrets under the guise that you're protecting your partner from something. And while you don't need to be brutally honest by saying, "Your shirt is ugly," withholding information because you think your partner is fragile is detrimental.

Not telling your partner that your job is in jeopardy will prevent them from unnecessary worry. But holding on to that information prevents them from supporting you and it keeps you both from having time to develop a solution together.

Sharing Your Partner's Secret With Other People

If your partner confides in you, don't share that information with other people. Show them that you are a safe person to confide in and you won't tell even your closest friends or family members.

If the secret will become obvious to people around you, talk about what they're comfortable with you sharing. Whether your mother asks you why she needs to watch the kids so you can attend counseling together or your neighbor asks why your partner's car is home during the day while they're taking a leave of absence for depression, don't share things your partner wants to keep private between the two of you.

If you need support for something—like your partner has an addiction or a mental health issue—join a support group. An in-person or online group that keeps information confidential can give you emotional support without breaking your partner's confidence.

Being Brutally Honest

I've heard people in my therapy office say, "I'm just an honest person. That's all." But they're actually mean to their partners sometimes and they justify their unkind words by calling it honesty. You don't have to announce that your partner's breath smells bad. Keeping some things to yourself doesn't mean that you're keeping a secret.

You can keep opinions that would unnecessarily hurt your partner to yourself, under the category of kindness. Of course, if your partner is about to go to a job interview and they ask if their outfit looks OK, telling them that their shirt is wrinkled is the kind thing to do. So consider whether the information is helpful or just plain hurtful before sharing.

Conversation Starters

Here are some questions to help you start thinking about secrets. If your partner is open to discussing mental strength and welcomes a conversation, ask them these questions. If you disagree with their answers, don't argue. Just listen with the intention of learning. If they're interested in your answers, share those too but ask them to respectfully listen as well.

- How were privacy and secrecy handled in your family when you grew up?
- What's an example of a time when you told me something and it was hard for you to tell me but you did it anyway?

- What's an example of a time when you're glad I confided in you about something?
- What are some of the privacy rules we have that you appreciate?
- If I had been holding on to a secret for a long time and I wanted to come clean, how would you want me to share that information with you?

Interview with Jenn Mann

A huge part of healthy communication involves sharing sensitive information, resolving conflict, and keeping open lines of communication. So I knew talking to Dr. Jenn Mann about healthy communication skills would be interesting. Dr. Mann is a psychotherapist who became well known when she hosted VH1's shows *Couples Therapy with Dr. Jenn* and *Family Therapy with Dr. Jenn.* She's written multiple bestsellers, including *The Relationship Fix: Dr. Jenn's Guide to Improving Communication, Connection & Intimacy.* She's been a licensed therapist for almost thirty years and has a private practice in Beverly Hills, California. I wanted to hear her thoughts on relationship secrets.

In your work with couples, how often do secrets seem to be an issue?

Secrets are very common issues with couples. A big part of secrets is figuring out boundaries. Where do I end and you begin? Many people struggle to figure out what is appropriate or important to share in order to be connected and emotionally intimate versus what is appropriate for me to have privacy about.

What are some of the biggest or most common secrets people seem to keep from one another?

Some of the most common secrets that couples keep from one another are: number of sexual partners, sexual experiences in their past, childhood trauma, adult trauma, and embarrassing experiences. People worry that their romantic partners will judge them or won't love them anymore.

Have you ever worked with someone who was too brutally honest? If so, did you find ways to help them tame it down so they weren't hurtful?

Sometimes people are too honest in their relationship. Your partner does not need to know every time you find someone else attractive, every feeling you have, every temptation you face, etc. In an adult relationship, it's important to have boundaries. It's also important to be a kind and gracious partner.

What are some of the most common issues you see in therapy that arise from secrets?

Couples should not ask questions that they do not want to know the answer to. Too often people get themselves in trouble by asking a question that they don't really want answered. Do these jeans make my ass look fat? Do you really want to know that? If you're asking, you probably don't like the way they look and you should take them off if that's not working for you. Stop looking for validation from your partner when you can't provide it for yourself.

If someone tells you something that their partner doesn't know, how do you respond as a therapist? Let's say they're having an

**emotional affair with a coworker and they say they don't want to
tell their partner because they're afraid it could hurt their feelings.
How do you proceed?**

When someone tells me something that their partner doesn't
know, as a therapist, my goal is to help them express themselves
to their partner in a way that will increase the odds of them getting their needs met. Complaining to your friends or even your
therapist is not going to change the dynamic in your relationship
unless you're willing to communicate with your partner, ask for
what you need, and share your feelings. Your partner may or may
not be capable of providing what you want, but they should at least
know what your needs are, so they stand a chance of being a good
partner to you.

If a client tells me that they are having an emotional affair with
a coworker and they don't want to tell their partner, I try to help
them understand why they are reaching out to this other inappropriate person and help them to shift that emotional connection back
to their partner. A lack of connection is the number one reason
why partners cheat or have emotional affairs. Sometimes couples
just need to rebuild that connection. That requires conscious effort,
time, and commitment on both ends.

**How can people manage the shame that can make it difficult to
"come clean" when they're harboring a secret?**

Shame is a normal and sometimes even healthy response to
hiding something that you don't feel good about. There are times
where you have done something you feel ashamed of and other
times when something has been done to you that you feel ashamed
about. One thing to keep in mind is that the longer something we

are ashamed about is held inside, the bigger it tends to become and the harder it becomes to talk about. Trying to tell a safe, loving person is the best way to deal with shame.

For people who want to start being more honest in their relationships, what tips do you have?

For people who want to start being more honest in their relationships, I recommend therapy. It is important to have clarity about your views, needs, and opinions in order to express them. If you're struggling to be honest in your relationship, you need to ask yourself, what is holding you back? Is it something from your childhood? Is it the way your partner is reacting to your truth? Is it assumptions you are making that may not be accurate? Sometimes we need a professional to give us a reality check or help us develop the tools and skills to be more honest in our relationships.

CHAPTER 3

They Don't Hesitate
to Set Boundaries

Thirty-four percent of couples disagree on the rules and
boundaries they should set with extended family.
—Couples by the Numbers Survey

Jen was a bubbly twenty-nine-year-old who felt overwhelmed and guilty
about her financial situation. During her first appointment at my office
she said, "I know it's going to stress me out to pay for therapy but maybe
it will only take a few sessions to help me figure things out." She told
me she'd made poor financial decisions in the past but now that she was
married, her husband, Ethan, had to deal with the financial mess she'd
created too.

She had huge student loan debt and regretted going to such an expen-
sive school. Throughout college, she racked up credit card debt and she
had a hefty car payment now too. She could barely pay her own bills,
which meant she couldn't contribute to household expenses.

Ethan didn't express concerns about her financial situation when they
were dating. But once they married, he seemed much less tolerant of the
bills as they rolled in.

Jen explained, "Ethan sometimes gets mad and says he spends all
his hard-earned money paying off my stupid decisions. Then I just feel

guilty that he has to do that." Sometimes, he made those comments in front of others, which fueled her shame.

One time, when they were eating dinner with Ethan's family, his dad suggested Ethan and Jen take a cruise. Ethan smirked and said, "A vacation would be nice. But unfortunately, Jen took so many vacations in college with her credit cards that I'll be paying for her sophomore spring break trip until I'm thirty-five." Jen was mortified.

Another time, their friends invited them over to see their new home. Ethan commented on how beautiful it was and said, "It'll be a while before we get to buy anything. Jen's credit is so bad the bank wouldn't even loan us enough money to buy a tent!" Jen pretended to laugh, but she said she felt embarrassed.

She feared she was ruining her marriage. She had never talked to Ethan about it, however. When I asked her why not, she said, "He's expressing how he feels. He has a right to be mad at me." She thought Ethan said those things because he didn't want anyone to think he'd made "stupid" financial decisions. He was financially savvy and he'd never had any debt.

When I asked Jen what she wanted to accomplish by being in therapy she said, "I want to make sure I don't ruin my marriage." So we set to work on figuring out the steps she could take to do just that.

I'll share Jen's steps a little later in the chapter (her solution involved setting better boundaries). But before we get there, take a minute and think about the boundaries you set with your partner and with people outside your relationship.

Quiz

You and your partner have some rules you've established regarding how you treat one another. You probably haven't talked about those rules—

but instead, they've just evolved. Take a minute and think about the boundaries between you and your partner and see how many of these statements describe you.

- ❑ I struggle to recognize how my partner wants to be treated.
- ❑ I find myself trying to guess what my partner wants sometimes because they don't tell me.
- ❑ Instead of asking directly for something, I complain to my partner in hopes they'll get the hint.
- ❑ I sometimes spy or snoop on my partner or they spy on me.
- ❑ I don't like how my partner treats me sometimes but I don't speak up.
- ❑ I don't share my opinions very often with my partner.
- ❑ I have trouble saying no to things my partner asks of me.
- ❑ We sometimes argue about what should be kept private and what should be shared with one another.
- ❑ I feel responsible for my partner's emotions sometimes.

If any of those statements sound familiar, it might be a sign that there's room for improvement in establishing boundaries within your relationship. Now, let's talk about the boundaries you and your partner have with other people. See how many of the following statements sound like you.

- ○ My partner and I disagree about how involved extended family should be in our lives.
- ○ I complain about people who infringe on our relationship or try to meddle in our private business.
- ○ I think my partner's friends take a toll on our relationship.
- ○ I think my partner shares too much information about our relationship with friends or family.

○ My partner and I disagree on how much information we should share about each other.

○ I have trouble finding opportunities to talk to my partner privately.

If any of those statements sound familiar, you may have room to improve in the boundary department as a team. Even if your partner doesn't want to establish a boundary, that doesn't mean you can't take action.

Starting Point

Throughout the next few sessions, Jen and I discussed her options. Her first idea was to get a second job. Increasing her income would mean she could contribute to the household expenses. But having an extra job might not solve the problem.

After all, her debt was only one piece of the puzzle. The real problem (as she saw it) was that Ethan was embarrassed and frustrated by their financial situation. If she worked an extra job, he would then have to explain to other people why she was working nights and weekends and she ultimately decided he might be even more embarrassed by this. She also worried that working a second job may make her so tired that she'd be less effective at her first job, jeopardizing her career.

Another way to tackle the financial problem would be for Jen to set some boundaries with Ethan and for the two of them to establish better boundaries with people outside of their relationship. It wasn't something they'd ever discussed so it took time for Jen to figure out what she wanted her boundaries to be and how she could start working on those boundaries with Ethan.

Like Jen, you might find that you aren't sure what your boundaries are. Essentially, they are the rules you set to protect your inner peace. You need boundaries within your partnership, and you and your partner also need boundaries with people outside your relationship. Healthy boundaries are essential to helping you feel your best and ensuring your relationship has the room to thrive.

And while many of us might be quick to complain about a meddling in-law or a friend who always asks for favors, we spend less time establishing healthy boundaries to prevent the problem from happening again. Fortunately, though, establishing some healthy boundaries can go a long way toward helping you grow stronger as an individual and as a couple.

It's not that you either have healthy boundaries or you don't, however. Boundaries range from too rigid to too loose.

When your boundaries with your partner are too rigid you'll risk becoming more like cordial colleagues rather than romantic partners. You might hide your feelings and keep the conversation superficial.

If your boundaries are too loose, you might worry so much about your partner's needs that you abandon your own. You might walk around on eggshells to prevent your partner from getting upset or you might never ask for the things you want because you don't want to appear too needy.

If you want to share a social media account and are both on board with that, no problem. If, however, you want separate accounts and don't want your partner to read your private messages, that's OK too. Unless there's been a betrayal in the relationship, you might appreciate having freedom on social media.

Of course, social media is just one small example of an area in your life where you and your partner need to decide on boundaries. There are other types of boundaries you might set within your relationship. Here are some examples of different kinds of boundaries you might set:

- **Physical**: If your partner is in the bedroom with the door shut, do you knock or is it OK to just walk in? If your partner walks away during a disagreement, do you follow them?

- **Financial**: How much money do you feel comfortable spending on something before talking to your partner first? Will you share all your money or keep some money separate?
- **Social**: When scheduling activities with friends that don't involve your partner, at what point would you talk to your partner first? If the plans were on the weekend? If the plans involved spending money? If the plans were during a time when your partner was home?
- **Sexual**: Have you communicated the things you aren't comfortable doing with your partner?
- **Emotional**: If an ex reaches out to you on social media, is it OK to respond? What if an ex reaches out to your partner?
- **Time**: Are there times when you need to be by yourself? If so, how do you communicate that to your partner?

Think about your boundaries with your partner as well as the boundaries the two of you have with people outside the relationship and answer the following questions.

- ○ Are your boundaries with your partner too rigid, healthy, or too loose?
- ○ Are your boundaries with people outside the relationship too rigid, healthy, or too loose?
- ○ Do you think your partner's boundaries with you are too rigid, healthy, or too loose?
- ○ Do you think your partner's boundaries with people outside the relationship are too rigid, healthy, or too loose?

Invite your partner to answer the same questions. You might find that while you think your boundaries are just right, your partner might think they're too loose. Or while you might think your partner is too rigid with boundaries outside the relationship, they might think their boundaries are healthy.

If your partner is willing, compare your answers and listen to one another's thoughts. Don't argue with what you hear or try to justify why that's not true. Just listen to one another's opinion, regardless of whether you agree.

Why We Hesitate to Set Boundaries

Jen grew up in a home where she was taught to be polite—even if she didn't like someone else's behavior. Her parents tolerated intrusive behavior from extended family but then complained about it behind closed doors. She learned speaking up was rude.

So it never occurred to Jen that she should set boundaries with Ethan or that they should establish some firmer boundaries regarding what information was being shared with the outside world. She didn't want to hurt anyone's feelings—but she realized that she was hurting her marriage by not setting boundaries.

There are many reasons why you might struggle to set boundaries. Maybe no one ever set healthy boundaries with you so you struggle to set healthy boundaries with others. Or perhaps you worry that you'll anger or upset people if you set limits. Take a minute and think about whether any of these statements describe you:

- ○ I worry that people will think I'm mean if I set a boundary.
- ○ I am afraid someone wouldn't respect my boundary and then I wouldn't know how to enforce it.
- ○ I'm afraid of abandonment.
- ○ I don't know what I want.

○ I'm not sure what's reasonable when it comes to how people should treat me.

○ I want to keep the peace.

○ I grew up in a home with poor boundaries.

○ No one respects my boundaries so I give up.

○ Other people have criticized my boundaries so I stopped setting them.

If any of those sound true, it's understandable that you may have difficulty establishing boundaries. Of course, you may have some additional reasons why it's hard to set boundaries as well. Understanding those reasons can help you develop a strategy for moving forward.

Mental Strength Exercises

Jen tried talking to Ethan a few times but she felt like she wasn't making much progress. She invited him to attend a session with her so she could talk more about boundaries in the office. During that appointment she said, "Ethan, I know you're upset about my financial situation. But I can't go back and change it. I don't want you to disparage me in front of your friends and family anymore. Our financial situation is no one else's business. Putting me down hurts my feelings and adds to my embarrassment. I need to know that we're a team and that we're working on solving this problem together."

She told him that if they both agreed that someone else should know about their financial situation, they needed to talk about it together first before revealing any information.

Behind closed doors, Ethan was willing to tackle the financial situation together. He agreed that as a married couple, it was both their responsibilities to pay off the debt. But, in front of other people, he felt like he needed to refer to their debt as "Jen's debt." He was embarrassed sometimes that they didn't have a lot of extra money and his jokes were a weak attempt to save face in front of other people.

He asked how they should explain why they can't attend a friend's destination wedding or what they should say when family asked them to do things they couldn't afford. He didn't want to lie.

They spent a few minutes talking about their options. Jen said, "Let's just say we're working hard on some specific financial goals right now so we'll have to pass." No one had to know whether their goal involved paying down debt or retiring at forty. It was an honest answer they could agree on.

They decided to set aside an hour each Sunday night to sit down and address their finances so they could make sure they were working together as a team and setting healthy boundaries with outside people. They also agreed to meet with a financial planner who could assist them in making healthy long-term decisions about their money. While Ethan was confident he was good with money, this would give them both some assurance that they could work together on their financial goals.

During Jen's final session with me, she said, "I feel like Ethan and I are finally on the same team and that he's not going to try and blame me or embarrass me. It feels good to know that we can work together on this."

Set Boundaries Within Your Relationship

Just because you're in a committed relationship doesn't mean you can't have privacy. Like we discussed in Chapter 2, you can still have your own friends, your own social media accounts, and time to yourself that doesn't involve your partner.

But the two of you get to decide what rules you want in your relationship. There's no right or wrong way to have boundaries.

Boundaries are personal. So what's right for you and your partner might not be right for another couple. But here's a look at some examples of healthy boundaries a couple might set within the relationship:

- Knock on closed doors before entering.
- Ask permission to look at my phone.
- I'm OK holding hands in public but am not comfortable with other public displays of affection.
- I'm going to need to talk to my ex about co-parenting issues on a regular basis.
- Don't ask me what I talked to my therapist about.

Spend some time thinking about any boundaries you may want to set in the relationship to become the best version of yourself. Then, communicate that boundary with your partner in a positive way.

You might say, "I've noticed I'm frazzled lately and it's because I'm not taking care of myself. I've decided that when I get home from work now, I'm going to go on a thirty-minute walk and during that time, I'm not going to use my phone."

Think about whether there are times when it feels like your partner is infringing on your space and consider whether you need to set a boundary. Also, ask your partner if there are any boundaries they would like to set with you. When everyone is clear on their expectations, you don't have to guess what one another wants.

Set Boundaries Outside the Relationship

Developing healthy boundaries within your relationship is only half the battle. You and your partner also need healthy boundaries that protect you from outside forces. This might prevent a meddling family member from intruding on your relationship or it might ensure that you aren't giving away resources you share (loaning someone money without first talking to your partner).

Without healthy boundaries, friends may demand too much of your time, family may want a lot of attention, other people's opinions might affect your connection, and relationships with others might cross the line into dangerous territories.

You may think listening to your mother tell you how much she disapproves of your partner over and over again doesn't really hurt anything. But allowing someone to speak ill of your partner can affect how you feel about them.

While there is some research that shows the "Romeo and Juliet effect" may have some temporary merit, the rebellious love that thrives on disapproval from a parent doesn't last. That's why it's important to set boundaries with parents and in-laws. Don't let them meddle in your relationships. It's also important to be aware of the impact your other networks (including your social network) have on your relationship. If your friends, colleagues, and online connections express frequent disapproval of your partner, their opinions will impact how you see yourself, your partner, and your relationship.

That's why boundaries with the outside world are essential. Listening to your mother lecture you about what a loser your partner is will take a toll on you. Spending time with your single friends who try to convince you that you'd have more fun if you were single too can create tension in your relationship. If you're in a healthy relationship, limiting unhelpful influences from the outside world is key.

Boundaries shouldn't just be reserved for people who aren't happy with your relationship, however. Your mother-in-law might have great intentions—but insisting that she visit every day might still take a toll on your time together even if she's a great person. Your brother might think your partner is a great person but letting him crash on your couch for a month might be bad for your relationship.

Of course, it'd be great if you and your partner always agreed on how to set boundaries with other people. But life is messy and relationships are complicated. There will likely be many times when you disagree about how to handle well-meaning friends, struggling family members, nosy neighbors, and attractive coworkers.

> Life is messy and relationships are complicated.

Think about how you might respond to the following scenarios. Your response can give you insight into your boundaries:

- Your mother-in-law says things to your kids like, "Your parents really shouldn't worry so much about sugar. Eating a few sweets won't hurt anything."
- Your cousin says, "You shouldn't let your partner go on all these business trips. Sometimes people on business trips get themselves into trouble."
- Your friend asks, "Can you loan me a few hundred dollars to cover my rent? I had some unexpected expenses and I'm running a little short."
- Your partner meets up to talk to a friend who is having a "personal crisis." Do you ask what the crisis is?
- Your child asks to sleep in your bed tonight.
- A cousin going through a divorce asks, "Can I stay at your place until I get back on my feet?"
- Your friend calls every evening and your partner says it's infringing on your time together.

If your partner is willing, ask them how they might respond to those scenarios. Consider how their answers differ from yours.

There isn't a right or wrong way to answer. But understanding how you differ in certain areas can help you plan for circumstances where you may need to set a boundary. That isn't to say you'll always agree on a boundary—you won't. But awareness of your differences can help you have conversations about areas where you're willing to compromise and areas where you aren't.

Consider whether there may be some areas where you could establish tighter boundaries with the outside world. Doing so can protect your relationship from outside influences that may create problems for you.

Address Boundary Violations

When you set a boundary, you've drawn a line that you don't want crossed. When someone crosses that line, you might be tempted to move the line. But changing your boundary line just because someone crossed it isn't a good idea.

That's not to say you can't make some exceptions to the rule or that you can't shift your boundaries over time. Boundaries should be flexible.

Let's say you and your partner agree to stop lending money to a relative because you know they are struggling with a drug problem. But then, your partner says they gave them $30 to buy food. If you're uncomfortable with that idea, talk about why you think giving money to someone with an addiction is a poor idea.

Here's another example. What if you tell your partner that you don't want your fertility issues discussed with extended family, and you find out that they told their parents? That's a boundary violation. Addressing it might involve saying, "I asked you not to talk to your family about our fertility issues right now as I am having a hard time and I don't think it's their business. But I overheard you telling your mom about my doctor's appointment and I'm upset about it. Please don't talk to anyone about this right now." You may want to find a way to balance your need for privacy with your partner's need for emotional support.

You don't always have to talk about boundary violations. You can communicate your boundaries with your behavior instead. If you've told your parents that you don't want them to argue in front of the kids and an argument breaks out when you're at their home, pack up the kids and leave. You don't have to explain. Instead, say, "Time for us to go," and walk out. If you do this a few times, you'll show your parents that you mean what you say and they might choose to stop arguing in front of the kids—or you might choose to stop bringing the kids over for a visit for a bit if it's an unhealthy situation.

You don't necessarily need to cut someone out of your lives just because they've crossed a boundary. People often test the limits a few times to see how you'll respond. If you remind them of your boundary, they may grow to see that you're not going to back down and they may change their behavior.

Who's Motivated?

Take a minute to think about who thinks there's a problem and who is motivated to create change. Then you can decide how to approach your situation best.

1. You struggle to set boundaries.

You might be tempted to "keep the peace" by refusing to set boundaries in the first place. But avoiding boundaries comes at the expense of your inner peace.

If you think, "I don't want to make the other person feel bad," or "They won't listen and then I'll feel worse so there's no use in trying," it's a sign you should set a boundary.

Boundaries should help you feel physically and emotionally safe.

They shouldn't be about trying to force someone to change their behavior—not even if you think their actions are self-destructive.

If you don't want anyone to smoke in the house, by all means, establish that boundary. But don't create that boundary just because you want your partner to quit or because you don't want your brother-in-law to visit. Creating a boundary that is meant to change someone else's behavior won't work.

Your boundaries can be flexible. And most of the time, you don't have to establish them in an emergency situation. You can always say, "This is what I'm choosing to do for right now," and then you can do something different later if you want.

2. Your partner struggles to set boundaries.

If you think your partner gets taken advantage of by friends or family or you suffer consequences because they refuse to set boundaries, establish your own boundaries.

It's best if your partner sets the boundaries with their own friends and family. So have a conversation about it and encourage them to try.

It's OK to start small. If your partner's parents have been meddling for a decade, asking them to take a giant step back might be too much. But if your partner can let them know that from now on you won't be discussing your parenting practices over dinner, that could be a step in the right direction.

Share how you feel about your partner's lack of boundaries—whether you're anxious, frustrated, or overwhelmed. And offer to problem-solve some strategies for setting boundaries that would help you feel more comfortable.

If your partner struggles to set boundaries, they will also likely struggle to handle boundary violations. You can help by pointing out your observations and inviting them to weigh in. Say something like, "I know it probably feels awkward to talk to your sister about the fact that she came over again when we weren't home after we asked her to stop doing that. But I think it's important for you to say something so she realizes that we are serious about this. What do you think?"

3. Your partner thinks you struggle to set boundaries.

Listen to your partner's concerns. Do the boundaries (or lack of them) affect them directly? Or are they worried about you?

For example, if they think your boss asks too much of you, it may not really affect them but they may encourage you to set boundaries because they care about you. However, you might be concerned that setting a boundary could harm you (like perhaps you'd get fired). So it's ultimately up to you to decide how to proceed. You might find that your lack of boundaries indirectly impacts your partner (like they're tired of hearing you complain about your job). In that case, you may decide to stop complaining about work so much.

If they're concerned that your lack of boundaries has a more direct effect, listen closely. You might not want to tell your mom that she should knock on your door before coming into your house. But if it upsets your partner, perhaps it's a boundary you could consider setting.

4. You both struggle to set boundaries.

If you complain a lot about the same things or people, it's a sign you probably need to set a boundary with someone.

If you agree on the boundary, work together to decide how to proceed. Should one of you have a conversation with the person? Should you both sit down and talk to the person? Should you both just begin to change your behavior to make the boundary clear to other people (like leaving family events as soon as political conversations get underway)?

Start with small steps and remember, setting boundaries takes practice. But if you support one another's efforts you'll make the process easier for both of you.

How Boundaries Help You Grow Stronger

Jen came back for a six-month checkup after she ended therapy. She said that overall things had gone well with Ethan since she created some boundaries.

They had a few issues they had to work through—like they disagreed about how much money to pay toward her debt and there were a couple times when Ethan still referenced her debt to his family. But overall, she felt like she and Ethan were finally working together as a team.

She said, "I feel like we can now attack the debt, not each other. I didn't really even realize how much Ethan's comments to people about my debt were affecting me and our relationship until he stopped doing it."

Jen knew that there would always be new situations that would pop up that would require her to continue to revisit boundaries. Most recently, several people had asked them when they were going to have kids—and that was something she also didn't think was anyone's business and she wanted to make sure Ethan agreed that they didn't need to announce their wishes or their plans to other people.

Overall, she felt more confident about herself and her relationship now that she was clear on how she expected to be treated. And she felt optimistic that she and Ethan could work on whatever future issues they encountered as long as they kept talking about boundaries.

Boundaries with your partner establish how you expect to be treated. They should demonstrate self-respect and allow you to become the best version of yourself.

Healthy boundaries can help you thrive as an individual while also helping you feel safe and secure in your relationship. That safety is key to giving you the freedom you need to build mental strength.

Troubleshooting and Common Traps

Disagreeing on external boundaries

You may never agree on all your boundaries. But it's important to talk about your feelings. Consider your disagreement an opportunity to problem-solve and work together on a project. It's a time to practice talking about your feelings, listening to how your partner feels, and to see if you can find creative solutions that you can both live with.

You don't like a boundary your partner has set

You don't have to like boundaries or agree with them to honor them. Respecting a boundary shows that you respect your partner's feelings. So while you may feel hurt or even embarrassed by doing so, honoring a healthy boundary is good for you, your partner, and your relationship.

> **You don't have to like boundaries or agree with them to honor them.**

Confusing boundaries with controlling behavior

Healthy boundaries involve self-respect, not controlling someone else. If your partner does not want you to talk to an ex, that may be a healthy boundary to honor. But if your partner doesn't want you to talk to your family, that may be a sign of abuse. A controlling partner may want to isolate you from anyone who is likely to point out that their behavior isn't normal.

Setting boundaries when emotions are running high

We all say things we don't mean when we feel emotional. "I'm never going to your parents' house ever again!" or "If you ever do that again, I'm not going to talk to you!"

The more emotional you feel, the less logical you will be. When you calm down, you'll likely see your threats were over-the-top and irrational.

When you make a mistake and establish a boundary that you don't want to keep, apologize (if you've announced it) and create a healthy boundary (if it's warranted).

It's best to avoid this situation altogether by waiting until you feel calm to establish a boundary. A boundary is rarely an emergency.

And you can always create a temporary boundary. You might say something like, "We aren't able to say yes to that right now. We're going to need to take our time to think about this," or "We're going to press pause on this for now until I feel calm enough to make a good decision."

Conversation Starters

Spend a few minutes answering the following questions for yourself and then, if your partner is agreeable, ask them the same questions. It can be a great way to start thinking more about creating healthy boundaries for your relationship.

- What's a boundary we've set for ourselves that you think is healthy?
- When is a time that you had trouble setting a boundary in life but you're glad you finally did?
- How did you find the courage to set that boundary?
- What's an example of a boundary I've set with you that you try hard to honor?
- What are some warning signs we might see that would signal we could use better boundaries with each other?

- What are some warning signs that we might see that would signal we need better boundaries with other people?

Interview with Nedra Glover Tawwab

To further the conversation about boundaries and how they affect couples, I turned to the world's top boundary expert, Nedra Glover Tawwab. Nedra is a licensed therapist, *New York Times* bestselling author, and a sought-after relationship expert. She has provided relationship counseling for fifteen years and she's the founder and owner of Kaleidoscope Counseling, a group therapy practice. Her books include *Set Boundaries, Find Peace,* and *Drama Free.* She's garnered a huge social media following by helping people discover how to set boundaries without feeling guilty, so I wanted her to offer some more insight on what she's discovered about boundaries through all of her work with couples.

What do you think are some of the biggest misconceptions people have about boundaries?

Many people think that boundaries mean estrangement or cutting someone off completely. While cutoffs are a type of boundary, it is not the only type of boundary. Healthy boundaries are flexible and allow room for change or growth.

What is the most common boundary problem you see with couples?

Unspoken expectations. Your partner cannot read your mind and it is unhelpful to expect them to. Practice asking for what you need together.

Can you share an example of a couple you've encountered who struggled to set boundaries either with each other or with people outside of the home?

One couple argued frequently about chores, time management, and even if they had a future together. They would often spend hours apart after disputes. Their communication during conflict was almost nonexistent.

Needs and expectations should be communicated at the beginning and during every relationship.

I see a lot of people who struggle with their relationships with in-laws. From meddling mothers-in-law to overbearing fathers-in-law, a partner's parents can be an issue. What are some problems you see with in-laws and why do you think those relationships can be so tough to navigate?

Parenting style differences and not respecting privacy are two common problems. These relationships can be difficult to navigate because in-laws are the family you marry into. As an outsider, you may see things very differently than your partner and in-laws.

What do you say to someone who says it's tough to set boundaries because they want to be "nice"?

Boundaries are about you and your needs. Sometimes we may fear that setting boundaries will cause backlash or not be well received, but often the story we're telling ourselves isn't true. Setting healthy boundaries is being kind to yourself.

CHAPTER 4

They Don't Become Martyrs

Forty-seven percent of people feel resentful about all the work
they do and sacrifices they make for their relationships.
—Couples by the Numbers Survey

Kevin called my office to set up an appointment for couples therapy.
He said that he and his wife, Leah, argued a lot and needed to find
ways to communicate better. When they arrived for their first appointment, they sat on the couch next to each other—which was a good sign.
Sometimes one person sits in the chair as far away from their partner as
possible, which can be quite telling about their feelings. But they sat next
to one another as they politely waited their turn to share their respective
viewpoints.

Leah thought Kevin didn't value family time enough and Kevin
thought Leah expected way too much from him.

Kevin owned a construction company and Leah was a stay-at-home
parent to their two boys. Kevin's long days as an entrepreneur made it
difficult for him to attend his kids' after-school activities but he did his
best to be there for every single one.

He thought Leah didn't appreciate the sacrifices he made for their
family. He earned a good income and did his best to be present for
family activities.

"She complains if I'm twenty minutes late to a soccer game," he said.
"She doesn't care that in order to make it to the game, I had to skip three

meetings, make business calls during halftime, and had to rush back to work as soon as the game was over."

But Leah's take was, "After he takes an hour or two to attend the kids' events, Kevin reminds me how much work he is going to have to make up—as if I should feel guilty that he went to his kid's game. He talks about how hard he works to support us but doesn't recognize that because he's working all the time, I'm left to do everything else!"

So while Kevin thought Leah should applaud his efforts, Leah was tired of hearing how overwhelmed he felt. "It's as if he doesn't think it's overwhelming to have to manage our household and raise our kids practically on my own because he's working all the time. Sometimes I feel like a single parent but all he wants to do is tell me about how rough he has it at work," Leah explained.

Leah said Kevin seemed annoyed whenever she asked him for help. She said, "Just the other day I asked him to put some boxes in the attic and he said, 'Why not? I do everything else around here.' But he doesn't do everything around the house. I do!"

Although they were still allowing one another to talk without interrupting, Leah was clearly getting more exasperated with each sentence.

Kevin admitted he got upset when she asked for his help recently but he said he was annoyed because she disrupted his concentration when he was working. He said, "She acts like every little thing is an emergency. I have a lot of work to do so it's not really a priority for me to do her odd little jobs!"

Kevin spent weekends doing paperwork for the company. And although Leah offered to help, he refused. Leah, who had a degree in business, was more than capable of managing the paperwork but Kevin insisted he do it himself because it'd be "easier that way."

Kevin also turned down opportunities to do fun things even when his paperwork was done. If friends invited them out for a night, he'd often say he had things to do around the house. He said things like, "My life isn't like yours, Leah. I have a job and other responsibilities too."

Leah said, "We fight all the time about who has it 'toughest.' But I think Kevin makes things tougher on himself on purpose just so he can show me how tough he has it!"

Kevin denied this, saying that Leah didn't understand how much pressure he was under as a business owner and he was frustrated that Leah was ungrateful for all the things he did.

Fortunately, they agreed to try couples counseling to address the issue, and we started scheduling weekly appointments. I'll share what happened with Kevin and Leah a little later. But first, think about your own relationship and the sacrifices each of you make.

Maybe you can relate to Kevin—you feel like you're forced to do everything in the relationship. Or maybe you can relate to Leah, where you feel like you're with someone who refuses help yet insists they have to do everything. Most of us feel a little resentful at one time or another because we're putting in more work than our partners.

Quiz

Take a minute to review the following statements. How many of them describe your experience?

- ❑ We argue about who suffers the most.
- ❑ I sometimes feel resentful about how much I do for the relationship.
- ❑ We argue about who contributes the most to the relationship or the household.
- ❑ I think I've sacrificed more than my fair share of things in life to preserve the relationship.
- ❑ My efforts aren't appreciated.
- ❑ I don't think my partner understands how much I really do for the relationship.

- ❑ When my partner offers to help me, it's never enough.
- ❑ I constantly abandon my own needs and wants to put our relationship needs or the family's needs first.
- ❑ I frequently complain about having to do everything.
- ❑ It's tough to accept help from my partner.

If some of those statements sound true, you might feel resentful about all the sacrifices you make. And if you don't address that resentment, things might get worse. Fortunately, there are steps you can take to address this.

Starting Point

Kevin and Leah were stuck in an unhealthy pattern. When Kevin complained about how much he was suffering, Leah insisted she was suffering just as much. They couldn't validate one another's feelings because they were too caught up arguing over who had things worse. So while they were able to stay quiet while the other one was talking (they had an incredible ability to avoid interrupting one another), they weren't really listening to each other. Feeling invalidated made their pain worse and they both grew more resentful of one another by the day.

Healthy relationships require sacrifice. In some cases, that might mean a big sacrifice. You might give up your dream to be a rock star so you can get a job that pays the bills. Other sacrifices are minor—like perhaps you go for a walk with your partner after dinner each evening even though you hate walking around the neighborhood.

Martyrs insist on showing their partner they're suffering the most.

Becoming a martyr is different. Martyrs insist on showing their partner they're suffering the most. They want their partner to know they don't ever get to be happy because they're giving up everything for the sake of family. Even when they're encouraged to do something kind for themselves, they refuse.

Their behavior often triggers guilt in those around them who aren't sure how to help—and family members feel confused when their offers to assist are rejected.

Being a martyr is tough because you'll never feel as though your efforts are recognized enough. Being in a relationship with a martyr is just as tough because it's impossible to remove the burden your partner insists on carrying, yet you'll have to endure hearing them insist on suffering out loud.

Martyrdom is a continuum. On one end of the spectrum, you find people who refuse to make sacrifices. These are the individuals who say, "This is my life. You can step into my world but don't expect me to change how I do things."

On the other end of the spectrum, you'll find individuals who say, "I have to do everything and I never get any help!" When someone offers to help, they resist, or complain that the help they received wasn't enough. And they're angry and resentful about how much they do.

In the middle, you'll find people who make healthy sacrifices with joy. That doesn't mean they're always thrilled about the things they give up. But they recognize that what they're giving up is a choice and they're making that choice because they want to, not because they have to.

Take a minute and consider the following questions:

- Do you make enough sacrifices for the relationship?
- Do you make too many sacrifices for the relationship and it's caused you to grow resentful?
- Does your partner make enough sacrifices for the relationship?
- Does your partner insist they make too many sacrifices?

If you feel like a martyr sometimes, you're not alone. But it's important to address the situation before things go too far. If you're thinking that there's nothing you can do because you have to make all these sacrifices, don't worry. There are several different ways to tackle the situation and we'll discuss those a little later in the chapter.

Why We Become Martyrs

When Kevin arrived at their children's soccer game twenty minutes late, he expected Leah to say something like, "Thank you so much for making this happen! I know you must have gone through a lot to try and be here for the boys during work hours!" Instead, Leah lectured him for being late.

In turn, he would then list all the ways in which going to the game set him behind and tell her he would have to work late because he'd sacrificed to take time off. He thought the fact that he still squeezed in as many of the kids' after-school or weekend activities as possible went above and beyond the call of duty. He also felt frustrated that Leah didn't appreciate he spent his weekends doing paperwork for the business.

We discussed his resistance to letting Leah help. At first, he said it was just easier if he did it. But he eventually said he thought his role was to earn money and if he let Leah help, that would mean he was failing to do his job.

Since Leah never acknowledged his hard work, he felt he needed to prove to her that he was making huge sacrifices and suffering along the way. At times, he took on more struggles on purpose just to show Leah he was sacrificing and suffering.

Like Kevin, sometimes people get confused about healthy sacrifices and they overdo it. Then, they aren't sure how to stop.

Someone working two jobs to support the family may keep working both jobs even when they're a little more financially stable because they think bringing in money is how they add value to the relationship.

Another person might have some unhealed childhood wounds—like they grew up caring for a parent who had a health problem. Perhaps they had to give up after-school activities and time with friends to care for the parent—and now as an adult, they're desperate to continue doing for others because they can't recognize their own needs.

Martyrdom can also stem from the idea that suffering somehow makes you kind or improves the world. And while there are people who do voluntarily give up comforts to help others, their actions become unhealthy when they become bitter about it. Then, they're not actually doing things for others.

Evidence suggests a little suffering is good for us. Studies have found that moderate adversity throughout your life might make you more resilient to certain stressors. But there's no evidence that daily suffering makes you a stronger, better person. Give yourself permission to enjoy life, accept kindness, and ask for help.

Martyrs often suffer for no real reason. Staying up until 2 A.M. to clean the house doesn't necessarily make the world a better place.

They might be looking for recognition too. They may put themselves in harm's way to look like they've pulled off a heroic feat in the end—like taking the last flight home for the day on a business trip and then showing up in the office the next day and making sure everyone knows they barely had a chance to sleep. Or they might say yes to lots of voluntary things only to then complain that they have so much to do that they can't possibly find time to eat or go to an appointment.

Martyrs believe they don't deserve to be happy, and they reject anyone's attempts at showing them kindness. They may think if they suffer long enough and loud enough, they'll finally gain something they're missing in their lives but as time passes, it may become apparent that they won't find what they're looking for by being a martyr. Yet, it's a tough role to step out of if you've invested a lot of energy into always offering to take the raw deal.

I've also seen people who think if they can prove they've suffered the most, they should get their way with a big decision. "If I work at a horrible job for a decade because it pays well, then I deserve to be able to move back to my hometown to be closer to my family," or "If I give up everything to be a stay-at-home parent, then I deserve to be able to spend a lot of money on myself."

Mental Strength Exercises

Kevin and Leah chose to break the pattern they were stuck in. With the help of therapy, Leah learned to validate Kevin's feelings. Rather than tell him he didn't need to work so much, she started acknowledging the pressure he felt.

For several weeks, she just acknowledged his feelings. And Kevin appreciated being heard. Then, Leah began to offer help and Kevin worked on learning to accept it.

In the therapy office one week Leah said, "You work long hours and it's stressful for you. I want to help. But when I offer to help, you won't let me. It leaves me feeling bad that there's nothing you want me to do and we both get frustrated. I'd love to work together to find a way to stop this pattern that we're in."

For the first time, Kevin acknowledged that he has trouble accepting help and Leah shared that she wanted to help him reduce the load he's carrying—if he in fact did want help.

We developed a plan. Kevin would work on asking for help. Rather than make a complaint, he would make a request. Instead of saying, "I'm so stressed out!" he could identify something Leah could do to help and then ask for that help. He might say, "Can you please file these receipts?" or "Would you be willing to help me with paperwork for a few hours?"

Leah would help when he asked for it. And slowly, she started doing regular bookkeeping for the business. When he shared some of his work, they had a little more time together in the evenings before they went to sleep. Leah always pointed out how much she enjoyed it when they could spend time together.

Kevin had to trust that asking for help and allowing Leah to assist didn't mean he wasn't doing his job. And Leah learned to stop expecting him to attend every single activity the boys were involved in. If he missed a baseball game or he showed up late to an event, he wasn't a neglectful parent. It meant he was a hardworking father. Leah also recognized that she could acknowledge Kevin's stress without diminishing her own. They weren't in competition over who had the most work or who had the hardest life. Instead, they could cooperate and empathize with one another.

Part of the solution involved changing the way they thought about things. But it also meant changing the way they treated one another. By the time they ended treatment, they were communicating better, supporting one another more, and no longer arguing about who had the most work to do.

Look for Patterns of Martyrdom Outside the Relationship

Being a martyr isn't always contained to a romantic relationship. But it can still affect you as a couple.

You might be the workplace martyr who insists you have to do all the work for every project. Or you might be a martyr when it comes to helping your parents because you don't think your siblings will pitch in—and if they did, they won't do it right.

You might also do everything for your adult child—like doing laundry for your thirty-year-old. Even if your child asks you not to help, you might continue doing things for them if your self-esteem depends on it.

If you have a pattern of doing too much, refusing help, and complaining about how much you have to do, you might need help from a professional. If it's your partner who could use a little help, talk about it. Explain how their choice to try and sacrifice everything impacts you.

Reframe Your Thoughts

When you think things like, "I have so much to do and my partner refuses to do anything!" take a step a back and examine the truthfulness of the thought.

Do you really have to do everything? Perhaps the dishes could wait until tomorrow or maybe you don't have to do all the laundry tonight. You might choose to do those things, of course, but you don't *have to* do them.

Also, pause and look at whether you asked your partner for help. Are you just assuming they won't help? Did you outright ask for assistance?

You might find you can replace your unrealistically negative thoughts with more realistic statements. Here are a few examples:

- ✗ **Unrealistic thought:** No one ever helps me.
- ✔ **Realistic thought:** Sometimes people are willing to help, especially if I ask for it.

- ✗ **Unrealistic thought:** I can't let my partner help because they never do anything right.
- ✔ **Realistic thought:** I could let my partner help and they may do things differently than I do.

- ✗ **Unrealistic thought:** I have to get all this done tonight and my partner doesn't care.
- ✔ **Realistic thought:** I can choose to do this work tonight if I want. I may feel more pressure to get it done than my partner does.

When you're feeling bad, your thoughts will become exaggeratedly negative. And the more negative you're thinking, the worse you'll feel. You can interrupt the pattern just by examining your thoughts and replacing unrealistic statements with more realistic ones.

Practice Asking for Help—And Accepting It

A common problem involves using complaints instead of requests. Instead of saying, "Can you help me clean this mess up?" you might be more likely to say, "This is such a big mess! It's going to take me all night to clean!"

You might think you're dropping strong hints or that they should get the message and make an offer. But your partner isn't a mind reader.

Unless you tell your partner what you need, they're going to be left trying to guess what would help. Let's say you're complaining that your boss gives you too much work. Do you want your partner to give you advice on how to set a better boundary with your boss? Or are you looking for emotional support and validation?

Or if you complain about how much cooking you have to do for a holiday, are you hoping your partner will pitch in and offer to help cook or are you hoping they will agree not to invite their entire family over for a meal?

There are many ways to solve a problem. Tell your partner what would be helpful to you. This can prevent unnecessary frustration and ensure that their offers have a better chance of being useful.

Who's Motivated?

Take a minute to think about who thinks there's a problem and who is motivated to create change. Then, you can decide how to approach your situation best.

1. You want to stop acting like a martyr.

If you have martyr-like tendencies, consider what you gain from being the martyr. Do you want to look like the hero? Does your work-horse status make you feel valuable? Do you just want your pain to be seen and heard?

Now, consider what your commitment to being a martyr is costing you. I guarantee it's damaging your relationship in some way. You may be complaining too much or showing bitterness toward those who offer help.

Ask yourself, "What would it mean if I allowed someone to help?" Would it mean I'm incompetent? Lazy? Average? Weak?

Once you identify your fears, begin addressing them head-on. Ask yourself, what's the evidence my fear is based in reality? What's the evidence my fears are exaggerated or irrational?

Next, have a conversation with your partner. Let them know you realize you often insist you have too much to do or that you have to suffer more than everyone else. And share that you want to work on that.

Develop a plan together if you can. You might decide that you'll identify one thing your partner can do each day to pitch in. Or, when your partner offers to help, you'll accept it.

Ask your partner to hold you accountable as well. It will take some courage but it could be crucial to helping you make changes. They might be able to gently point out when you're acting hostile or when you're not accepting the support that is being offered.

2. You want your partner to stop acting like a martyr.

If you think your partner acts like a martyr sometimes, take a compassionate approach. This can be tough, especially when they resist your kindness. But they're working hard to show you that they're suffering.

Make it clear that you understand and that you believe them—they're in emotional pain. Acknowledge their hard work and validate their feelings even if you think it's a little out of proportion to the situation.

You don't have to agree with your partner's feelings to validate them. Instead of saying, "You don't need to make the house look perfect before your mother comes over," say, "I know it's important to you to get things in order before your mother comes. And I get it that it's frustrating for me to pitch in because I don't organize things the same way you do."

> **You don't have to agree with your partner's feelings to validate them.**

Make an offer to help, but only offer once. Don't argue or insist on helping. If your partner says no, say something like, "Let me know if you change your mind."

Show appreciation for what they do and encourage them to cut themselves some slack sometimes. You might offer some kind words when they take time off to do something fun or say something like, "It's great to see you relax. You deserve a break." If they insist they aren't having fun or they tell you that they don't have time to relax, don't argue.

If your partner is open to it, problem-solve together. Sit down and talk about the fact that your partner feels like all the responsibility falls on them. Discuss how they might relieve some of their workload or how they might get some help. Remember, your assistance might not always be the solution. They might prefer someone else help them—and that's OK too.

3. Your partner thinks you should stop acting like a martyr.

If your partner has suggested you have a bit of a martyr complex, you might have denied it—at least at first. This is tough to hear. Your response might have been, "I don't *think* I have to do too much, I really *do* have to do too much!"

But even if you don't believe that your sacrifices are doing more harm than good, if your partner thinks they are, consider the possibility.

Ask them what things you do that cause them to think that. Are you bitter? Do you work too much? Do you make snarky remarks about how what you want in life doesn't matter?

Even if you don't feel like a martyr, you should still be aware of those behaviors as they can damage your relationship.

Be open to the idea that perhaps your sacrifices come with a bit of hostility or perhaps you refuse to delegate because no one does anything right. Becoming aware of how you come across might inspire you to make a few changes.

4. You both want to stop acting like martyrs.

If the two of you get into contests about who suffers the most or who has the most to do, no one is going to win. There's no prize for suffering the most, doing the most work, or sacrificing the most happiness for the sake of the relationship.

You might need to just agree that you both work hard and you both make sacrifices but there's no need to compare apples to oranges. Let's say you're suffering because you agreed to move to a city you didn't want to live in so that your partner could take a job that requires them to work long hours. That doesn't make you a champion of sacrifice. Instead, everything you do as a couple will likely require some sacrifice from both of you.

Validate one another's feelings. When your partner talks about how bad their day was, instead of responding with something like, "Oh yeah? Well, my day was even worse. Listen to this . . ." you can say, "That does sound like a stressful day." Share about your day too, but no need to one-up one another.

How Refusing to Be a Martyr Makes You Stronger

Kevin and Leah weren't acting like a team. Kevin insisted on being a martyr—and Leah responded by trying to prove that she was suffering endlessly too. It was as if both of them were carrying heavy weights and when they got tired, they complained their load was too heavy but refused to allow one another to lighten the load. And when Kevin complained the weight he was carrying was too heavy, Leah lacked empathy because the load she was carrying was also heavy. The key to lightening their loads was to work together.

Once Leah acknowledged how much work Kevin was doing, he felt understood. And then, he became more open to the idea of letting her help him with work on the weekends. Their relationship grew stronger when they tackled a problem together. Rather than argue, they freed themselves up to take productive action as a team. At their final appointment, Kevin said he felt less stressed and happier. And Leah said she felt relieved and less frustrated. They both agreed they were now focused on cooperating, rather than competing to see who could suffer the most.

A healthy relationship involves teamwork. Of course, there will be times when one person does more than the other. And there will be certain areas where one partner will do more throughout the whole relationship. But being a martyr isn't about who does the most or who sacrifices the most—it's about attitude too. The person who is a martyr might not even do more work than the other. But they might insist they do or show resentment about the things they do.

And when one person is a martyr, it leaves both people feeling discouraged and let down by the other.

If you insist on suffering as a martyr you'll never feel heard or understood enough. Your partner will likely grow exhausted from trying to remove the burden and they'll feel frustrated that they aren't allowed to help.

When you give up the need to always be the hero or to always prove that you've suffered the most, you and your partner can work together as a team. And each of you will be motivated to contribute to the relationship without keeping score.

Troubleshooting and Common Traps

Your thoughts about not getting enough help might be rooted in reality

There may be times when you're not being a martyr but you're legitimately overwhelmed by all the tasks you need to do. If you need help, ask for it. Avoid passive-aggressive attempts to get help—like sighing loudly or sulking. Instead, ask for what you need. If your partner declines, decide what to do next—keep working on something on your own, ask someone else for help, or step away from what you're doing.

You disagree on what needs to be done

Sometimes the reason one person feels like a martyr is because the couple doesn't agree on priorities. One partner might do most of the housework because they think the house should be spotless while the other person has a much higher tolerance for clutter or a mess.

Or one person might do more with the kids because they think the kids need more entertainment than the other partner does. If you disagree on how much work to put into certain things, have some ongoing conversations about it. You might never agree on exactly how much effort to put into something, but you may be able to find a solution so you can work as a team without one person feeling like they need to do everything.

You Refuse Kindness from Each Other

If your partner offers you the better seat when you're watching a play or they offer to give you the last piece of cake, don't automatically decline. Allowing your partner to show you kindness is good for everyone.

People feel good when they're kind and helpful—especially to their partner. If you always turn down your partner's offer to help, you take that opportunity away from them. So give yourself permission to accept acts of kindness from your partner and remind yourself, you don't always have to be the one who suffers more or who gets the worst end of everything.

Conversation Starters

Take a few minutes to answer these questions. If your partner is interested in building mental strength, use these questions to get the conversation started.

- What's an example of a time when I accepted help from you and you were glad that I did?
- What's an example of a time that you accepted kindness from me even though that may have been a little hard to do?
- What's a good example of a time or an area of our lives when we've shared the workload?
- What do you think was helpful to us during that time or in that specific area that helped us share the load?

Interview with Andrea Bonior

Healthy relationships require some natural give and take but it's common for one individual to do more. I wanted to hear Andrea

Bonior's perspective on this. She is a psychologist in private practice who has written several books, including the wildly popular *Detox Your Thoughts*. For fifteen years, she was the voice behind a *Washington Post* advice column called "Baggage Check." Now, she hosts a podcast that's also called *Baggage Check*, where she talks about psychological topics such as stress, relationships, and depression. She shared her insights on common issues she sees surrounding martyrdom in relationships.

Sometimes people grow resentful because they think they have contributed more than their fair share to the relationship. Can you share a story or case study where you've seen this happen? Did it get resolved?

I have definitely seen this resolved, but I think the biggest predictor of whether that can happen is whether the person carrying the resentment is able to be vulnerable in talking about it, without simply escalating their anger or finger-pointing, and whether both members of the couple are truly motivated to work on it.

For instance, I was working in individual therapy once with someone who just had so much pent-up frustration with her partner. It was a very classic problem, as in my client was carrying the majority of the mental load between the two of them, having to initiate, plan, and strategize so much of what needed to be done day to day for keeping up their home, their social lives, and extended family relationships, and caring for their young baby. It's a very common dynamic where on the surface, the division of labor looks somewhat equitable, but one person is actually doing the project managing of that division of labor—which means they are carrying the mental load of always being on top of it, even if they eventually delegate tasks to their partner.

So, my client was carrying around so much frustration, but also a little bit of confusion about the frustration, because she felt like she should be grateful that her husband did more than what some of her friends' husbands did, and she also felt like when she gave him tasks, he did them, so she felt like she had nothing to complain about. But in reality there was a nonstop cycle of planning and strategizing and initiating all the tasks, and that planning all fell to her, and that was what was totally unequal.

So, we strategized about how to talk about it, to pick a good time for the conversation, and not be accusatory but rather to talk about her feelings. And to express love and appreciation, and also explain that she needed him to take custody of certain things and become the project manager of them—relieving her of the mental load. That it wasn't enough for him just to be given the traditional "honey-do" list, even if he was good at completing it.

When it was put in these terms, he was surprised at first, but he eventually got it. And he started to take more pride in being in charge of things himself, rather than just waiting to be told what to do.

What do you say to someone who insists they have to do everything in the home or in the relationship because if they don't, it just won't get done?

I try to help them see that they are setting themselves up for a situation that is not fair to them, nor to their partner, and that it will rarely be sustainable. When the imbalance is so extreme, with one person doing so much more than the other (whether because they think they have to because it won't get done otherwise, or for some other reason) it is really rare to just get used to it without consequences.

Typically, resentment starts to corrode the relationship, and gets in the way of emotional intimacy, and even trust, respect, and attraction. And the partner who is not doing much is aware of the imbalance too, but feels helpless to change it because it has been so ingrained—and they often feel judged and belittled.

What words of wisdom do you have for someone who finds themselves in a long-term relationship with a martyr?

I think it's worth giving serious thought to how this is affecting your relationship, and whether this dynamic is sustainable. It's not healthy for either of you to feel like there is this level of imbalance, whether it's in the actual work being done or the way the partner wants credit for it! Think about having a conversation about the way it makes you feel, and the ways it takes a toll on your connection. And ask if they are willing to work on it—really work on it—together.

Do you think that someone who insists on being a martyr learned to do so in their family of origin? What might be some of the root causes?

I do think it could trace back to childhood. Not always, of course, but sometimes. I think a lot of times it has to do with people never really feeling appreciated or validated. And so they are always trying to get that validation from others—maybe it's hard for them to find it themselves. Or, deep down maybe they fear that they don't have anything to offer unless they are trying to run everything or give so much to others. They worry people will leave them otherwise. Sometimes it has to do with gender roles too, and what their expectations are about who runs the show.

Self-care is important but a lot of people feel guilty about doing nice things for themselves. How can people practice self-care when they're in a relationship and what are some ways in which people can take care of themselves?

I think a lot of times, we look at self-care strategies like time alone as automatically detracting from a relationship. So we might feel guilty spending time on our own if we have a partner. But everyone needs some solo time—and sometimes two members of a couple might need different levels of solo time, and neither one of them is wrong—just like one partner may need an hour more sleep each night than the other. Think about what you need to stay energized and nourished mentally, and try to value it in the same way as things like physical needs (that you most likely wouldn't deny yourself!).

If someone feels like they've already given up a lot for their partner and their family, what can they do about the resentment or anger they already feel?

I think they need to be realistic about whether or not they are actually allowing their partner to try to make amends and make things better or more equitable. Because I think sometimes we fool ourselves and the reality is, we want there to be an imbalance because it allows us to stay angry—and maybe that's easier than letting go of our anger and moving forward. Or maybe we've gotten so comfortable with this dynamic that although we are angry, we kind of like the idea of the other partner always feeling a little bit like they owe us something, so they can't ever make up for it—and we can't really imagine letting go of that.

But of course, this isn't everyone. Many of us are just plain resentful because we have reason to be! And that resentment can't go away if the imbalance keeps persisting. Because you can't heal from the anger or the resentment if you feel like your partner doesn't get it, and doesn't understand your viewpoint, and doesn't validate it. So it really takes having some genuine conversations where you try to empathize with each other—which of course, professional support can help with.

CHAPTER 5

They Don't Use Their Emotions as Weapons

Thirty-seven percent of people think their partner uses
emotions like anger and sadness as a manipulation tactic.
—Couples by the Numbers Survey

Jillian was a thirty-five-year-old teacher who started therapy because she wanted to learn to communicate better with her husband, Marcel. They'd been together for five years and married for three but during that time, she thought their communication was getting worse. She said, "I don't want to trigger him but sometimes, it seems like everything I say or even the way I say it sets him off."

Marcel had endured a rough childhood. Jillian wasn't sure of the details and Marcel didn't like to talk about it. But she knew he'd been abused and neglected and the last thing she wanted was to do or say anything that would make his life worse. But she felt like she was walking on eggshells around him.

Whenever she tried to address an issue, he was quick to say, "You know I hate conflict!" So, she stopped confronting him or talking about anything serious because she didn't want to upset him.

But Marcel did things she found upsetting. For instance, he refused to visit Jillian's family. He said Jillian's mother was too outspoken. This was distressing to Jillian—she liked spending time with her parents, and she always had to decide whether to stay home with Marcel or attend family gatherings alone.

Jillian said, "I spend a lot of time guessing what Marcel wants. He doesn't tell me so I try to guess by his mood if he needs space or if he needs me to coax him to go do something and get out of the house."

Marcel said phone calls made him anxious so Jillian scheduled his appointments for him. But getting him to attend the appointments was tough. If he didn't feel like meeting with the doctor or didn't want to see the chiropractor when his appointment time rolled around, he'd tell Jillian to cancel on his behalf.

Jillian didn't invite people into their home often because she never knew what kind of mood Marcel was going to be in. If he was in the mood to be alone, he might lock himself in the bedroom rather than eat dinner with their guests. Or he might get up and walk out the door without saying a word. Jillian was left explaining to their guests that Marcel was working through some things but she felt embarrassed by his behavior.

"I don't always guess correctly what he needs, though," said Jillian. "The other day I pushed him too hard to get up off the couch and go outside. It sent him into a depressive state for like three days."

Jillian hoped therapy could help her better understand trauma and Marcel's needs, so she could find ways to be more supportive of him. But I didn't think the problem was that she misinterpreted Marcel's behavior. It wasn't her responsibility to cater to Marcel's ever-changing moods.

But I didn't tell Jillian that right away. I wanted her to see for herself that she didn't need to continuously adjust her behavior based on Marcel's moods.

Jillian eventually discovered that Marcel was using his emotions to manipulate her—I'll explain more about that later in the chapter. But first, consider whether there may be times when you have used your emotions as a way to try and manipulate your partner—and whether you suspect your partner has done the same to you.

Quiz

Take a minute to think about how many of these statements sound familiar.

- ❑ I've cried during a conversation to make my partner stop talking about a difficult subject.
- ❑ I have expressed anger during a conversation with my partner because I wanted them to change their viewpoint.
- ❑ I have tried to use guilt to make my partner change their behavior.
- ❑ I have accused my partner of being selfish to get them to change their behavior.
- ❑ I tell my partner I can't discuss certain topics surrounding our relationship because the subject matter is too upsetting.
- ❑ I try to get out of doing certain things by telling my partner I'm too anxious to do them.
- ❑ I use the silent treatment when I'm angry.
- ❑ I remind my partner that I'm too fragile to handle certain things.

Now, review these statements to see whether they sound true for your partner. If these statements describe you or your partner, you might sometimes use your emotions as weapons. Fortunately, there are steps you can take to manage and express your feelings in a healthy way while also getting your needs met.

Starting Point

I spent the first few sessions with Jillian talking about how much responsibility she wanted to accept for helping Marcel manage his moods and deal with past trauma. Initially, she thought it was her job to make sure Marcel always felt good. But she acknowledged that was an impossible task. As hard as she tried to help Marcel, she wasn't able to make him happy all the time.

We talked about his mental health as well. Jillian realized that trying to make him happy all the time wasn't actually being supportive. She could support his efforts to get professional help instead. She also learned she didn't have to allow his emotional expressions to control her behavior.

But her most telling insight may have been when she said, "I'm starting to think he's better at managing his emotions than he lets on. He pretends he can't keep things in check just to get out of doing things. I think I'm being manipulated." Once she drew that conclusion, she wanted to learn how to become less reactive to Marcel's behavior.

A healthy relationship allows you to express your feelings appropriately while also showing respect for the other person's feelings. But some individuals use their feelings as a weapon.

They show anger because they want to end a conversation. Or they cry because they want to get their way. They express their emotions in an attempt to manipulate the situation.

Sometimes the emotions are completely feigned. Someone might not actually be angry but if they raise their voice and pretend to be, they know the conversation will end. At other times, the emotions are genuine, but their expressions are exaggerated.

It's not just emotional expressions that become weapons, however. Some individuals plant feelings within their partner. They work hard to cause the other person to feel guilty or selfish. Then, they prey on those emotions to their advantage.

If we looked at the emotional expression spectrum, on one extreme end you'll find people who hide their emotions, which isn't healthy either. Research shows hiding your emotions also hurts your relationship.

Researchers from the University of Genoa, Italy, found that the more one partner hid their emotions, the more the other person avoided a close attachment to them. That, in turn, led to more concealed emotions and decreased relationship satisfaction.

Smiling when you're sad and insisting you're not angry when you are is bad for your relationship. But so is exaggerating just how awful you feel.

Healthy emotional expression is good for your mental health and your relationship. That means talking about your feelings and expressing yourself in a way that is congruent with how you feel. You might take a break from a conversation when your emotions become too intense or you might conceal your emotions a little when it's not socially acceptable to show them (like not jumping for joy when your least favorite colleague gets transferred).

Now that you have a better idea about what it means to avoid using your emotions as a weapon, take a minute to answer the following questions.

○ Do you sometimes use your emotions as a weapon against your partner?

○ Do you suspect your partner sometimes uses their emotions as a weapon against you?

Why We Use Our Emotions as Weapons

As Jillian reviewed the way Marcel expressed himself and managed his emotions—storming off, refusing to make phone calls, isolating himself when guests came over—she realized his actions were effective ways for him to get his needs met. If he sulked, she catered to him. If he got mad, she backed off. If he said something was too hard, she did it for him.

Jillian had grown up watching her mother appease her stepfather, who had a drinking problem and a bad temper. She'd seen her mother go to great lengths trying to prevent him from blowing up. Her mother worked hard to anticipate what would set him off but she didn't always get it right.

While she didn't know the details surrounding Marcel's childhood, she suspected he'd grown up watching people weaponize their emotions. Perhaps his behaviors also helped him survive everything he'd been through, somehow.

For instance, Marcel may have learned in childhood that his emotional expressions were a good way to get what he wanted. Some kids learn at an early age, "When I show explosive anger, people spring into action." Or, "When I show people I can't control my temper—and they can't control it either—they work on controlling themselves so they don't anger me."

Or too, he may not have known how to deal with conflict or how to communicate how he was feeling. Jillian and I weren't sure—Marcel wasn't my client. But what we did know for sure was that Jillian could change the dynamic in the relationship by changing her behavior.

She didn't need to walk on eggshells around him. Marcel could feel angry without acting aggressive. He could feel sad without sulking. And he could manage his anxiety with healthy coping strategies. Perhaps, if she stopped making his manipulation effective in their home, Marcel would look for new coping strategies that might serve him better.

Like Marcel, many people use their emotions as weapons simply because it works. If you insist you're too anxious because you want to get out of doing something or you raise your voice because you want your partner to stop talking, those strategies might be effective ways to get what you want.

You also might find you use your emotional expressions to control others because you feel like your real emotions are out of control. Trying to control other people with your emotional expressions might feel like a good way to control your internal chaos.

Difficulties managing your emotions might not be your fault, but it's your responsibility to find healthy ways to express your feelings. Those emotional expressions shouldn't be used to manipulate your partner's behavior. Fortunately, you can learn healthier ways to express your emotions and meet your needs.

Mental Strength Exercises

Jillian hesitated to hold Marcel accountable for his feelings at first. She thought he was fragile and if she held him to higher expectations, he would fall apart under the pressure.

But we talked about how Marcel managed his emotions in other areas of his life, such as work. Jillian acknowledged that Marcel must handle his emotions OK when he was on the job as he'd worked for the same company for over five years without any problems that she was aware of.

He also seemed to manage his emotions well around his mother and his siblings. And Jillian didn't think the family necessarily gave him any special treatment. In fact, his mother often asked for his help and Marcel always pitched in. He attended family gatherings and, according to Jillian, Marcel's family was dysfunctional but Marcel seemed to manage himself well around them. He appeared to be better than his siblings at regulating his emotions, so he was often the voice of reason when dealing with his own family. Jillian said, "I think their dysfunction is familiar to him—so he almost becomes the leader in the family and he rises to the occasion to make sure things are OK when there's an issue. It's like he's a different person with them than he is with me."

She had proof that he could handle his emotions if he wanted to. Which meant he must also have had some skills to handle conflict and keep his feelings in check.

That wasn't to say he was lying when he struggled with those things at home. Instead, it just might mean they'd gotten caught up in unhelpful patterns. Jillian had the power to disrupt those patterns by changing her behavior.

Whenever Marcel would say he couldn't handle something, she would believe him. But believing him didn't mean she had to allow herself to be treated poorly.

She developed a plan that involved strategies such as:

- Being proactive before company came over. She let Marcel know if he disappeared while she was entertaining his friends, she'd assume he needed ten minutes alone. If after ten minutes he didn't return, she would go knock on the door and invite him to rejoin the conversation.

- She would go to her family events regardless of whether Marcel went. She would invite him and encourage him to go to the big family gatherings, where his contact with her mother would be limited.

- She would no longer walk on eggshells if she had a concern. She would regularly discuss issues with Marcel. She was open to either discussing them as they came up or having a once-a-week meeting to review them. If Marcel walked away from a conversation, she would give him an hour and then they would revisit the conversation.

- She would allow Marcel to schedule his own appointments—unless he specifically asked for help. She would let him be responsible for making the calls and getting himself to his appointments and he could accept the consequences if he didn't show up.

As Jillian started making these changes, Marcel initially insisted it wasn't fair and that she clearly didn't understand his needs. But Jillian held firm and let him know that if he couldn't handle his anxiety or manage his temper, those were opportunities for him to seek professional help. Over the course of several months, Jillian said Marcel started to change as she changed how she responded to him.

By the end of our time together she said he was taking more responsibility for his emotions. He could ask for help when he needed it but was no longer using his inability to manage his emotions as an excuse to get out of doing things he didn't want to do.

Create Emotional Rules for Your Home

You probably have some unwritten rules for how emotions are expressed in your home. Is it OK to slam doors when you're angry? Some families slam doors all the time. In other households, that might feel like a violation of sorts.

Or how about sadness? If someone goes to their room to be alone, would they be encouraged to retreat to their own space to work through their emotions? Or would you worry that the person is isolating themselves and they wouldn't be allowed to withdraw? Some families accept the person needs space while other families would insist they come out of their room.

Even happiness and excitement may have rules. Do you cheer loudly for a sporting event on TV? Or would you stay neutral even during an intense game?

People express their emotions differently and at different intensities based on factors like culture, personality, and life experience. And when couples get together, they figure out how much emotion the other person expresses and how those feelings are expressed.

You don't necessarily have to be on the same page. One of you is likely more exuberant than the other and that's OK. But you do need to know what one another is comfortable with in the home.

You don't have to tell your partner to show less emotion. But you could say, "When you get really excited about the game and start yelling, it sends my body into a state of panic for a second. I'm going to get some help with that from a therapist but if you could also let me know when you're watching a game ahead of time, that'd be great. I'll put on my noise canceling headphones and listen to a podcast in the other room."

You might also point out behaviors that you've tolerated that you might want to change. For example, you could say, "I notice we slam doors in this house whenever we're angry. I wonder if we could find another way to tell someone that we're upset without being so disruptive?"

Consider the unofficial rules in your home. Are you comfortable with them? Are there any you'd want to change? If your partner is open to a discussion, talk about your rules and if there are any they'd like to change.

Take Responsibility for Your Feelings

You affect how your partner feels. Just the sound of your voice might help them feel better after a long day or a hug from you might boost their mood. But it's their responsibility to have additional coping skills that can also help them so they don't depend on you to regulate how they're feeling.

It's important to take responsibility for your feelings while also allowing your partner to take responsibility for theirs.

Respect your partner's emotions. If a conversation becomes intense, take a break if they need it. Or, if they're too anxious or too sad to tackle something, your role may be to step in and help. It takes trust to know that they're not just exaggerating their emotions to manipulate your behavior.

> It's important to take responsibility for your feelings while also allowing your partner to take responsibility for theirs.

The last thing you want to do is imply that they don't actually feel all that bad. Invalidating your partner's feelings could be quite damaging to the relationship. Give them the benefit of the doubt.

But that doesn't mean you have to allow their behavior to dictate your behavior. Separate the behavior from the feeling. They're entitled to whatever emotion they have. They are, however, responsible for what they do with that emotion. You might develop rules like this:

- It's OK to be angry, but it's not OK to scream at me.
- It's OK to feel sad, but it's not OK to ignore me.
- It's OK to feel frustrated, but it's not OK to call me names.

It's essential that you know your emotional limits as well. Make it clear when you're reaching your limit. Say something like, "I am really stressed out right now and I'm not able to have this conversation. I am happy to revisit this issue when I have the emotional capacity to do so."

If you reach your limit often, you may need to work on charging your batteries. That could mean starting a new morning routine so you can feel less anxious during the day. Or it may mean going to therapy to heal old wounds so you aren't quite so limited in what you can handle.

Develop a Plan Together

Your emotions should factor into the decisions you make as a couple. But it's important to consider both of your feelings as you discuss your options.

Let's say you received a job opportunity that requires you to move several hours away. You feel excited about it and you'd love to start packing today. Your partner feels sad about the possibility of moving and they want you to decline. How do you decide what to do? Does your level of excitement need to outweigh your partner's level of sadness about moving? Would you opt out of moving because you don't ever want to do anything that your partner says will bring them sadness? Do you suggest you compromise somehow, like you'll move to the new place and return home on the weekends?

There's not a scientific formula to follow when it comes to making relationship decisions like this. There are too many factors to consider. But it is important to talk to your partner openly and honestly about your feelings—as well as how you think both of your emotions should be taken into consideration to tackle issues.

Who's Motivated?

Take a minute to think about who thinks there's a problem and who is motivated to create change. Then, you can decide how to approach your situation best.

1. You use your emotions as weapons.

If you use your emotions as a weapon, it can be a difficult habit to break. Always insisting you can't do things because you're too stressed out when the truth is, you just didn't want to do them, or acting as though you can't handle things—when you just don't want to handle them—has likely been effective for you. Otherwise, you wouldn't keep doing it.

It's OK to say that you're choosing to stay home and care for yourself. Or that you're opting out of doing something because you are tired. But the exact language you use is important. There's big difference between, "I can't do that," and "I'm choosing not to do that."

You may need to address some underlying issues—like the fear of rejection. You might find it's easier to insist you can't do something than it is to ask for help. If you ask for help, your partner might say no.

Or you might feel unworthy of taking care of yourself or you might worry that caring for yourself is selfish. So rather than say you prefer to stay home, you might insist you can't go because you have too much anxiety.

If you struggle to experience and express your emotions in a genuine and authentic manner, practice identifying and expressing yourself in new ways. With practice, you might find it gets easier. If not, talking to a therapist, listening to mental health podcasts, or learning more about emotional regulation skills may help.

2. You think your partner uses their emotions as weapons.

When your partner expresses an emotion, validate how they're feeling. Even if you suspect they're exaggerating or being a little dramatic, don't say that. Instead, make it clear that you see they feel angry, anxious, or sad.

Support them in finding ways to care for themselves when they have intense emotions. Rather than talk them out of feeling bad (which won't work), encourage them to find a healthy way to manage that emotion (like walking around the block when they feel anxious).

It's not your job to rescue your partner from uncomfortable feelings.

It's not your job to rescue your partner from uncomfortable feelings. They're responsible for how they feel and you don't have to allow their behavior to change your choices. If your partner raises their voice, you're not obligated to change your mind about something.

Instead, you might pause the conversation and at another time when they're calm, bring up that you notice the subject is upsetting but you really want to work through it.

Or, if they have so much anxiety they depend on you to do a lot of things for them, have a conversation about how you can support their efforts to address their anxiety. Encourage them to get help with a professional and offer to be involved in their treatment.

3. Your partner thinks you use your emotions as weapons.

If your partner thinks you're overly dramatic, take a minute and consider whether it's a possibility.

Also, consider whether you and your partner just have different ideas on how emotions should be expressed. Perhaps you get excited when you see the neighbor's dog sitting on his lawn looking cute. Meanwhile, your partner might be the kind of person who wouldn't even break a smile if they just won the lottery.

So you might agree that you show emotions differently. That doesn't mean you're being manipulative, however.

Talk about your partner's expectations in how they think you could handle your emotions. If you're anxious about attending a huge gathering on their side of the family, do they expect you to go at all costs, or would they understand if you said your anxiety was just too high?

Have regular check-in conversations about your emotions. Identify your feelings and share them with your partner. They may better understand you when they know you're nervous or when they are aware that you're sad. Keep in mind that feelings often get lost in translation. What your partner sees might not match up with how you feel. Your irritability might stem from sadness. Or what looks like impatience might be anxiety. So talk about your feelings, discuss your expectations, and problem-solve together.

4. You both want to stop using your emotions as weapons.

If you've gotten into a competition over who has the most hurt or you both use emotions as an excuse to get out of having to do something, talk about it. Take responsibility for your share. When you take responsibility for your behavior, your partner is more likely to accept responsibility for their share.

Discuss difficult subjects for small chunks of time. For example, if you disagree on budgeting issues, don't expect either of you to shift your emotions in a single conversation. Agree that you'll both think about your options and then revisit the conversation at an agreed upon time.

Make it a habit to talk about your feelings. You might decide that each day over breakfast or each night before bed, you'll each say an emotion you felt that day and why you felt it. This could help you better understand one another's emotions while also building your own emotional vocabulary.

How Managing Your Emotions in a Healthy Way Makes You Stronger

When Jillian grew to see that Marcel was competent and capable of managing his emotions, their relationship soared. But, it took a while to get there. In fact, things got worse before they got better.

When Jillian stopped catering to Marcel, his emotional expressions increased. But over time, when he saw that she wasn't going to back down, he learned new ways to manage and express his feelings. He discovered that he could take care of himself, talk about his feelings, and confide in Jillian when he was genuinely overwhelmed.

Jillian learned to talk to Marcel about his emotions too—so she didn't have to guess how he was feeling. If he was feeling anxious about people coming to their home for dinner, they could discuss it ahead of time and come up with a strategy they both agreed to try. For example, they decided he would go to his room for a few minutes and regroup but then would return to socialize with their guests. And if there was something he really didn't want to do, he could communicate that to Jillian ahead of time. During her last appointment, Jillian said, "Once I stopped letting Marcel's weapons work, he changed. And I get the idea he actually feels better about himself now that I've made it clear that I believe he's capable of doing things differently."

A key component in a healthy relationship is trusting the other person. This means you trust that the words coming out of their mouths are true and you trust that their behavior is in line with what they say.

If you and your partner stop using your emotions as weapons, you learn about your own tolerance as well as theirs. You'll discover when to challenge one another by saying, "I know this is scary but I think you should do it anyway," versus when to say, "This is a lot for you right now. Why don't you let me step in and help out?"

Troubleshooting and Common Traps

Not believing the other person's genuine expression of emotions

Accusing your partner of being overly dramatic or telling them that their emotions are nothing more than shallow manipulation tactics will harm your relationship more than almost anything else. So give your partner the benefit of the doubt that their emotions are genuine. That doesn't mean you have to tolerate behavior that is out of line, but you can acknowledge that the emotions behind the behavior might be authentic.

Confusing feelings with behaviors

Emotions aren't bad. Just remember you have choices in how you express those emotions. So, while it's OK to feel angry, becoming aggressive isn't OK. And while it's OK to feel anxious, calling your partner repeatedly while they're at work isn't OK. No matter how you feel or how intensely you feel those emotions, you have choices in how you respond to them and how you express them.

Dealing with a mental health issue

If you or your partner is dealing with a mental health issue, like depression, anxiety, or PTSD, your emotional expressions may be difficult to manage. Personality disorders, such as borderline personality disorder, can increase the likelihood that someone will use their emotions as a weapon. If it's your partner who is struggling, encourage them to get professional help if they aren't doing so already. Be patient with them in the meantime.

If you suspect you might be dealing with a mental health problem, seek treatment. Getting your symptoms under control could go a long way toward helping you feel better.

Conversation Starters

Take a minute to review the following questions. If your partner is interested in learning about mental strength too, use these questions to get the conversation started about your emotions.

- How can you tell when I'm feeling sad?
- How can you tell when I'm angry?
- How can you tell when I'm happy?
- What's an example of a time when you appreciated that I took your feelings seriously?
- What's an example of a time when we've both managed our feelings in a healthy way despite the difficult circumstances?
- How do you think we were able to do that?

Interview with Eli Weinstein

The biggest reason people attend individual or couples therapy is because there's difficulty managing an uncomfortable emotion, like anxiety, sadness, or anger. So I wanted to talk to Eli Weinstein about how he helps people in his therapy office learn emotional skills. Eli is a licensed clinical social worker who treats individuals and couples at his private practice in Las Vegas. He is also the host of a podcast called *The Dude Therapist*, where he tries to help listeners understand themselves and others a little better. I was a guest on his podcast and I appreciated our conversation so I asked him to share how he addresses emotion regulation skills in his therapy office.

What are some of the most common reasons couples come into your therapy office?

One of the more significant issues is the struggle to put aside our focus to let someone else's views, ideas, values, and thoughts into our own lives. This can lead to unmet expectations or communication failure due to our limited perspective, which causes a blockage to our compassion to see the other person for their needs and wants. We find it hard to keep our things in line; we need help to balance someone else's into that mix.

How much of your work with couples involves helping one or both manage their emotions better?

That's the majority of my work. We must learn to regulate ourselves to be our best partners for our loved ones. The emotions we struggle to balance and manage can lead to inner pain and a narrative of resentment, anger, and frustration. This can lead to a lack of kindness/compassion because we are running on pure emotions and letting them run wild and control our mindset.

Do you have a story or case study from your office you can share that involves one partner (or both) whose trouble managing their emotions was affecting the relationship? How did the treatment go?

A familiar story that happens often is the difference in how someone expresses their emotions and how the other partner can view that as an attack or personalized frustration when in reality, it's just venting and letting off the steam of daily life. But sometimes, the person venting doesn't realize how intense it comes off, causing the other partner to feel a lack of safety. Both parties are uncertain about why they feel upset, and neither knows how to express this struggle with the other, leading them to hold things in, emotions bubbling under the surface, waiting to explode with aggression and toxicity.

The focus of treatment was to see themselves for how their actions, behaviors, and words (that includes tone, body language, and choice of words) can impact the other and the other's perception of being attacked and learning to create the distinction between perception/feelings and reality (which comes from awareness of the perspectives and habits of the other) and knowledge of what's going on inside the other partner.

What skills or strategies do you use to help people learn how to manage their feelings better?

1. Learning to be aware of yourself and the space created due to your power, presence, and speech. How do I impact my space and surroundings?

2. Can I make minor tweaks to create a safer, more effective zone for my partner to express and feel comfortable sharing without judgment or backlash? If I can't, what can be done?

3. Pausing between stimulus (thought + feeling) and expression. If we can take two to five seconds before speaking, we can add three key factors to expressing emotions (or any communication, for that matter).

Can I:

Validate- Can I help my partner to be seen + respected at this moment? I heard them and listened to their concerns, stories, and statements.

Compassion- Can I have a kind and compassionate focus on the person I love and care about when I speak to them?

Present- Does this statement, question, or thought impact the now? Does it have a purpose for this conversation, or is it connected to associated feelings/situations that won't help the now?

Aware- Can I focus on the person across from me to truly pay attention to their needs and wants and see what they are asking me now? Stop reading into or making assumptions of perceptions . . . but focus on and be aware of what they are saying and how I can achieve or give them that.

People grow up with very different ideas about appropriate ways to express emotions at home. One partner may have grown up in a home where it was normal for doors to be slammed or loud disagreements to occur. Another person might not be used to such expressions of anger. How do you help couples who have very different ideas of how to express an emotion like anger?

You are 100 percent correct that we all have different backgrounds and precedents that might have been set on the expectations and perceptions of how a household should feel and a relationship should run. So talk about it early and in-depth. Something that helped me when I first got married that I tried to practice (and go over on our anniversary) is called the "Import + Export" list.

The exercise goes like this:

Set a time when you both are calm and relaxed. Talk about your expectations, hopes, and realities for your relationship, home, and family. This is not the time to judge or question each other or your past. But talk through what you want from your backgrounds (import) and what you didn't like and hope to avoid repeating (export).

For me, it was slamming doors and doing our best not to yell (export), but I want our home to be filled with people and open to whoever wanted to come (import).

Take an hour or two. Do it as a date night.

P.S.: Do it on paper with a pencil, so you can edit it, tweak things, and add/remove. The key is not to make this a bible or ten commandments. This is an ever-evolving document between the two of you. My wife and I look through it every anniversary to see if we are sticking to our word and have our lives changed (maybe even our values and perspectives); now that we have kids we need to adjust the list. Feel free to pull it out and talk things through. Keep evolving, keep talking, and keep growing together.

How do you know whether someone should seek individual therapy to work on an emotional issue or if they should attend couples therapy to work on the issue together?

First off, everyone can benefit from individual therapy so they have a place to learn, grow, and gain reflection and introspection of the self. We all have things we need to tweak and polish. No one is perfect, and everyone deserves an objective opinion filled with compassion, no judgment, and care.

When it comes to couples therapy, I feel couples should start as early as possible; sometimes, in the beginning stages of relationships, we begin to set things in stone (habits, the way we communicate, how we deal with one another, quirks and behaviors). It never hurts to have someone to challenge bad habits/behaviors and teach you tools and tips to grow together to have a longer and healthier perspective and practice within your relationship. Be sure to handle the crisis before the crisis happens or feels too much to handle, because from my experience, it can sometimes be too late to pull away from all the settled stuff that has been building for years.

CHAPTER 6

They Don't Try to Fix Each Other

Thirty-six percent of people say their partner tries
to fix the things they don't like about them.
—Couples by the Numbers Survey

When Janice showed up for her first appointment, she said, "I need help talking some sense into my husband, Ken!" She was a well-put-together sixty-year-old woman who said she was relieved to finally have someone to talk to. She was tired of Ken's behavior and needed to know how to change him.

She described Ken as an overweight sixty-two-year-old who had diabetes. For the last six months or so, he'd been stopping by a bar on his way home from work almost every night. He told Janice it was the only time he got to talk to his fellow coworkers about the ridiculous changes they'd gone through at work. They were under new management and some of the "old-timers" hated the new rules.

Janice thought it was great that Ken could unwind with his work friends. But she was concerned about how the alcohol was affecting his blood sugar. When he was drinking, he was less careful about what he ate and less likely to test his blood sugar.

She reminded him that he shouldn't be drinking. But he always brushed her off. She was also concerned that he was drinking on the weekends now too—something he hadn't done for most of their marriage.

"He used to be a social drinker," she told me. "But he started drinking at home more often during the pandemic. I wouldn't worry so much about his drinking if he were a healthy person but with his health issues, even a drink or two is too much!"

When I asked Janice what steps she'd taken to try and address the issue so far, she said, "I've told him to cut back, dumped his alcohol down the drain, told him how much his drinking hurts me, and told him to go to AA meetings. Nothing has worked. I need another plan to get him to stop drinking before this gets completely out of hand." She said Ken always accused her of overreacting and they got into frequent arguments about this.

Janice said, "I am afraid he's going to permanently damage his health if I don't fix this now." What she didn't yet realize was that she couldn't "fix" Ken. She could, however, change how she responded to Ken's drinking and work on their relationship even if Ken wasn't on board.

You'll hear more about how Janice worked on the relationship a little later. But for now, perhaps you can think of some ways in which you've also tried to fix your partner at one time or another. Maybe it didn't involve a substance abuse issue, but perhaps you tried to fix a habit that you don't like. Or maybe you tried to get your partner to change a character trait that you thought was holding them back. Either way, trying to fix someone else—even your partner—can backfire.

Fortunately, though, there are healthy ways to deal with your partner's habits that you don't like and there are strategies that can help you cope when you feel like they aren't doing enough to live up to their greatest potential.

Quiz

Take a few minutes and see how many of the following statements sound true.

- ❑ I try to trick my partner into making healthy changes (sneaking vegetables into their food or hiding their alcohol).
- ❑ I give my partner unwelcome feedback on their behavior.
- ❑ I sometimes feel more like my partner's parent or coach.
- ❑ I think I've made my partner's life better because I've helped them improve so much.
- ❑ I sometimes lecture my partner about their unhealthy habits.
- ❑ I invest a lot of energy trying to convince my partner they should change their habits.
- ❑ I spend a lot of time talking to other people about how I'd like to get my partner to change.
- ❑ I feel sorry for my partner sometimes.
- ❑ My partner has so much potential and I want to help them reach it.

Now that you've reviewed these for yourself, read through them again and think about how many might describe your partner's behavior. If several ring true about you or your partner, you may be spending a lot of energy trying to fix one another.

Starting Point

Janice felt desperate to get Ken to stop drinking. She worried about his health and feared his drinking would get worse. And she was concerned about the toll it was taking on their marriage too.

Her anxiety often turned to anger, and she yelled at Ken when he returned home from work late (which meant he'd stopped by the bar). Even though yelling and lecturing didn't deter his behavior, it didn't deter Janice from trying those tactics over and over again.

Like Janice, you may have seen things in your partner that you were tempted to fix. Perhaps it wasn't quite as serious as the health issue Janice was concerned about, but maybe you felt desperate to do something because your partner was suffering, making poor decisions, or engaging in self-destructive behavior. It's tough to watch someone you love in distress.

It's healthy to want to bring out the best in your partner. You want them to feel happy and fulfilled. When you see areas that could use improvement, it's normal to want to pitch in and help out. But, it's tempting to cross the line and try to fix the other person.

You might want to motivate them or convince them that whatever they're doing is a bad idea. In fact, you might want to do the work for them to spare them the pain of having to change. From nagging to punishment, your efforts to fix your partner can damage the relationship. They can also backfire.

It's important to recognize when you should step in and help versus when you should step back.

What would you do if your partner suddenly came to you and said they'd just read an article that stated eating nothing but carrots for thirty days straight improves health, and they can't wait to try it? Hopefully you'd say that sounds unsafe and discourage them from doing it as it could have serious health implications.

You might also intervene if your usually confident partner suddenly says, "I'm going to turn down this promotion because I'm too stupid to do the job." Hopefully, you'd have a conversation about their fears.

In a healthy relationship, your job is to provide emotional support—and to introduce logic when your partner is struggling to think clearly. Strong emotions can cloud their judgment even if they're level-headed most of the time.

But your job isn't to "fix" them. You aren't a surgeon who is going to repair them. You also aren't their coach or a trainer who needs to educate, motivate, and correct them. You're not their parent who needs to teach or discipline them.

Fixing someone involves a pattern of behavior—not just those moments when you're offering an alternative viewpoint. Constantly rescuing someone from their poor choices or trying to save them from themselves isn't healthy.

Find that healthy balance where you provide support and share your opinion without trying to force them into making changes they don't want to make. Attempting to fix your partner changes the dynamic of the relationship and damages it. Take a minute to really think about answers to these questions:

- ○ Are there things about your partner that you try to fix?
- ○ Does your partner try to fix things about you?

If there are things you try to fix about one another, you're not alone. But there are better ways to influence your partner and bring about change without trying to fix them.

Why We Try to Fix Our Partners

Janice's anxiety was palpable each week she came to therapy. She loved Ken and the thought of him ruining his body with alcohol was almost more than she could bare. She said, "He's hurting himself and our relationship and I don't understand why he won't stop." She was terrified Ken was going to develop another irreversible health condition—or worse yet, die. But she knew that her attempts to talk him out of drinking were failing.

No one wants to see their partner suffer. So it makes sense we go to great lengths to stop them from doing things we think are self-destructive. It might be a single event. You might try to talk your partner out of having a cosmetic procedure that you think is risky.

Or, you might be trying to save them from death by a thousand paper cuts. Smoking one cigarette isn't going to kill them. But smoking every day might. You might grow more and more desperate each day as you try and talk them out of smoking another cigarette.

And while talking to them about your concerns isn't bad, your attempts to get them to quit may turn unhealthy if you become obsessed with getting them to stop.

But it's not just saving someone from physically hurting themselves that leads to "fixing." Maybe you want to fix your partner's "shyness." Or perhaps you've been tempted to fix your partner's poor decision-making, chronic lateness, or quirks that cause you to cringe. If you see them continually making what you perceive to be social blunders, you may want to help them out so they don't embarrass themselves or accidentally offend others.

You might also want to fix the things that affect you. If they're always running late or they make poor financial decisions, it's going to disrupt your life. So it's understandable that you want to fix those habits.

For some people—like Janice—the desire to fix centers around a single issue. For others, the desire to fix is more encompassing. These are the people who act as if they're the construction foreman and their partner is a job that needs to be tackled.

There are also people who have a history of trying to fix all their partners. They get into relationships with people who have unmet needs—substance abuse problems, pending legal difficulties, mental health problems, financial issues, and other chronic crises. And they find a sense of purpose in trying to fix people who may not necessarily want to be fixed.

Mental Strength Exercises

Early on in Janice's therapy, I asked her to identify steps she could take to get Ken to stop drinking. We wrote down the ideas she brainstormed and I encouraged her to keep throwing out potential solutions, no matter how farfetched the ideas seemed.

She thought she could try cutting off Ken's access to the credit cards or hiding his wallet so he couldn't buy alcohol. But she knew those things wouldn't work in the long term. She said she could contact Ken's coworkers and tell them to stop inviting Ken out after work. But that would only upset Ken and they probably wouldn't listen. She even thought of showing up at the bar when he was there and telling everyone to stop serving Ken because they were killing him. But she knew she'd embarrass Ken and that wouldn't change his behavior. Eventually she said, "Short of locking him in a room without access to alcohol, I don't know what else would make him stop. And don't think I haven't thought of that!"

My point in having her brainstorm these far-fetched options wasn't because I wanted her to follow through with any of them. I wanted her to see that Ken's behavior wasn't something she could stop. After our discussion, she acknowledged that even if she did develop some strange movie-plot-like plan to address his drinking in a grand way, Ken wasn't going to create lasting behavioral change as a result.

We discussed what tactics she had tried and the current behavior pattern they had fallen into. When Ken returned home from work late (after presumably being at the bar), Janice yelled at him as soon as he walked through the door. She would tell him to check his blood sugar and he often refused, saying he was a grown man and he didn't need her to remind him of such things. From there, they argued until they retreated into separate rooms for the evening.

So we decided to change that up. On the evenings when Ken returned home right after work (which was usually about two nights per week), Janice would greet him at the door with a huge smile and a hug and say how happy she was to see him. They'd have dinner together and after they ate, she'd spend time with Ken watching their favorite shows and talking about their day. At the end of the evening, she'd tell Ken that she enjoyed their time together.

On the nights when Ken arrived home late and she assumed he'd stopped by the bar, she would eat dinner at the scheduled time and put his food in the fridge if he wasn't home. When he walked through the door, she'd calmly say, "Leftovers are in the fridge. I'm going to go read for a while." No yelling and no carrying-on, even if he smelled like alcohol.

To Janice's surprise, the new approach led to positive results. She and Ken no longer argued. And she felt like she was doing something more proactive than she had before, which helped her relax a bit.

Over the course of several weeks, Ken started coming home in time for dinner a little more often and she felt like the change in her behavior was shifting Ken's behavior without her mentioning alcohol or his health. Once their relationship improved a bit, we discussed how she could talk to Ken about her concerns.

We reviewed what she wanted to say and how she wanted to say it. She planned the conversation for a time when she thought Ken would be most receptive. One night, after dinner, she asked him about his health. She said she was curious to know how the alcohol was affecting his blood sugar. Ken said he hadn't noticed a huge difference in his diabetes, but he said he did notice that he was gaining a little weight and had less energy. Janice took that opportunity to encourage him to schedule an appointment with his doctor, just to make sure everything was OK. Ken agreed to at least think about doing so.

Janice didn't expect Ken to change his behavior overnight. But she thought she may have planted a seed that would perhaps get Ken to think about his health a little more. She didn't want to stop him from spending time with his coworkers after work—but she did hope that he might start opting for less alcohol and more sugar-free drinks.

Once Janice realized she couldn't stop Ken from making his own choices, she looked like the weight of the world had been lifted off her shoulders. Instead of feeling like it was her job to take care of Ken, she started taking care of herself. During her last therapy appointment, she said, "I came here thinking I had to fix Ken. I thought there was something more I should be doing to intervene. I feel much better now that I'm focused on how to respond to him, not how to control him."

Express Your Concern in a Loving Way

Lecturing, nagging, begging, and manipulating won't work. In fact, offering advice to someone who isn't interested usually leads to a defensive response. When you say, "You know what you should do? You should stop going to your mother's house altogether!" your partner isn't thinking about what you've said—they're thinking about their argument against what you just said.

You might even reinforce their position. If you tell your partner, "You should go to sleep sooner," they immediately think of all the reasons why they want to stay up late—I have too much to do, I like watching TV before bed, I don't need much sleep anyway, etc. As they think about all the reasons why they enjoy that habit (or feel they need to do it), their desire to keep doing that thing actually gets reinforced.

People change for different reasons.

People change for different reasons. One person might be motivated to quit smoking because they want to save money. Others might quit because they don't want to get wrinkles or because they don't like smelling like smoke. So don't waste your energy telling your partner why you think they should quit or change their habit.

Think about it like this too. When you were a kid and an adult lectured you, what were you thinking about during that lecture? You probably weren't thinking, "This person is so smart. They're making amazing points right now and telling me things I hadn't even thought of. I'm so glad they're enlightening me. I'm going to change my behavior right away."

If you're like most people, you sat through that lecture thinking about how much you despise the person lecturing you. And you might have been plotting your next move to make it stop—like, "I'll apologize, promise to never do it again, and stare at the floor so I look sad." You weren't really thinking about changing your behavior—you were just looking for a strategy to make the lecture stop.

So skip the lecture but do offer your concern in a carefully planned conversation. Try saying something like, "I love you and you know I sometimes worry about you too. Lately, I've noticed you haven't been wanting to do fun things and you spend more time in bed. I wonder if you might be struggling with something, like depression?" Don't offer advice or a solution as that will likely lead to a defensive response. Instead, start by asking whether they might share your concern.

Then, just listen. If your partner insists they're fine, don't push the conversation further. But if they're willing to talk a bit, just practice listening and asking some questions about how they think they might handle the situation. They may have already been thinking about seeing a doctor or joining a gym but perhaps they feel guilty about spending the money on it or maybe they had been trying to convince themselves that their struggles weren't a big deal.

Your partner might think about what you've said at another time or they may have a conversation with someone else about the issue (like their doctor, or someone who has had a similar struggle). They might not change right now, but perhaps they'll decide to make a change down the road.

Focus on Influencing Your Partner, Not Fixing Them

When is the last time you created a major change in your life because someone told you to? I'm not talking about a minor shift in your work habits or a slight change in your routine. I'm talking about a major change.

If you're like most people, you might say never. If you did make a big change based on what someone else said, think about what inspired that change. Did your doctor tell you that if you didn't make a big change you were going to die? Those words do often inspire change.

The threat of losing something can also inspire change. If your partner threatened to leave you or your boss threatened to fire you, you might have gotten things together fast. But short of threats of death, abandonment, and unemployment, a short conversation doesn't usually lead to an immediate big change.

Instead, we often make change incrementally. Adding a new habit means you have to give up another habit. Let's say you decide to start going to the gym. You may have to give up time with your family or time you used to spend watching TV. You have to factor those things in when you're giving up a habit. Until you're convinced that the benefit of the new habit outweighs the pain of giving up the old habit, you won't want to change.

A good way to help other people see the benefits of adopting a new habit is observation. If your partner sees how staying calm helped you succeed, they might be less likely to keep losing their cool. But it's important not to rub this in their face. Saying something like, "See how I did that, honey? I just stayed calm and persuaded the manager to give us an upgrade and it worked. You should try that," sounds condescending and will likely lead to a defensive response.

You'll be more influential just by allowing your actions to speak for themselves. If you get up and go to the gym every day with a positive attitude, your partner might become a little more motivated to work out too. They might never leap out of bed at the crack of dawn to exercise, but maybe they'll feel motivated to go for a walk during their lunch break.

Instead of criticizing your partner for a behavior you don't like, offer kind words about the behavior you do like. For example, if you tell your partner, "You should quit working so much in the evenings," you might get into an argument. But on a night when you are spending time together enjoying one another's company, you might say, "I love it when we can go for a walk and talk about our day together. It's so nice to spend time with you."

You don't even need to bring up the behavior you don't like as that may seem like a backhanded compliment. If you said, "I'm glad you finally took a night off," your words may sting and have the opposite effect. Instead, reinforce the positive behavior you'd like to see more often by showing your appreciation for it.

Look for Wishes and Dips

Ambivalence about change is completely normal. One day, your partner might say, "I really need to stop getting so frustrated with the kids. I'm going to work on that." Two days later, they might say, "Well, they don't listen unless I raise my voice so I guess that's the only way to get anything done around here!"

Motivation doesn't come in a straight line.

Motivation doesn't come in a straight line. It's going to wax and wane. Even if your partner really wants to do something—like they seem intent on starting a new exercise plan—they will have days when change feels too difficult.

If your partner seems stuck in an unhealthy cycle for a long time, they likely still exhibit wishes and dips. Here's what those look like:

- **Wishes**:Your partner might talk about wishing things were better or wishing they could have something that their problem prevents them from having now. For example, they might say, "I wish I could get my weight down a little so I could get off this medication," or "I wish I could find the time to apply for new jobs so I could find something that I like better."
- **Dips**: When there's a dip in desire to keep up their habit, your partner might say things like, "If I didn't spend so much money on vaping, I wouldn't have so many student loans to still pay off," or "If I could cut back on how much time I waste looking on social media, I might actually have a chance to get something done around here."

Wishes and dips are considered "change talk." They indicate your partner is thinking about making a change. When you hear a wish or a dip, it's your chance to show some curiosity. You might ask a question like, "What do you think we could do to make that happen?" or "How could we get that started?" Then, see if your partner has any ideas or suggestions about how they want to proceed. Remember, don't offer advice and avoid lecturing them. Let them develop their own solutions.

Who's Motivated?

Take a minute to think about who thinks there's a problem and who is motivated to create change. Then, you can decide how to approach your situation best.

1. You try to fix your partner.

Just because your partner recognizes they have a problem doesn't mean they want to fix it, let alone want your help in fixing it.

Reminding them that their habit is damaging to their body, their psychological health, or the health of your relationship isn't likely to spark change. People know that eating too much junk food, skimping on sleep, and using social media too much is bad for them—but that doesn't make them stop. I'm sure you can come up with a habit in your own life that isn't the healthiest—but you do it anyway.

If your partner has a problem, your words might not affect their choices. If a doctor, friend, or someone else points out the same thing you've been concerned about, your partner might listen. That's not to say you didn't do enough—but they may have needed to hear the message from someone else for one reason or another.

In the meantime, focus on everything you can do to be the best person and the best partner that you can. Take care of your health, nurture your spiritual life, engage in your social life, and do things that are good for your psychological well-being.

If your partner has an issue that is taking a toll on you, get professional help. Whether they have a serious issue like a gambling problem or depression, or you disagree with the way they parent or spend money, get support.

If you have a habit of trying to fix people, get professional help. It's a tough habit to break—you might find your self-worth depends on fixing people or you might be trying to make up for a mistake that you made or secretly punishing yourself for something. There are often some deep-rooted issues that can lead to a pattern of trying to fix others.

2. Your partner tries to fix you.

If your partner tries to fix you, it can feel frustrating and even downright demoralizing. So it's important to address the issue. If you don't want your partner to keep trying to fix you, speak up.

Hold a conversation about what you notice. Talk about how you feel and what would actually be helpful to you. Remember, your job isn't to fix their tendency to fix you. But, you don't have to sit through lectures or critiques.

You might say, "Honey, I know you are concerned that I have some self-esteem issues and you give me advice based on what you think I should be doing differently. But right now, those things aren't helpful. I'd appreciate it if you'd stop giving me advice."

There's a chance your partner doesn't recognize what they're doing. If they disagree that they are trying to fix you, offer to point out examples as they come up. Then, each time your partner attempts to "correct" your behavior, say, "This is an example of how I feel like you're trying to fix me sometimes."

If they're trying to address a behavior that directly affects them, listen to what they have to say. If, for example, they're trying to fix your spending habits, it may be because they feel stressed out about the budget and they want you to change your behavior because they're suffering the consequences.

3. Your partner thinks you try to fix them.

There was a couple who used to live next door to me that I used to bump into when we were outside with our dogs. When the woman would say something, like a joke or a comment about the news, her husband was quick to say something like, "She grew up in foster care so she doesn't always know you shouldn't say stuff like that," or "Don't take it personally that she just walks off mid-conversation sometimes. She didn't learn a lot of social skills as a kid."

He would also correct her frequently by saying things like, "Oh honey, don't let the dog go too close to the tree because he'll get the leash wrapped around it," or "You could have negotiated a better insurance rate. You should have said . . ."

When I talked to him individually, he said things like, "I have to teach her about life since she missed out on so many basic things growing up." Meanwhile, she said things like, "He thinks I'm unintelligent and incompetent."

It was uncomfortable to watch as he tried to correct almost everything she did. But just because she did things differently than he did, didn't mean she was wrong.

If your partner thinks you try to fix them, listen carefully to what they have to say. You might be inserting yourself into their choices in some unhelpful ways, regardless of whether you agree with that assessment. Ask them to point out specific examples of the things you do or the times when you try to fix them.

4. You both try to fix each other.

Your partner can bring out the best in you. They can also show you a whole new way of thinking—and a whole new way of life. But that's only the case when you cooperate and work together as a team.

If you tell your partner you want to work on facing your fear of public speaking, they can hold you accountable, check in with you on your progress, encourage you to challenge yourself, and help you find strategies that work for you. But only if you are open to that help. Similarly, you can help them if they want the assistance.

If you're intent on fixing one another, however, and neither of you is invested in change, you're going to experience a lot of conflict.

Whether you're trying to change your partner's eating habits or your partner is trying to convince you to let loose more often, attempting to force change drains your energy and damages the relationship.

Have a conversation about the importance of focusing on self-improvement at your own pace and in the areas of life that you want to change. Discuss how you can support one another in reaching your goals. And if there's something your partner wants you to change and you don't want to change that thing right now, say that. Be clear about saying, "My sleep habits just aren't a priority for me right now but I appreciate the concern."

How Accepting Your Partner Makes You Stronger

Janice initially thought she was saving Ken—and her relationship—by trying to get him to stop drinking. But the more she argued, begged, and tried to change him, the more he resisted. And the more problems their relationship encountered.

Once she stopped trying to fix Ken, she focused her energy back onto responding to his behavior, not changing it. She improved her communication skills—which was also helpful outside of the specific problem they had, and even beyond their relationship.

When people try to fix their partner, they shift from a partnership to a parent/child or teacher/student dynamic. And when one person acts like the parent or the teacher, the other person falls into the role of being the child or the student.

I've seen it happen over and over again in my therapy office. One partner will try and get the other to change and suddenly, the other partner starts acting like a rebellious teenager. Instead of quitting smoking or suddenly becoming financially responsible, they start hiding their behavior the same way a teenager might.

Part of developing a healthy partnership means accepting that your partner is their own person. It's not your job to fix the behaviors you don't like. It's your job to manage how you respond to those behaviors.

You can still have a good relationship with an imperfect partner. And you don't have to try and mold them into becoming a "better" person. You can hold out hope that they might create change at a later time while also accepting that it isn't your job to change them.

Interestingly enough, when the "fixer" decides it's not their job to fix the other person anymore, the person often begins to take responsibility for their actions. An unintended outcome might be that the other person gets better—as does the relationship.

Troubleshooting and Common Traps

Tossing Around the Label "Codependent"

People are often labeled codependent if they become overly involved in trying to convince a loved one to give up a destructive habit. When the term was coined, it was specifically used to describe the wives of men with substance use disorders. But, "codependency" isn't a mental illness.

The behavior exhibited by people who are described as "codependents" is often a survival skill. A mother of three children who calls in sick for her husband (who has a hangover) might be avoiding the consequences she and the children would face if he lost his job. She might be trying to be a good mom given the circumstances she's in. The label "codependent" implies she has a "sickness" that encourages her husband's substance use.

Over time, the use of the word "codependency" has expanded and is often used to describe a multitude of symptoms or problems. But since it's not an actual mental health issue, there's little agreement about what the signs or symptoms are or the treatment. So while someone might be quick to label you or your partner as codependent, take caution with that label. It may reinforce the idea that you're either "codependent" or you're not, or it may imply you have an illness and your behavior isn't your fault. The truth is, we all likely cross the line and try to fix someone once in a while, but it's a behavior we can choose to stop.

Stealth Attempts to Fix Your Partner

If you're concerned about your partner's salt intake and you switch to some low-sodium products without telling them, you're not necessarily doing any damage. But, if you find yourself going to great lengths to trick them into giving up their unhealthy habits, it can start to consume your life.

I've seen desperate partners go to such lengths to try and change their partner's behavior. One man I worked with used to dilute his partner's alcohol with water in hopes she wouldn't drink so much. Or another woman I worked with used to get her family to make comments about how many hours her husband worked in an attempt to make him feel guilty for working so late every night. If you find yourself resorting to drastic measures and trickery, talk to a mental health professional as the situation is going to take a serious toll on you if it continues.

You Disagree with the Approach

Sometimes couples agree on an issue but have a very different idea about how to create change. Let's say you're concerned about your partner's health, and you think the solution is for them to take medication, and they want to just try going to the gym more. Don't force them to adopt your way of change. They may need to experiment with a variety of things to figure out what works best for them. The important thing is that they're trying something and you can support them in their efforts even if you don't think it's the best way to reach a goal.

Conversation Starters

Take a minute to review the following questions. If your partner is open to learning about mental strength, ask one another the following questions to get a conversation started.

- What's an example of a time or situation when you've been tempted to fix something about me but you didn't?
- What's an example of a time that you've appreciated that I didn't try to fix you?
- If I see a self-destructive behavior or a problem with your behavior that you don't see, how would you hope I would respond?
- How can we make sure we support one another and challenge each other to be our best without trying to force the other one to change?

Interview with Julie Hanks

It's common for people to come to couples therapy in hopes the therapist will fix their partner. So I decided to talk to Dr. Julie Hanks about how this plays out in her therapy practice. She is a licensed therapist, coach, author, and relationship expert. She's also the executive director and owner of Wasatch Family Therapy in Utah, and she has twenty-eight years of experience counseling women, couples, and families. She's written two books: *The Burnout Cure* and *The Assertiveness Guide for Women*. I wanted her perspective on how people try to fix their partners.

How often do people come into your therapy office with their partner because they're hoping you'll be able to get their partner to change?

I've rarely met a couple in my office who wasn't hoping to get their partner to change. It is quite rare for me to see a couple where they both take responsibility for their part in a difficult relationship dynamic.

What are some common things people want their partner to change?

Common things people want their partner to change are often related to money, sex, parenting style, in-laws, and emotional connection. However, often these areas are topics that represent deeper emotional longings or relationship patterns that are less obvious.

So often people think if their partner just did something differently or if they just changed, the relationship would be great. Then, they spend a lot of energy trying to fix the other person or convince them to change. Why do you think there's such a tempting tendency to think everything is the other person's fault?

Many people are stuck in black-and-white, all-or-nothing thinking. "It's all my fault" or "It's all my partner's fault,"; "I'm the healthy partner" or "He/she's the sick partner." This binary way of thinking leads them to protect themselves from blame or being bad, wrong, or sick, to avoid feeling shame or thinking "I'm a bad person."

Many people don't have a strong enough sense of self to tolerate looking honestly at how their own thoughts, feelings, and behaviors are contributing to dysfunctional relationships. To look honestly at their part in the relationship dynamic, and not go immediately into shame, takes a level of emotional maturity that many people haven't developed yet.

What tips do you have for someone who knows they devote too much energy to trying to fix their partner rather than work on themselves?

I would encourage the person focused on fixing their partner to explore their own fear. I would ask, "What do you think it would be like if you let go of trying to change your partner?" "What is your biggest fear about primarily looking at yourself and your part in this relationship?"

I would help the individual explore why they want their partner to change and look at what unmet childhood needs they are seeking to meet through their partner. This doesn't mean letting their partner off the hook. It means owning their own needs, learning how to meet their own emotional needs, or learning to reparent themselves, and making requests of their partner (instead of demanding that their partner change).

Another tip is to turn their complaint about their partner around and see how it applies to them. For example, the complaint "My partner disengages with me emotionally when we disagree on parenting" becomes "In what ways do I disengage with my partner when we disagree?"

What about someone on the receiving end of that? If they feel like their partner is trying to fix them, what can they do?

The people closest to us have the most to teach us. Those we live with often see our blind spots, or areas where we need to grow of which we are unaware, very clearly. If you have a partner who is trying to change you, consider whether what they are highlighting is one of your blind spots.

I would teach the person to identify and share with their partner the impact of him/her trying to change them. "I feel hurt and scared when you nag me consistently to spend less money because I think you're trying to control me. It would mean a lot to me if we could sit down and go over finances together, and if you could get more curious about why this is such an intense topic for you."

CHAPTER 7

They Don't Communicate with Disrespect

Thirty-six percent of people say their partners are
sometimes rude, condescending, or disrespectful.
—Couples by the Numbers Survey

When Trevor and Haley showed up to their first appointment together, it was clear that they could only agree on one thing: they were constantly fighting. "We can't have a normal conversation anymore," Trevor said. Haley agreed, but that's where their common ground ended.

They'd been married for six years and their arguments had increased over time. And they argued about everything from household responsibilities and money to parenting and extended family.

During that first appointment, their body language spoke volumes. Haley sat in the chair with her arms folded tightly across her chest. Trevor sat on the couch on the edge of his seat the entire session. When I asked them what they hoped to accomplish in therapy, Trevor said, "We need to learn how to communicate better. Haley doesn't know how to have a conversation without yelling."

Haley rolled her eyes and said, "I have to yell because you can't listen. Besides, we don't need to talk more, anyway. You need to learn to do more around the house! The more we talk about problems, the less time you'll have to get things done."

As I went through the list of questions we ask everyone during the first appointment, I got a glimpse of some of their communication patterns. They raised their voices, used sarcasm, interrupted, blamed each other, and put one another down repeatedly.

Before the end of that first session, I gave them a checklist of common disrespectful communication habits. Their first homework assignment was for each of them to keep track of their own disrespectful communications. I asked Trevor to check off the disrespectful behaviors he exhibited each day and for Haley to check off the disrespectful behaviors she exhibited each day.

Both of them initially insisted they wanted to keep track of when the other person was disrespectful to *them*, not the other way around, but I told them that wasn't the assignment. They weren't to give any input on what went on each other's lists either. I didn't want one of them saying, "You better be putting this on your list!" during their conflict.

They returned the following week with their lists. Both of them had checked off plenty of disrespectful behaviors they exhibited each day. We discussed what it was like to look down at their lists and realize just how many times they were disrespectful to each other. Haley said she was surprised to see how often she was rude and Trevor said it was "eye-opening" to see the list on paper. Fortunately, they agreed to start weekly therapy to address their communication patterns. I'll explain what happened in their treatment a little later in the chapter.

While you might not have a long list of disrespectful things you've done to your partner every single week, you've likely been disrespectful at one point or another. It might have been something minor, like a long sigh while your partner was explaining something. Or maybe it was more passive—like you never looked up from your phone the last time your partner was telling you about their day.

Respectful communication is vital to a good relationship, but it's often the first thing to go out the window when a couple is struggling.

And poor communication erodes the connection fast. Fortunately there are skills and strategies that can help you get your needs met without damaging the relationship.

> It's crucial to distinguish disrespectful behavior from abuse. These are a few examples of verbal abuse but it's not an exhaustive list. If you or your partner becomes abusive at times, seek professional help. Here's what constitutes abusive behavior:
>
> - Threats
> - Intimidation
> - Screaming
> - Swearing
> - Shaming/humiliating

Quiz

Take a minute to review the following statements and see how many of them sound like you.

- ❑ I roll my eyes at my partner.
- ❑ I say mean things to my partner.
- ❑ I call my partner names.
- ❑ I make disparaging remarks about them.
- ❑ When they ask me not to say certain things about them or to them, I do it anyway.
- ❑ I share embarrassing things about them in front of others even though I know it bothers them.
- ❑ I have mean-spirited nicknames for my partner.
- ❑ I use sarcasm with my partner often.
- ❑ I raise my voice sometimes.
- ❑ I use a disrespectful tone of voice.

Now, review the statements again by thinking about how many of those statements sound like your partner. If you or your partner use disrespectful communication take action immediately before your communication efforts degrade further.

Starting Point

During Trevor and Haley's second appointment, we established ground rules for their therapy sessions. We were going to discuss tough subjects and tackle uncomfortable issues. My office needed to be a safe space, and repeating their disrespectful communication patterns during their sessions would compromise that.

They agreed to the rules. There would be no yelling, no name-calling, and no put-downs. If someone was disrespectful, we'd pause to address it right in the moment.

If they could shift the way they communicated—even if it were only in my office, for one hour per week—they might be able to start making some healthy relationship changes.

How partners communicate often reflects the way they feel about one another. Individuals who speak highly of their partners tend to have deep feelings for them. On the other hand, individuals who disrespect their partners often have underlying disdain for them.

Of course, it's not always that simple. For example, someone with an anger management issue might be disrespectful when they're upset. Their words don't reflect their overall feelings about their partner, but instead reflect their inability to regulate their emotions.

Disrespectful communication sometimes involves active behaviors—like name-calling. But there are also passive disrespectful behaviors, like not looking up from your laptop when your partner tries to tell you something.

While all disrespectful communication can damage the relationship, certain patterns can be big red flags. Relationship researcher John Gottman identified four communication styles that can predict the end of a relationship. He refers to them as "the four horsemen." Here's what they look like:

1. **Criticism**: While giving your partner constructive feedback can be helpful, attacking their character isn't. Calling your partner selfish or lazy, for example, leads to an escalating pattern of unhealthy communication.
2. **Contempt**: While criticism attacks someone's character, contempt includes an air of superiority. It often involves sarcasm and mocking and is the single greatest predictor of divorce.
3. **Defensiveness**: In response to criticism, someone may blame the other person. If their partner asks if they picked up the dry cleaning, they might bring up the time their partner forgot to pay a bill. It escalates the situation.
4. **Stonewalling**: In response to contempt, someone might disengage to end the attack. They may engage in another task or turn away from their partner to show that they aren't going to have a discussion.

Even if your relationship has degraded to the point that you recognize the four horsemen, don't despair. It's not too late and you aren't destined for divorce. You can create positive change by shifting the way you communicate.

Here are a few more examples of disrespectful communication:

- Using your phone when your partner is talking to you
- Not consulting your partner before making a major decision
- Interrupting
- Name calling

- Teasing your partner when they ask you not to
- Using the silent treatment
- Lying
- Making insensitive jokes

Here are some examples of healthy communication:
- Active listening
- Maintaining a conversational tone
- Apologizing
- Using humor appropriately
- Staying calm

Take a minute to think about your communication with your partner, then answer the following questions:

○ Do you communicate disrespectfully toward your partner?
○ Does your partner communicate with you disrespectfully?

If you or your partner are disrespectful, it's essential to break out of that habit as treating one another poorly is one of the fastest ways to degrade a relationship.

Why We Communicate with Disrespect

Trevor and Haley were kind to one another when they were dating—and they got along better in the early years of their marriage. But as life got busier, they became increasingly impatient with one another. Their disrespectful communication increased over time and when one of them was unkind, the other returned the barb with their own jab.

You've seen how quickly a conversation can go downhill. Whether it's a miscommunication in a workplace meeting or it's a snide comment at a family event, one disrespectful comment can lead to a huge disagreement.

When conversations like that are repeated in the home between romantic partners, disrespectful communication can quickly become the norm. And it's tough to turn things around and start communicating in a healthier way.

Whenever you spend a lot of time with someone, it's easy to get annoyed by their habits. Anything from chewing too loudly to repeating the same story for the zillionth time might feel like they're tap dancing on your last nerve.

That annoyance often becomes evident in communication. You might sigh loudly and roll your eyes or say, "Do you have to make a call every time you get in the car? You yell into your phone like it's a tin can on a string!"

The words you use, the body language you display, and your tone of voice are all just a few ways you communicate with your partner.

But why is it that the person we are closest to sometimes becomes the person we speak to with the most disrespect? A 2014 study published by the Association of Psychological Science examined this idea. The researchers coined the term "everyday aggression" after confirming that we're most likely to take out our aggression on the people we encounter in our everyday lives. The study drew three conclusions:

1. The people we interact with most frequently are most likely to anger us.

2. We have the power to hurt people with direct action (like a verbal attack) or nondirect action (like the silent treatment).

3. The way we hurt people depends on our relationship with them.

It's likely the people we spend the most time with have the greatest chance of annoying us. We also sometimes get a little too comfortable in knowing that someone close to us won't leave us if we are rude. Over time the disrespect escalates as each partner hurts one another's feelings and those issues are left unaddressed.

Mental Strength Exercises

We tackled Haley and Trevor's communication from two different directions. We addressed the unresolved issues that contributed to their disrespectful communication. And we looked at improving their communication so they could better manage their unresolved pain.

Stories of hurt feelings emerged as we discussed how resentment had built over time. Haley was a stay-at-home parent for about six months after their daughter was born. They had planned for Haley to stay home until their daughter started school, but Trevor became worried about their financial situation and encouraged her to find work. Haley reluctantly returned to work, but was angry that Trevor went back on their plan.

Haley never told Trever that she felt resentful about this. He thought she was on board with the plan the entire time.

Two years later, when Trevor started talking about wanting another baby, Haley said she wasn't ready. She wanted to keep working a few more years to save enough money to stay home longer with their next child. Trevor was resentful she wanted to wait, but he didn't speak up.

We uncovered several more examples of unresolved wounds each of them felt were inflicted by the other over the past few years. Even though they never verbalized their feelings, they certainly showed one another how they felt.

During our sessions, they shared about the pressure they felt, their fears, and their frustrations. They realized they were afraid to disappoint the other and neither asked for what they needed.

As we discussed some of their unhealed wounds, we also reviewed the communication patterns they had gotten caught up in and healthier ways they could express themselves. Things went smoother once they could say how they were feeling without fear of upsetting the other.

As their relationship improved and their communication became more respectful, we decided to schedule a booster session in three months. We knew there would be times when they felt impatient and times when they were stressed out—and that could lead them to resort to their old patterns if they weren't careful. Their new ways of communicating would take consistent practice and if they weren't careful, they could slide back into their disrespectful habits.

Reflect and Validate

Listening to your partner is the best way to diffuse almost any situation. Many of the disrespectful behaviors people exhibit during a disagreement (raised voices, interrupting, and belittling) occur because someone isn't feeling heard. When people don't feel heard, they often resort to trying to show you how upset they are because they don't feel understood with their verbal attempts to communicate.

One of the best ways to improve your communication is to become a better listener. But good listening isn't just staying quiet. It involves demonstrating a better understanding.

Reflective listening shows that you are intent on trying to understand. Essentially, it involves summarizing what the other person said and asking them to confirm that you understand.

Imagine your partner is telling you how frustrated they feel about their job. Rather than give them advice about what they should do or insist they're overreacting, reflect back what you heard without adding in your own opinions.

Say, "I just want to make sure I understand. Your boss is telling you that you have to start holding weekly meetings to give updates on the project. And you don't have time to get the project done and you think adding more meetings to your schedule isn't fair because it's making even more work for you. Is that right?"

If they add more facts, reflect that back too. When they agree that you have the facts correct, validate how they feel. Say, "It's understandable that you'd feel frustrated" or whatever other feelings they may have said they're experiencing. When you say, "That's understandable that you'd feel that way," you're validating that it's OK for them to feel whatever emotion they are experiencing.

If they've said they're upset with you, say that's understandable as well. You don't have to agree with your partner's feelings to validate them. Once you have listened and validated them, then, talk about how you see things. But if you listen first, they're much more likely to listen to you when they're done talking.

Address Your Unhealed Wounds

If you and your partner have a pattern of unhealthy communication, you likely have emotional wounds you haven't healed. And you've likely continued to hurt one another for a long time.

Of course, some of your unhealed wounds might not be from your partner. But your emotional pain could spill over onto the person who is closest to you.

> You might have some emotional pain that is just spilling over onto the person who is closest to you.

Fortunately, you can work on healing from the things that hurt you. If you have an unresolved issue with your partner, talk about it. While talking about something that happened in the past won't change things, being heard by your partner might go a long way toward helping you feel better. But, if you don't think you can have a productive conversation with your partner, you may want to see a couples counselor (alone or together). A therapist may help you find ways to communicate your pain to your partner in a healthy, productive way.

Broach the subject by explaining to your partner that you want to change the way you communicate. Keep the focus on you and what you plan to do differently. Here are some components you may want to incorporate into your conversation:

- State your feelings.
- Accept responsibility.
- Apologize.
- Say what you're going to do differently.

When you put it all together it might look something like this:

"I feel sad when you come home late and sometimes I'm frustrated when you aren't here to help me with stuff around the house. But then when you do come home, I lash out and say mean things. I am sorry that I am rude toward you. I'm going to work on myself because the last thing I ever want to do is treat you poorly."

When Haley decided to address her past emotional wounds, it sounded like this:

"I was frustrated about having to go back to work after we had our baby. I was disappointed I couldn't stay home longer. But I didn't tell you how I felt at the time. Instead, I begrudgingly went back to work because I knew you worried about money. I'm sorry I didn't talk about it at the time. I want to make sure that in the future, I tell you how I'm feeling so we can work together and I won't hold a grudge."

When you're in a lot of emotional pain, it's tough to think rationally and hard to have a delicate conversation. If you spend some time planning how you can talk about it, you'll increase the chances that you'll be able to express yourself in a helpful way.

You might feel a little silly practicing to have a conversation with your partner. But there's a good chance you practice for other important conversations in your life—like a job interview or a wedding toast. So why wouldn't you practice an important conversation with your partner?

Say It with Respect

There are many ways to say the same thing. And a slight change in wording makes all the difference.

If you want your partner to take out the trash, you could make your request in several different ways:

- "Do you think you could at least take the trash out tonight?"
- "Could I interrupt your TV show for one minute to remind you to take the trash out?"
- "Would it kill you to take the trash out tonight?"
- "I've done everything else tonight. Do you think you could at least take out the trash?"

Making a request like that may not get you very good results. Even if your partner does take out the trash, you might have a tension-filled evening or an argument. You might get a better response by using one of these requests:

- "Can you please take out the trash tonight?"
- "I'd really appreciate it if you could please take out the trash."

Of course, even the statements that include the politest words might still be expressed in a disrespectful manner. If you speak with a condescending tone or you sigh loudly and roll your eyes, you'll be sending a much different message than if you speak with respect.

Before you say something, or respond to a request, pause and think about what you're going to say and how you are going to say it. If your emotions are running too high to say something in a polite manner, hold off until you can be respectful.

Take a few minutes to think about the difference between these disrespectful and respectful communication examples:

- ✗ **Disrespect:** Stop repeating yourself. I heard you the first time.
- ✔ **Respect:** This must be important to you because you've said it more than once. Do you feel like I'm not understanding you?

- ✗ **Disrespect:** Why would you buy that many boxes of cereal all at once? All those boxes everywhere make us look like hoarders.
- ✔ **Respect:** I get frustrated sometimes that we have so much food that it doesn't fit in the pantry and then it ends up sitting out on the countertop and our kitchen feels disorganized.

- ✗ **Disrespect:** You can't do this one little favor for me when I do so much for you? I never ask you to do anything and whenever I do you act like I'm trying to get you to move a mountain when it's something that would just take you two minutes. You're lazy. That's what the real problem is.
- ✔ **Respect:** I would love it if you could do this. I know you have a lot going on but I'm not able to get it done and it would mean a lot to me if you would do it.

The good news is, communication is a skill you keep learning and sharpening over time. You'll get opportunities to practice those skills every single day and better communication skills at home translate to all other areas of your life too.

Who's Motivated?

Take a minute to think about who thinks there's a problem and who is motivated to create change. Then you can decide how to approach your situation best.

1. You communicate with disrespect.

If you know you've been communicating with disrespect, you have the power to turn things around right now and create a much healthier relationship.

Take a few minutes to consider the last few times you were disrespectful. Do you say disrespectful things out of habit? Or out of anger? Or both?

If you do it out of anger, learn to recognize when your anger is on the rise. In the anger management class I used to lead, people would often say, "I go from being completely calm to exploding in five seconds." But that's not usually the case. They just hadn't learned to recognize when their anger was on the rise so they could take appropriate action before they got explosively angry.

When your anger and frustration is growing, your body responds. You likely experience physical symptoms, like your face feels hot or your heart beats faster. You might start sighing loudly too. These are signs that you should do something to calm down now, before you say or do something that could damage your relationship.

Some couples create a plan—for instance, they allow one another to call a time-out when a conversation gets intense. The person who needs a break might have a signal they use that shows things are getting too heated to discuss right now so they go for a walk to calm down. When they feel calmer, they return to the conversation.

If your disrespectful communication stems from habit, start by raising your awareness of when you're being disrespectful. Whenever you catch yourself doing or saying something rude, stop the conversation and acknowledge what you just did. Say something like, "That sounded disrespectful. I'm sorry. Let me start over."

At the end of every day, write down the ways you communicated with disrespect. This list isn't meant to shame you, but it's meant to raise your awareness and help you develop a plan to do better tomorrow.

Look for patterns in your communication. You might be disrespectful when your feelings are hurt or when you're stressed out or when the subject of your family comes up. When you recognize those patterns, develop a plan to proactively communicate with respect.

2. Your partner communicates with disrespect.

If your partner does something that you perceive to be disrespectful, point it out in a gentle, healthy way. Start with the positive. Identify a specific problem and then show a willingness to listen.

Say something like, "I enjoy our conversations so much. I know you're probably listening even though you're looking at your laptop but I feel like you're distracted. It hurts my feelings because I think you don't want to listen to me."

Your partner may minimize your feelings or insist your interpretation of events isn't accurate. They may even claim the issue you raise isn't a problem by saying something like, "Oh, I'm good at multitasking. I can respond to emails and listen to you at the same time."

They may also identify a problem you can solve. For example, maybe they lose their train of thought when you interrupt them while they're working. Perhaps you could ask if you could have a minute of their time (as opposed to jumping in with a story) and then wait until they're ready to listen.

If your initial conversation doesn't go well, calmly point out concerns in real time. When your partner picks up their phone when you're in the middle of telling a story, pause and ask, "Can I have your undivided attention for a minute? This is important to me."

Alternatively, you might point out other behaviors in the moment, like, "I noticed you rolled your eyes when I brought up going to my mother's house. That hurts my feelings. I would love to hear what you are thinking."

That type of response is likely to work better than if you yell, "Don't roll your eyes at me!" When possible, point out what you notice and invite your partner to explain.

3. Your partner thinks you communicate with disrespect.

It's common that one person thinks they're being polite and respectful while their partner interprets their tone as condescending and patronizing. So it's important to be aware that your partner may hear your communication much differently than you are intending.

Have some open and honest conversations about the specific things your partner finds disrespectful. Remember, you don't have to agree with their opinion. You can still agree to change your behavior.

Maybe you smile when you're delivering bad news. It might be your attempt to soften the blow. But it comes across as if you're taking pleasure in their misery.

Or maybe you lower your voice when you're offering criticism. You think you sound calm. Your partner feels like you're talking down to them as if they're a child.

Take your partner's concerns seriously. Thank them for sharing the specific examples of times when they felt your communication was disrespectful. That's hard to do. You might be tempted to make an excuse, point out why your behavior was justified, or just point the finger back at them to show that you feel disrespected at times too. But those things aren't helpful.

Take a deep breath and simply acknowledge how they feel. Remember, listening to them is a first sign of respect. Validate them and discuss your plan for change.

Here's an example: "I'm sorry that I pick up my phone and reply to messages sometimes when you're talking to me. I don't even realize I'm doing it and I know that is rude. I'll work on getting better about that."

Of course, don't say that you're going to work on something if you don't mean it. But, if you make a genuine, concerted effort to change your communication patterns, your partner will notice and your relationship will improve.

4. You both communicate with disrespect.

It's common for both individuals to communicate with disrespect over time. It often starts with small communication issues that snowball into bigger ones.

There's often an attitude of, "If you don't show me respect, don't expect to get any respect in return." And that mentality causes communication to degrade as each partner refuses to be the first one to use respectful communication.

The key to creating change is to focus on communicating respectfully, regardless of what your partner says or does. When each of you makes that commitment, positive things will start to unfold almost immediately.

You might develop some strategies for breaking the pattern before it goes downhill in each conversation. Calling a time-out, taking a deep breath, or even saying, "Let's start over," could help you get back on track. You can take a break from conversations when emotions run high. This is a great way to practice using boundaries that you have set.

When you've messed up and a conversation doesn't go well, revisit it at a time when you're both ready to talk. Take responsibility for your share and review what you could do differently next time to make your conversations more effective.

How Respectful Communication Makes You Stronger

When Haley and Trevor returned for their booster session, they both reported that things were going much better. Trevor said, "I now realize that we were like two third-graders arguing over who is more likely to become an astronaut. Our arguments never got us anywhere."

But once they found helpful and effective ways to communicate, they realized conflict wasn't a bad thing. They could work together to get their needs met. Their resentment toward one another decreased and they were able to cooperate. But they didn't get to that point overnight. They had to put in the work to create positive change.

When Trevor and Haley changed the way they communicated, everything changed—including their feelings for one another. They developed a pattern that included empathy, compassion, and kindness. They were able to be assertive with one another to get their needs met without crossing the line into disrespect.

At the end of the booster session, Haley said, "I feel better about our relationship but I also feel better about myself. It's like I feel more empowered in other areas of my life too."

It wasn't surprising that Haley said improving her communication improved her overall well-being. Contempt isn't just bad for the person on the receiving end. It's also unhealthy for the person harboring it. Studies show harboring contempt is a predictor of illness and poor well-being. Learning to let go of contempt and empowering yourself to communicate in a healthy manner goes a long way toward helping you become a stronger and better version of yourself.

Troubleshooting and Common Traps

Passive-Aggressive Communication

There will probably be times when you communicate with your behavior more than your words. And you might do this on purpose.

Slamming things around just to show your partner how frustrated you feel without saying a word doesn't do any good, though. Neither does staying up half the night cleaning just to prove to them that they're lazy.

When you find yourself being passive-aggressive, pause and ask yourself what you're feeling and what you're really trying to communicate. Then ask yourself how you could communicate better—without hoping your partner catches the hint or feels bad for you and changes their behavior. Speak up and ask for something if you need it.

Hissing Through Your Teeth

If you try to paste on a smile to hide your underlying anger, your partner is going to know. It doesn't matter what words come out of your mouth if you're essentially "hissing through your teeth." Saying, "Nope, that's fine!" when you really mean, "You don't care about my feelings, otherwise you wouldn't do this to me!" isn't a good idea. If you're upset, do something to calm down for a bit and then revisit the conversation. It's OK to say, "I'm going to need to take a minute to collect my thoughts," before offering a response.

Be Mindful of Electronic Communication

I've worked with some couples who communicate better by email or text message because they have time to think about what they want to say and how they want to respond. For them, electronic communication might mean that they are less emotionally reactive and they can hold serious discussions better when they aren't face-to-face.

But for other couples, texting creates a lot of added stress because they misinterpret the tone or have different expectations—one person expects an immediate response to a text message while the other does not. So consider how to use electronics to enhance your communication and set limits on what conversations you'll have over text if it's causing problems for you.

Even a question like, "Did you forget to pick up the milk?" can be interpreted a lot of different ways. Are you mad? Are you accusing me of being forgetful? Are you passive-aggressively trying to get me to go to the store again? Or, are you just wondering if I genuinely forgot? So work with your partner on figuring out how you communicate best and if you struggle with electronic communication, you might decide that phone calls and face-to-face conversations work best.

Conversation Starters

Take a minute to review the following questions and answer them for yourself. If your partner welcomes the conversation, invite them to answer the questions too. It's a great opportunity to put your respectful communication skills into practice.

- ○ What are examples of times when I've communicated respectfully toward you even though I may have been emotional?
- ○ What are examples of times when you've worked hard to keep your communication respectful?
- ○ What's a time when you've been impressed by our ability to communicate well about a difficult subject?
- ○ What do you think helps me communicate respectfully?
- ○ What helps you communicate respectfully when it's difficult to do so?

Interview with Dr. Mark Goulston

A slight shift in communication can sometimes make a big difference in the overall health of a relationship. No one knows this better than Dr. Mark Goulston, one of the best communication experts I know. He is a psychiatrist who spent more than twenty-five years as a psychiatry professor at UCLA. He's also a former FBI and police hostage negotiator who has been relied upon in some of the highest-stakes situations requiring an expert in communication.

Dr. Goulston has authored many books, including *Just Listen, Talking to Crazy,* and *Get Out of Your Own Way.* He's the host of the *My Wakeup Call* podcast and he has been a guest on my podcast several times. He has an incredible ability to help people feel understood and he's great at teaching new communication skills so I wanted to hear his thoughts on how couples can better communicate.

What do you think are some of the biggest misconceptions couples have about communication?

That your partner can read your mind, that your partner should be able to anticipate your needs, that if your partner really cared about you they should understand you better than they do, and that a partner giving you input or a suggestion is telling you you're wrong or stupid.

What are some of the most common ways you've seen couples communicate disrespectfully?

By yelling at each other, continuing to harangue the other person if they're not doing what you want them to do, stonewalling each other, using the words "always" and "never" frequently, and failing to apologize, thank each other, or congratulate each other.

Do you have a quick case study or an example of someone who communicated disrespectfully with their partner that you can share? What happened and did they learn to change their communication habits?

In one couple, the woman thought her male partner was telling her that he was right and she was wrong.

When I asked the man, "Are you telling her that she's wrong and you're right?" he replied, "Absolutely not. What I am saying to her is that I'm not *always* wrong! I'm not a moron! I'm not incompetent! I wouldn't be as successful as I am in the world if I was always wrong."

I asked him, "What's really going on?" He finally said, "Once upon a time she trusted me, had confidence in me, respected me, and even liked me. I get all of those responses from people in my job and my friends, and the person I need and want it from most and get it least from is her. I know I sound frustrated and even angry, but that is not what I truly feel. What I feel is hurt and I'm afraid to let her know, because I'm afraid of discovering something that deep down I believe. And that is that she just doesn't care."

When I asked her what was going on with her, she replied, "Yes, I'm frustrated with him, but what I've really worried about is that deep down, under his being so sullen and moody around me, he felt contempt for me and that our relationship was over. I had no idea he was hurt, because our communication is that awful."

He then said, "I appreciate that and for what it's worth, I *can* act very childishly and can see how that invites some of the ways you treat me."

"So what do you both want to do going forward?" I asked.

"What if she and I check in with each other regularly—let's not let it slip—every week to see if we're still on track to keeping things good instead of lousy between us, and each of us will bring up anything that either of us has done to kick it off track?" he offered. She agreed and they both agreed to let me make a suggestion.

I said, "You're each going to slip from time to time. Do you each promise to not react by throwing all the progress you will have made down the drain? And you can do that by catching yourself and apologizing or you can each pause, after the other person says something lousy, and say, 'Whoops, I think you just slipped,' after which you will own up to it if you're the one who slipped, and say, 'Looks like I did. Sorry.'"

What's a strategy or a few strategies you use to help people become more effective communicators?

One of the best strategies to nip an argument in the bud is to stop and instead of escalating ask yourself, "What's it like for the other person right now?" What you'll discover is that you can be curious and angry at the same moment in time. What you'll also discover is that the other person doesn't like where the conversation is going any more than you do.

Many years ago, I did exactly that with my wife, who I've been happily married to for forty-four years. I stopped myself and realized she didn't like where our conversation was heading either. I said to her, "Do you like where this is heading?"

She stopped in her tracks and replied, "I can't stand it when this happens." I then said to her, "Neither do I. Do you have any idea how we can prevent it from going there?" At that point she smiled and said, "No, but you're doing good."

You talk a lot about the importance of listening—and how listening is more than just "being quiet." How can people listen to their partners better?

An activity I suggest people try once a day for a week that will completely change how they listen is the HUVA exercise. Each day, select a conversation where you want to be a better listener. After the conversation is over, rate yourself on a scale of 1 to 10 from their point of view in terms of HUVA:

1. H - how much they felt HEARD by you versus your interrupting them or being distracted

2. U - how much they felt UNDERSTOOD by you, by you're asking them to say more about topics that they seemed to be emotionally connected to

3. V - how much they felt VALUED by you, by your sincerely finding something positive in what they said and telling them so

4. A - how much they felt you ADDED value to what they said by possibly seeing something even more that they could be doing with what they spoke about.

Don't beat up on yourself if at first you're lousy at this. This doesn't come naturally, but will help build up both your listening and presence muscle.

CHAPTER 8

They Don't Blame Each Other for Their Problems

Sixty-four percent of people blame their partners for their lack of happiness.
—Couples by the Numbers Survey

When Casey entered my therapy office, she said, "I'm not even sure why I'm here. My husband is the one who needs help. But he refuses so I figured I'd show up but I'm pretty sure it's pointless." She and her husband, Andy, had been married for four years. They had one child together, who was two, and Andy had a twelve-year-old from a previous relationship.

When they got together, Casey told Andy she wanted two children. At the time, Andy agreed. "He's now changed his mind," Casey said. "He says he doesn't want any more children. So now my only options are to either strong-arm him into having another kid even though he doesn't want to, or get divorced so I can go have a child with someone else. I'm not getting any younger so I need to make this decision soon."

When I asked her about her overall relationship with Andy, she said it "wasn't bad." They mostly got along and he was a good father—so she didn't understand why he was no longer interested in having more kids.

It had been about a year since they began talking about Casey's desire to have another baby. Now, the topic consumed their relationship—and her life.

"We can't talk about it because we just argue but the subject comes up constantly," she said. "I just don't understand him. He either lied to me when he said he wanted kids or he's not a man of his word. So whatever he says now doesn't really matter."

When I asked Casey what she hoped to get out of therapy, she said, "Maybe talking about all this could help me sort things out so I can decide what to do next."

During the next few appointments, Casey made it clear that she believed that if she stayed with Andy, she was going to live an unhappy life. She couldn't be happy with only one child. It would be all Andy's fault that she was miserable and would spend the rest of her life being reminded that he was "selfish." But she also wasn't sure she had the energy to start over with someone new. That option felt overwhelming too.

I asked her about the possibility of a third option. She could accept the idea that Andy didn't want another baby and she could still have a wonderful, happy life with Andy and the one child they had together and Andy's child from a previous relationship.

At first, she resisted the possibility. If she stayed with Andy that would mean that she wasn't living the dream life she wanted. She said, "I'm not sure I want to settle for that."

Like many people who come into my therapy office, Casey was convinced that her happiness depended on having two children. If Andy made any choices that weren't in line with what she thought would make her happy, she would spend the rest of her life feeling miserable and it would be all his fault.

I'll explain what Casey decided to do a little later in the chapter. But before we get there, take a few minutes and consider how much responsibility you take for your happiness and how much responsibility you accept for the state of your relationship.

Quiz

Read over the following statements and see how many of them sound true.

- ❑ I blame my partner for my unhappiness.
- ❑ I blame my partner for forcing us to do something I didn't want to do.
- ❑ Our relationship problems are mostly my partner's fault.
- ❑ I would be happier if my partner did things differently.
- ❑ My partner's behavior makes it tough for me to enjoy life.
- ❑ My partner has an unhealthy habit or way of thinking that makes it impossible for us to get along.
- ❑ Most of our arguments are my partner's fault.
- ❑ Our relationship could be a lot better if it weren't for my partner's issues.

Now, read through those statements again and think about how many of those statements your partner might affirm. The more statements that sound true, the more likely you are to blame one another for your problems.

Starting Point

Casey showed Andy how unhappy she was with his unwillingness to have another baby any chance she could. She often turned happy moments into opportunities to remind Andy that they were missing out by not having another child. When their two-year-old said something funny or learned something new, she'd say, "I wish we'd gotten that on camera since we'll never get to experience stuff like this ever again."

It's tempting to make your partner the scapegoat. When you blame them for your stress, unhappiness, or relationship trouble, you don't have to take responsibility for your share. But when you decide everything is completely out of your hands, you also can't take responsibility for improving things.

While blaming your partner for everything is a bad idea, it's also not healthy to blame yourself for everything. I see this in my therapy office too. Sometimes people beat themselves up for past mistakes and assume all the problems in the relationship stem from their choices.

So while it's not healthy to be on the extreme end of either behavior—refusing all responsibility or accepting too much blame—it's important to take some responsibility for your happiness and the health of your relationship.

Take a minute and think about your answers to the following questions:

○ Do you blame yourself too much for the problems you and your partner have?
○ Do you blame your partner too much for your problems?
○ Does your partner blame themselves too much?
○ Do they blame you too much?

Fortunately, you can take steps to accept appropriate responsibility for your share while also holding your partner accountable for their share.

Why We Blame Each Other for Our Problems

Casey had developed a plan for her life and felt like any change to that plan meant certain misery. She blamed Andy for destroying the happy future she envisioned with a growing family. She thought he was selfish for not doing something that would give her joy.

She didn't think about things from his perspective. In fact, when I asked her why he didn't want another child, she couldn't come up with a reason other than "he's selfish." She wasn't sure if he was worried about the financial ramifications, the loss of freedom, or the fact he was getting older and just didn't have the energy to raise another child. Regardless of his reasoning, she was convinced she was going to be unhappy and it would be Andy's fault.

We'd all like to think that our problems in life are someone else's fault. In some ways, that lets us off the hook. Telling yourself, "I could have a great career but my partner made us move so often for their job that it was impossible," means you have an excuse for the lack of advancement in your career.

There may also be a biological explanation for why we are quick to blame other people. Brain imaging research from Duke University shows positive and negative events are processed in different parts of the brain. The prefrontal cortex processes positive events. It takes a while for those memories to get processed and the brain often concludes good things happen by chance.

The amygdala, which controls your fight-or-flight response, processes negative events. The amygdala processes events quickly and often concludes bad things happen on purpose. It happens so fast that we often don't notice the automatic assumption that the person closest to the problem must have caused something bad to happen.

If you arrive late, you are more likely to blame something beyond your control—like the traffic. If your partner arrives late, however, you are more likely to blame them for leaving too late.

So you might automatically blame your partner when the kids misbehave, when the taxes aren't done correctly, or when the car insurance lapses. If you don't evaluate the truthfulness of your thoughts and you don't give your partner the benefit of the doubt, you'll start resenting them for all the mistakes they seem to keep making.

Blame is a great defense mechanism.

Blame is a great defense mechanism. If you blame someone else for the fact that you messed up or the fact that you aren't happy, you can protect your ego. If you don't own up to your part in the process, you might convince yourself that you shouldn't feel bad that a mistake was made.

Mental Strength Exercises

After several weeks of meeting with Casey, I asked her to consider if there were any way for her to have a happy life with Andy and only one biological child. At first, she said no. She had always envisioned having two kids.

So I asked, "What if having one child were your only option? What would happen if you or Andy had a fertility issue or some other issue that made it impossible to have another biological child?" She said if that were her only option, she would accept it. She'd invest her energy into enjoying her life as they raised their child and stepchild together.

She said the main difference between that type of situation and Andy choosing not to have another child was that she would likely always feel that Andy prevented her from having the greatest life possible. She thought the fact that the person who was supposed to love her more than anyone would refuse to give her the thing she wanted most seemed like an unforgivable offense.

That was certainly one option. She could choose to believe Andy was causing her to suffer. But she could also choose to let go of that belief and take responsibility for her happiness.

We had a bit of a philosophical discussion about life and the cards we're dealt. And a scientific conversation about happiness and whether another baby was likely to actually be the one thing that would make or break her ability to have a good life. Much of the research shows happiness has very little correlation to life events and depends much more on our response to those events.

If, however, she chose to believe Andy was going to make her life miserable, she might make it so. If you expect horrible things to happen and for life to be awful, your beliefs might turn into a self-fulfilling prophecy.

I asked her how her anger at Andy might affect her ability to enjoy parenting their child now. She acknowledged missing out on some of the joys of parenting because she was so focused on having another baby.

We also talked about what life might be like if she divorced Andy—what that would be like for her child, her stepchild, and her future. She said, "I'm not convinced that path leads to happiness either. But I feel like I'm in between a rock and a hard place sometimes."

We discussed the ramifications of trying to make Andy have another child if he wasn't comfortable doing so. Did she really want to threaten divorce? Would she be happy if the only reason he agreed was because he was given an ultimatum?

She had choices in responding to Andy's reluctance to have another child. She could make the best of it or she could make everyone else miserable, all the while blaming him. I didn't put it that bluntly, but we spent many sessions talking about the various outcomes and options until she came to that conclusion herself.

Over several weeks and many discussions about life, happiness, and personal responsibility, the language Casey used to talk about Andy started to shift. Instead of saying things like, "Andy's selfish," she said things like, "Andy's funny." And rather than insist he was going to ruin her life, she spent more time describing him as a loving father. She talked more positively about their relationship too.

I pointed out my observation to her one week and she said, "I started looking at things from Andy's point of view. We talked about why he didn't want to have more kids and I understand more. I realize I didn't want anything to be my fault—including my misery. But I'm not going to blame Andy anymore and I'm going to focus on being the best person I can be to my family, even if my family isn't as big as I had once hoped it would be."

Casey was trying to avoid grief. She would rather feel angry at Andy than feel sad about not having another child. But once she allowed herself to experience sadness, she could choose to accept responsibility for her happiness moving forward. She didn't want to waste the time they had together feeling miserable and instead, chose to be grateful for the life they had together.

Stop the Downward Spiral of Blame

If you've been upset about something minor your partner said, only to find that ten minutes later you're convinced they don't care about you, you're not alone. A small infraction or a perceived slight can quickly turn into major blame if you aren't careful.

Negative thinking leads to a downward spiral and blame is no exception. You're likely to assign meaning to your partner's behavior and that meaning might cause you to quickly conclude they don't care about you.

Here's an example. Bill was going golfing with his friends. But he promised Sam he'd be back in time to attend her family's barbecue. He shows up late and didn't call to say he was running behind.

Sam is furious. Sam thinks:

Bill would rather spend time with his friends than me and my family.
Bill is insensitive.
Bill doesn't care about my feelings.
Bill never cares how I feel.
Bill doesn't care about me at all.

Within a matter of minutes, Sam's response to Bill being late leads to the conclusion that Bill doesn't care about her. While that's one possibility, there are many more. Perhaps Bill's game ran late and he couldn't find a good way to exit the situation with his friends. Or maybe traffic was terrible and he miscalculated how long the drive to the barbecue would take. Or maybe he underestimated how important this was to Sam. There are many possibilities but when we're upset, it's easy for our thoughts to become catastrophic in a matter of minutes.

Pause and catch yourself when the spiral begins. Take a breath and ask yourself whether your statements are actually true. If your partner left their shoes in the middle of the floor, does it mean they don't love you? If your partner didn't get the gift you wanted, does it mean they don't care about you? When you ask yourself those questions it often becomes clearer that your brain is taking some irrational leaps and blaming your partner for more than they deserve.

Accept Some Responsibility

Your relationship problems are never all one person's fault. You may not have caused the problems, but you do have some responsibility in how you respond to them. Right about now, though, you might be thinking, "But you don't understand! This problem *is* my partner's fault."

Even if the mess you find yourself in isn't your fault, digging yourself out might still be your responsibility. Accepting some responsibility for the problem empowers you to be part of the solution.

> **Even if the mess you find yourself in isn't your fault, digging yourself out might still be your responsibility.**

Here are some examples of how you can take responsibility for problems you experience that, on the surface, might seem like they're all your partner's fault:

- Your partner's gambling addiction isn't your fault. But it is your responsibility to manage how you respond to their addiction. Your share of the problem might be that you've been yelling, arguing, and even trying to hide their money from them as opposed to getting help for yourself. It is tough to live with someone who has an addiction and your responsibility might be to get support for yourself. That support might mean anything from a therapist to a financial adviser who can assist you in making healthy decisions.

- Your partner's affair isn't your fault. But, if you spend years yelling, accusing, snooping, and spying, you won't do yourself or your relationship any favors. You might decide your responsibility is to suggest your partner get treatment and for you to eventually go to therapy together if you want to try and work through the relationship.

- Your kids' behavior problems aren't your partner's fault. You might disagree on discipline strategies but you are responsible for parenting too. Your responsibility might be to stop yelling at your partner in front of the kids. Instead, you might work on developing a parenting plan that both of you can agree on.

As we discussed in Chapter 6, your partner doesn't always have to be completely invested in change for you to pave the way toward doing things differently. Just by accepting some responsibility, you can reduce your partner's defensiveness and increase the chances they'll want to create change. When they aren't investing their energy defending themselves, they're free to work on solving the problem.

So spend some time thinking about what you want to accept responsibility for. You may need to work on this for a while before you say anything out loud. When you feel like you can stay calm and have a productive discussion, talk to your partner about the responsibility you accept.

Develop a "We vs. the Problem" Mentality

You're going to face problems as a couple. When you do, you have two choices: either fight with each other or join forces to fight the problem together.

Adversity sometimes tears couples apart. Whether it's financial stress or the loss of a loved one, tough times can lead to intense emotions. There are many misunderstandings and hurt feelings that become compounded during a difficult time. When both partners struggle, providing emotional support to one another is challenging and they may even turn against each other.

I've seen this happen in my therapy office with grieving couples. In one instance, one partner worked hard to try and "move on" after they lost a child. He wanted to get life back to normal as soon as possible. His partner felt confused by his behavior—and she interpreted it to mean that he wasn't sad and she withdrew from him. The more she withdrew, the more he felt compelled to try and make things better and they got stuck in a cycle that compounded their feelings. It's common for couples to get into those types of patterns when they're dealing with big issues.

But when couples work together to attack a problem, adversity can actually draw them closer together. In fact, research shows a natural disaster can bring couples together. Researchers looked at what happened to the relationships of 231 couples who lived in Harris County, Texas, in 2017, when the area was struck by a category 4 hurricane that caused catastrophic flooding. The couples reported significant increases in relationship satisfaction that began before the arrival of the storm and lasted for a bit after the storm passed through.

It's likely that couples become happier with one another when they have a common enemy—like a hurricane. They can view that storm as a problem they need to work together to solve, like boarding windows or evacuating together. Then, following the storm, they can work together on cleanup strategies or they may need to address problems caused by the storm (such as finding temporary shelter or dealing with insurance if they received damage).

When we look at problems as something we can attack as a team, we can grow together while also challenging ourselves to grow as individuals. If, however, you blame your partner for the problem, you won't feel like you have any power to work together.

Who's Motivated?

Take a minute to think about who thinks there's a problem and who is motivated to create change. Then you can decide how to approach your situation best.

1. You want to stop blaming your partner.

Pay attention to the language you use. When you start thinking or saying that something is *all* your partner's fault, pause and take a minute to reframe your thoughts.

Also be on the lookout for thoughts or statements that begin with "If you'd just . . ." You might insist that if your partner would just stop eating out at lunch, your financial problems would end. Or, if your partner would just clean up in the evenings, you'd get along better.

When you aren't pleased with your partner's behavior, pause and ask yourself, "How do I want to respond to this?" Then look for ways you can take a team approach to tackling the problem together.

You may have made some mistakes in the past—like agreeing to things you didn't think were a good idea because you wanted to appear supportive. But now you feel resentful and blame your partner. You can't change the past but you can change how you respond to it.

You might not be responsible for a problem—but you may have made the problem worse by arguing about it. Perhaps you nagged too much, lectured harshly, or said, "I told you so," which only made things worse. Take responsibility for the things you did to contribute to the problem.

Start a conversation by acknowledging your part. Say something like, "I know we've been arguing a lot lately and I want to change that. I am sorry that I say mean things when I'm frustrated. I don't want to contribute to more problems and I'm going to work hard to control my temper better."

2. You want your partner to stop blaming you.

If your partner blames you, you've probably already said, "It's not all my fault!" at least once. But telling someone to stop blaming you won't work.

If you want your partner to accept some responsibility, accept your role in the problem first. Then, take a collaborative problem-solving approach. Finally, offer an explanation, not an excuse. For example, you might say, "The reason I'm late for dinner is because I'm trying to get my work done at the office so I don't have to bring work home." Show you understand why this is stressful by saying, "I realize the kids need to eat earlier so you can get them to bed. What can we do to address this?"

You might decide it's better to bring work home. Or maybe your partner can let the kids eat early and the two of you eat together on the nights you get home late. There are many different ways to solve the same problem and once you accept that yes, some of the problem is your fault, you'll be one step closer to working on a solution.

When you feel unfairly blamed, avoid the tendency to point out your partner's flaws.

When you feel unfairly blamed, avoid the tendency to point out your partner's flaws. If they call you out for spending too much money, don't remind them that they're not perfect either by pointing out that they broke their phone last month and had to buy a new one. Otherwise, you'll get into a contest over whose infractions are worse.

3. Your partner wants you to stop blaming them.

If your partner thinks you place too much blame on them, listen to their concern. You don't have to agree that you do blame them too much, but you can agree that it's not healthy if they're feeling that way.

Your partner may be blaming you for blaming them! And it doesn't mean you're actually blaming them too much—they might just feel that way. Sometimes people feel guilty about things even if they didn't do anything wrong.

Here's an example. Someone says to their partner, "We're running late." It's a fact and it's merely meant to be an observation. But their partner interprets that to mean, "He's blaming me because we're running late." She thinks his comment is a passive-aggressive attempt to get her to hurry and an argument ensues because she feels like she is being blamed.

You aren't responsible for making your partner happy all the time—but it's important to understand whether your partner might interpret your statements to mean they're at fault. Discuss how your message might come across differently then you intend and encourage your partner to ask questions like, "Are you implying this is my fault?" In turn, make sure you don't use sarcasm or passive-aggressive communication that implies your partner is responsible. If you want to address your partner's responsibility about something, be up front about your concern.

4. You both want to stop blaming each other so much.

As you've likely noticed, conversations can't be productive when they include statements like, "It's your fault!" "No, it's your fault!"

If you and your partner get into disagreements that sound like that, focus on yourself for a bit. Take a break and write down some things you are doing to contribute to the problem. Have your partner do the same. Resist the urge to write down what you think your partner is doing wrong. After a few minutes, discuss your lists with one another.

If you think your partner has left out some things, no need to point them out. Just listen to what they have to say and share what you're willing to take responsibility for.

You also don't need to declare what percentage of the problem is your fault. Take responsibility for the exact things you did that led to a problem, contributed to the problem, exaggerated the problem, or made things worse after the fact.

Start conversations by accepting your part, rather than accusing your partner of doing something wrong. You might start by saying, "I've been making things worse lately by complaining about how much you've been working. I'm sorry that I've started so many arguments. I want to get better at communicating with you." That's likely to inspire your partner to accept some responsibility too, as compared to if you start by saying, "You shouldn't work so much."

How Accepting Responsibility Makes You Stronger

Once Casey stopped thinking of Andy as the enemy who was purposely trying to make her life miserable, she was able to work on the relationship. They had a problem where they couldn't compromise—they were either having another child or they weren't. But she had to stop giving him the power to determine whether she was going to have a happy life.

Once she stopped blaming him and empowered herself to take control, she was able to start healing. She grieved for a while over the fact that she wasn't going to have that life she once pictured with two biological children. But, she didn't have to spend the rest of her life blaming Andy for making her miserable. She could still have a great life if she wanted to do so.

Once she made that shift, her relationship with Andy improved, her psychological well-being improved, and her relationship with her child and her stepchild likely improved as well.

When you accept responsibility, you are free to begin taking action. Ultimately, you'll feel your best when you accept responsibility for your life and your happiness.

Troubleshooting and Common Traps

All-or-nothing thinking

Too often, people assume something is all their fault or all their partner's fault. It's the childhood argument of, "Well you started it!" But, almost every problem can be traced back to a series of events. One thing goes wrong, the other person responds in an unhelpful way, and things often continue to go downhill from there. It's impossible to make things better when you're busy pointing fingers to decide who is "at fault," however.

Looking for allies

It's tempting to look for other people who can attest that something isn't your fault. And it's pretty easy most of the time to turn our friends and family members into allies who will assure us that we bear little to no responsibility in the situation. But collecting allies will only make things worse. This isn't a war and the last thing you want to do is turn your partnership into an all-out battle as both of you try to win people over. It doesn't matter if your mother agrees with you or your friend is on your side. It's between you and your partner and the outside person's opinion shouldn't carry any weight.

Conversation Starters

Take a few minutes to consider the following questions and how blame plays a role in your relationship. If your partner is willing to discuss these with you, go through the questions together.

○ What are some examples of times when I've taken appropriate responsibility for problems that we share?

○ What's an example of a time when you accepted responsibility for your share of a problem?

○ What's an example of a time when we both accepted our share of responsibility for a problem?

○ What do you think has been helpful during those times when we accepted appropriate responsibility?

Interview with Elliot Connie

While some forms of therapy go deep into childhood issues and healing old wounds, Solution Focused therapy is a short treatment that focuses on the here and now. It's a great strategy for dealing with blame because you can't blame your behavior on something your partner did in the past if you're focusing on what is going on right now. That's why I wanted to talk to Solution Focused therapist Elliot Connie about how he handles blame in his office. Elliot has a master's of science in professional counseling and he's written four books on the Solution Focused method. I knew he'd have strategies that could help people stop the blame game right away.

What are some of the biggest things you see people blame their partner for?

Everything. Couples will often initially blame each other for the fact that they're unhappy, blame each other for the problems that exist between the two of them, blame each other for their own mistakes, meaning, "I made this mistake because you did such and such a thing." I think the human experience is one where people look to blame other people for their own misgivings, their own problems, and their own symptoms.

If somebody's on the receiving end of that, what do you recommend that they do if they tend to get blamed for lots of extra stuff?

When someone's on the receiving end of blame, my first thought is, "How much of that is truth? And how much of that can you make a difference for?" Meaning if my partner blames me for them being unhappy, I can disagree with that. I am not responsible for you being unhappy, but I also can do something to provoke happiness.

I think sometimes in couples, there's this flawed thought that I'm only responsible for problems that I created, and that's actually not true. You have partnered with this person and that means you need to be a positive force contributing to their happiness, even for problems you didn't create. We fall into this trap.

When someone says, "X, Y, or Z is your fault," the first thing we think is, "But is it my fault?" If the answer is no, then it's like I disengage from the healing process. But I think we need to bypass that and think, "To what responsibility can I contribute?" Or, "To what part can I contribute to the healing process?" Which really is the only thing that matters.

When you have a couple and they're blaming each other a lot for stuff, where do you start or how do you work with them?

I ask them about the outcome they want to achieve from therapy, which is the foundation of Solution Focused Brief Therapy. What they're doing, up to and including their participation in the problem, is not relevant. I simply want to know, "What is it you want to gain from the therapy?"

Human beings are really silly. We do things that are not working, meaning they're not getting us our desired aim. It's like, "I'm going to do this thing and if it doesn't get me my desired aim, I'm going to do more of that thing, and if it doesn't get me my desired aim, I'm going to do more of that thing."

Before you know it, you're doing ten thousand iterations of the thing that is not getting your desired aim, when really you just should have done something different initially. The first thing I do is ask people, "What are you hoping to achieve from talking to me?" That immediately causes the conversation to shift and focus and turn toward efficacy, turn toward what's the transformation we're actually in pursuit of? I'm like a dog on a bone. That's the only thing I'm willing to talk about. That's the only thing that matters to me.

So then what do you do when you have a couple who brings up a past hurt? Sometimes I'll see couples where one made a mistake years ago, whether they overspent on their credit card or they did something that hurt the other, and these past hurts get brought up. Since you are focused on Solution Focused treatment, what do you do about those old wounds?

I ask them questions that help the old wound stay healed. I'll say things like, "That must have been terrible to discover they overspent on the credit card or made whatever mistake. How did you overcome it and stay in the relationship?" I ask questions like that because I want them to focus on: there might have been a mistake, but you have stayed and there must have been reasons that you stayed.

And I would also ask them, "At what points were you happy that you stayed? Because not only must there have been reasons that you stayed, there must have been moments wherein you were pleased that you did so."

How would you help a couple who said they wanted to get better at giving feedback without placing blame?

That's a good question too. It's so hard because I don't really think about blame. If someone said, "We want to get better at giving each other feedback without placing blame," I would say, "If you caught yourself doing that, what would it sound like?" And then they would say, "I would be saying this, this, and this, and not saying this, this, and this." And I would just help them describe how they would like to be doing it.

If a couple says, "Hey, we want to start having more positive or productive conversations." With the Solution Focused approach, how do you help?

I would say, "If you caught yourself having more positive and productive conversations, how would you notice you were doing it?" You ask really minute questions. "What would you notice about your partner that would let them know that they're having positive and productive conversations? How would you show your partner you were pleased to be having these conversations with them? If your partner slipped up and accidentally started talking in a blaming, problem way, how would you let them know that you have grace for them and you're not going to fall into that pattern? How would you let them know that it's safe for them to recover?" I would ask all of those questions that highlight that A, none of us are perfect, and B, we can all do this thing.

I know that you can have a significantly negative impact on your partner's day, and I know you can have a significantly positive impact on your partner's day. That's just the way relationships go.

If I told you right now I'll give you a million dollars if you go home and have a genuine knockdown, drag-out argument with your partner, you know exactly what buttons to push to do that. You'd be like, "Ooh, I know how to make that million dollars. I'm going to go home and I'm going to say this, this, and this."

And I also know if I gave you a million dollars if you have a genuine joyous moment with your partner, you'd also know how to do that too. You would be like, "Ooh, I know. I want that million dollars. I'm going to go home and I'm going to push these buttons." I think part of therapy, whether it's Solution Focused or not, part of therapy is to be able to push the buttons that ignite positive things.

CHAPTER 9

They Don't Forget Why They Fell in Love

Thirty-six percent of people say they wonder
why they even stay with their partner.
—Couples by the Numbers Survey

I knew very little about Mindy and Paul before their first appointment. My receptionist had fielded the call from Mindy, and the note in my calendar simply said: "Mindy is upset Paul doesn't clean the house."

When they arrived for the first session, I greeted them in the waiting room. They both smiled and followed me to the office, but before they even took a seat, Mindy said, "Can you please tell him that no one wants to be married to a slob? He thinks it's just me but seriously, who would want to be in a relationship with someone who can't pick up after themselves? Would you?"

I assured her that I'd never encountered anyone who said, "What really attracted me to my partner was how messy they are." But I added that socks being left in the middle of the floor didn't have to be the reason the relationship ends either.

Paul laughed a little and he acknowledged that he doesn't like to clean the house. He didn't care when things were out of order. He said, "When the house gets dirty enough, I clean it. Until then, I relax."

Mindy sighed loudly and said, "Paul, we have three kids. If you don't clean throughout the day, the house looks completely destroyed by the time the kids go to sleep!"

Paul and Mindy both worked full-time, and their kids had lots of activities that kept them busy. Mindy felt like every spare second she had went to cleaning the house. The stack of dishes, heaps of laundry, and scattered sports equipment felt like a never-ending job.

Mindy said their messy house was taking a toll on almost every aspect of their lives. She felt stressed out most of the time, had less time to spend with the kids, and it was impacting their social lives. "I don't let the kids have friends over because the house is such a disaster. I'd be embarrassed if their parents picked them up and saw the mess we live in." She didn't invite her own friends or family members over either and she often turned down social invites because she felt guilty if she went out while the house was a mess.

Paul thought his lack of tidiness was a minor inconvenience. But Mindy was at her wit's end. She said, "I feel disrespected by Paul. I spend all my spare time picking up while he watches TV or does fun things with the kids. And he doesn't seem to care."

Paul, on the other hand, thought Mindy stressed herself out too much. He wanted her to relax, have more fun, quit arguing with him, and stop "pestering" the kids about their messes.

By the end of the first appointment, it was clear that Paul had concluded Mindy was "a drama queen" and Mindy had decided Paul was "an inconsiderate slob."

The division of labor was a problem that could be solved. But until they addressed how they felt about one another, they weren't likely to reach any solutions together. So we didn't start therapy by addressing the division of labor. Instead, we started talking about why they fell in love in the first place.

I'll explain more about what happened with Mindy and Paul later in the chapter. Before we get there, take a few minutes to think about your relationship and whether you remember what made you and your partner fall in love.

Quiz

Review the following statements and see how many of them sound familiar.

- ❑ I sometimes wonder why I'm in this relationship.
- ❑ I occasionally daydream about how life might be better if I had a different partner (or no partner at all).
- ❑ I question what I was thinking when I got together with my partner.
- ❑ We lose sight of why we fell in love in the first place.
- ❑ We get so caught up in what's going on right now, we forget to look at the overall, bigger picture of our relationship.
- ❑ I focus mostly on what's wrong with the relationship.
- ❑ I spend a lot of time thinking about all the things I wish my partner would do differently.
- ❑ I feel irritated by many of the things my partner says or does.

Now, think about how your partner might respond to the statements. If some of the sentences sound true, don't worry. There are several things you can do that can help you remember why you fell in love in the first place—and that can renew your commitment to one another.

Starting Point

When Paul and Mindy returned for their second appointment, I didn't ask them how things had gone over the week—I knew the answer. They'd spent the week arguing about the condition of their home. So I started the session by asking them what first attracted them to one another. They both paused and thought for a minute.

Mindy said she was attracted to Paul because he was kind and funny. Paul said he fell in love with Mindy because she was fascinating. She had a fun outlook on life and a smile that melted his heart. Those descriptions were far from the "slob" and "drama queen" labels they were placing on one another now.

Relationships change as time goes by and it's easy to lose sight of why you fell in love. I'm not talking about literally forgetting your love story but instead just losing sight of how you once fell so deeply in love that you decided to create a partnership.

Those euphoric feelings you likely felt early in the relationship made it easy to cooperate. When you're falling in love, you assume your partner has good intentions. Their quirks are often cute and entertaining—and might even draw you in even more as you feel captivated by them.

But ten years later, late-night conversations about your dreams for the future might be replaced with arguments over the bills and disagreements about where you'll be spending the holidays.

And those stories that used to make you laugh might irritate you after you've heard them a zillion times. Those same quirks that you used to enjoy might now seem like bad habits that slow you down, gross you out, or get in your way. You might question whether you made the right decision or even daydream about how your life might be different if you'd picked a different partner.

The good news is, you can conjure up those positive feelings again by recalling why you fell in love in the first place. In fact, remembering why you chose your partner might be one of the most powerful tools you have to stay in love.

Take a minute to answer the following questions:

○ Do you ever forget why you fell in love with your partner?
○ Do you think your partner loses sight of why you fell in love?

Why We Forget Why We Fell in Love

Like many couples, Mindy and Paul felt their relationship was magical in the early days. But that was before they had to share the responsibilities of real life. Romantic nights out were replaced with helping kids with homework. Their dinner and movie nights now consisted of popcorn and Marvel movies in the living room. Although their relationship had a firm foundation, the stress of their daily lives was taking a toll on the connection.

Maybe you can relate to their story on one level or another. You fell in love during a certain time frame—when you were in college, before you had kids, or when you lived in a particular city. Over time, your circumstances changed and so did your feelings.

You might forget that the things you complain about most now are the exact things that initially attracted you to your partner. Perhaps you fell in love with your partner's ability to enjoy the journey and to savor every moment. That might have worked well for you when you were dating and weren't pressed for time. But now, that same tendency to savor the moment might irritate you when you're rushing out the door to make it to dinner with your friends on time or you're trying to catch a flight at the airport.

It's much easier to think about how your partner chews too loudly, complains too much, demands too much, and doesn't get enough things done than it is to think about what an amazing human they are. When you're busy, stressed out, and trying to reach your goals, you might focus more on your partner's perceived flaws or the behaviors you don't like.

One reason this happens is because emotions naturally shift over time. The intense emotions you feel at the beginning of a relationship aren't meant to stay that intense.

Researchers have found that when you're falling in love, your brain responds similarly to those of people who have a drug addiction. Brain chemicals, like dopamine, oxytocin, adrenaline, and vasopressin, are released throughout different points in your attraction to help you bond with your partner.

From obsessive thoughts and cravings for more time together to feeling euphoria when you are together, those experiences are the same things that happen to someone with a substance use disorder. Over time, however, a tolerance is built—like with a drug. If your partner breaks off the relationship, you'll experience symptoms similar to that of someone going through drug withdrawal—irritability, change in sleep habits, change in appetite, lethargy, and loneliness.

Knowing that your brain was "under the influence" when you got together might make it seem even more remarkable that you've made your relationship last. Those emotions change over time—and that's not a bad thing. It's tough to function well when you're in the early stages of love. As things level out a bit, you were probably able to think a bit more rationally. You might also feel less obsessed about spending time together.

As your emotions shift, sometimes your thoughts and your behaviors shift too. You might start focusing on all the things you dislike about your partner and on meeting your own needs, rather than working as a team to meet both your needs together.

As your circumstances change and your brain chemistry adjusts, it's normal to move into a new phase of your relationship that makes it a little more challenging to stay connected. That's why it's so important to remember why you fell in love in the first place. There's a reason you chose to make this person your partner and keeping that in mind can help you stay committed as you go through life's inevitable ups and downs.

Mental Strength Exercises

At the end of their second session, I gave Mindy and Paul a homework assignment—create a list of all the things they love about one another. I told them not to share their lists with each other during the week. And I encouraged them to think about the list throughout the week rather than just slap something down right before the next session.

They returned the following week with their lists and we reviewed them. Both of them had no shortage of reasons why they loved one another. Mindy went first. Her list included things like, "I love that Paul insists on reading each kid a story at bedtime." Paul smiled as she read his list. When he read his list, Mindy teared up a little as she heard Paul say things like, "I love that Mindy checks on her mom every day." After they read their lists, I asked how they had gotten along over the past week. They agreed they fought less than usual.

We discussed how thinking about what they loved about each other throughout the week had stirred up more loving feelings and reduced their conflict.

We took that opportunity to start discussing their discord over the division of labor. That was a good time to talk because they already felt more connected since they had shared their lists. This time, they were able to have a much more productive conversation.

I encouraged them to communicate what they needed from the other person. Mindy said she needed more help around the house. Paul said he needed some time to relax and the chance to clean on his timeline.

We reviewed what had just happened—they'd got into a better headspace about their relationship by recalling why they fell in love and suddenly, they could have a much more productive conversation about the household chores.

Obviously, that one conversation didn't cure their relationship problems or solve their differences about how clean their house should be.

But it showed them that conjuring up some loving feelings was possible, and when they felt more loving toward one another, they were better equipped to work together to solve problems.

We developed strategies that could help them feel emotionally connected and reduce their conflict moving forward. It would be important for them to recall why they fell in love in the first place. That's not a subject that they addressed often. They were more likely to talk about how much life had changed when they had kids or how things were different when they moved into a bigger house than they were to recall how their love had drawn them together and helped them stay together through the years.

They decided to start scheduling more fun things to do by themselves without the kids. They needed to schedule those activities in advance, so that would give them something to look forward to. Just talking about an upcoming opportunity could give them a chance to bond. Doing fun things together would also create more positive memories for themselves as a couple. Then, they'd have more happy memories to think about twenty years from now. After all, many of the days in their current routine blended together. But they'd never forget hiking a mountain, visiting a special museum, or exploring a new city together.

They also set aside time to eat dinner by themselves a few evenings per week. Rather than scarf down a meal alongside the kids, they'd feed them and after they went to bed, they'd spend some time together—just the two of them. And they wouldn't use that time to discuss the hustle and bustle of daily life. Instead, they'd use it to talk about the bigger-picture stuff—how they were feeling, what sorts of things they wanted to do in the future, and how they appreciated one another.

They also got clearer on a plan for dividing up the household responsibilities. Instead of just insisting Paul clean more, Mindy got specific about the chores she found time-consuming and Paul discussed how he could meet his need for relaxation by carving out some time every day to be by himself—while also still helping out around the house.

Look at Your Partner's Picture

Most therapists don't display family photos in their offices. We try to be somewhat of a blank slate for our clients. Having a picture of a child on the desk might create some extra sadness for a client who just lost a child. Or seeing family photos on the desk might cause a client to develop assumptions that could affect the therapeutic relationship. But one of my colleagues always kept a picture of his wife right next to his computer monitor.

One day he said to me, "Looking at Debbie's picture keeps things in perspective for me. No matter how rough my day is, just knowing I am going to see her after work makes everything feel better." He talked lovingly about Debbie and the things they did together during their time off. And whenever there was a work event that would take place outside of the usual work hours, he'd never commit until he talked to her first.

I have no doubt that Debbie's picture helped him feel good about himself and their relationship. There's research that shows just looking at a picture of your partner might be one of the simplest but most effective things you can do to keep the relationship spark alive.

A 2022 study found that viewing a spouse's picture increased infatuation, attachment, and marital satisfaction compared to viewing pleasant or neutral pictures. Ultimately, the authors of the study concluded that "Looking at spouse pictures is an easy strategy that could be used to stabilize marriages in which the main problem is the decline of loving feelings over time."

So something as simple as looking at your partner's photo might help you keep life and your relationship in a healthy perspective. Technology makes that easier than ever, since you can carry around a picture on your phone, which you likely have with you at all times.

You might even create a special folder on your phone that contains your favorite pictures of your partner. Include photos from a vacation, special times together, or those pictures where you find your partner especially attractive. Even if you see your partner every day, spend a few minutes each day looking at those pictures. Scrolling through them might increase your positive feelings.

Talk About Your Love Story

Recall those early dates you went on or when you first realized you wanted a long-term commitment. Bring up the hurdles you had to overcome to stay together or make it work.

Some couples have amazing love stories about how they knew from the first second they locked eyes that they were destined to be together. Other people have stories about the incredible challenges they had to overcome to be together—like forbidden love or being separated by war.

If your story isn't quite so exciting, don't despair. You still have a love story that led to the two of you choosing one another. And recalling the early days of your romance can go a long way toward rekindling some passion.

Spend time answering questions that remind you of why you fell in love. Here are some examples of questions you can ask each other:

- What first attracted you to me?
- When did you first know you wanted a long-term relationship?
- Who did you first tell about me and what did you say?
- What made you pick me?
- What makes me different from other people?
- What are some times when your love for me grew even more?

If your partner isn't into answering questions, answer them about your partner for your own sake. Remembering why you chose them is an effective exercise, even if they don't hear your answers. If telling them these answers feels too forced, get creative. Give a card or a letter or even an email every once in a while that shares some thoughts like "The Top 5 Reasons I Picked You."

If the two of you have a song, listening to your song can also be a powerful way to connect. Whether it's a song that you heard while you were on your first date and you've always considered it "our song" or it's the song you first danced to at your wedding, research shows couples who have "couple defining songs" tend to have more intimate relationships. Listening to their song was associated with more positive emotions, like happiness and love. It also stirred up happy memories, such as their wedding day or a memorable vacation.

Spend time listening to "your song" together.

Spend time listening to "your song" together. And if you don't have one already, nothing says you can't get one now.

Assume Goodwill

In the early days of your relationship—once you felt secure—you likely assumed your partner's intentions were good. If they showed up late, you may have told yourself that it was fine or they just got stuck in traffic. Or, if they weren't interested in going somewhere with you, you may have concluded they just weren't into that activity. But after being together for years, you may read into their behaviors a little differently.

Now—as we discussed in the last chapter—you might be more inclined to blame your partner for being irresponsible when they show up late. Or you might convince yourself that they never want to spend time with you if they turn down an opportunity to do something together.

But what if you became committed to assuming your partner's intentions are good (at least most of the time)? Assuming goodwill can help you become more forgiving when they forget something, say something you dislike, or do something you don't appreciate.

Your partner is an imperfect human who will hurt you sometimes. They will let you down, disappoint you, hurt your feelings, and surprise you in an unpleasant way. They will say and do things you don't like. That's what happens when you're in a relationship. But they may not do those things intentionally, and assuming goodwill can help you zoom out a bit and keep the overall relationship in a healthier perspective.

When your partner does something you don't like, notice your assumptions. If you're assuming something bad, pause and ask yourself, "What would I assume if I assumed goodwill?" Instead of labeling your partner as inconsiderate, you might remind yourself that they're taking care of themselves. Or, instead of saying that they're lazy, you might remind yourself that they're tired because they work hard. Assuming goodwill can help you have more compassion and it can help you respond with more kindness.

Who's Motivated?

Take a minute to think about who thinks there's a problem and who is motivated to create change. Then, you can decide how to approach your situation best.

1. You forget why you fell in love.

When you get caught up in the busyness of life and you forget why you fell in love or you start treating one another more like business partners, get proactive about recalling why you fell in love in the first place.

Set aside time to think about what you love about your partner and what made you fall in love. Just a few minutes each day can help you feel more connected.

You might keep a journal where you write down why you love your partner. Or create a habit to tell them one thing you really love about them each day. It turns an "I love you" into something more meaningful.

You could even create a list of the top ten reasons why you fell in love with your partner and read it over to yourself whenever you need a little reminder.

2. Your partner seems to forget why they fell in love with you.

Don't take it personally if your partner has been a little more irritable or less loving lately. It may have more to do with something they're going through rather than anything you've done or their feelings toward you.

That doesn't mean you have to sit still and idly wait for things to get better. You can take some kind and loving action that might shift things up and improve the relationship.

Pause and show appreciation for your partner. Bring up some of the reasons why you fell in love with them. Say something like, "Sometimes we get so caught up in the day-to-day stuff that I forget to take time out and tell you why I love you so much."

Focus first on modeling this for your partner rather than demand they too list all the reasons why they fell in love with you.

3. Your partner thinks you forgot why you fell in love.

Times have changed and your relationship may have shifted. So even though you feel just as in love as you once did, your partner might not necessarily feel loved all the time. Whether you're busy with your career, raising kids, or you've got some hobbies that you love, sharing your loving feelings all day might not top your priority list.

But it's important to help your partner feel loved. That's the key to a secure relationship. Take time to talk about your feelings and point out exactly what you love about your partner. Give your partner your undivided attention and ask them what would help them to feel more loved.

Resist the urge to be defensive and say, "I do that already!" Instead, just listen and show that you're invested in hearing what they have to say. Sometimes, just being heard can go a long way.

4. You both seem to forget why you fell in love sometimes.

If you both agree that you lose sight of why you fell in love sometimes, make it a priority to change this. The last thing you want to do is wait another five years before you address the issue. Start to tackle it right now.

Hold conversations about what brought you together in the first place. And work together to see if you can find ways to drum up those feelings or experiences in life now.

For example, if you fell in love with your partner's love for adventure, talk about how you might find some adventures again.

Work together to revitalize the relationship. You might do anything from setting aside one night a month to look through old pictures to planning an annual adventure with the couples you used to hang out with in college. A little nostalgia can stir up reminders about what got you together in the first place.

How Remembering Why You Fell in Love Makes You Stronger

By the time Mindy and Paul were done with therapy, they were more confident that they could tackle problems together. They knew they would probably never agree on exactly how clean the house should be or how often it should be cleaned. But they had more confidence about how they could work together to develop a plan they could both live with.

Of course there would be days they were going to argue about the division of labor again. But they now had more strategies they could rely on to keep the bigger, overall picture of their love front and center—which made the household chore arguments feel a lot more manageable.

Before they could solve the problem on the surface—the issues surrounding the household chores—they had to remember why solving the problem was so important to them in the first place. They loved each other and wanted to create a great life together.

Simon Sinek highlights this in his bestselling book, *Start with Why,* which has sold more than a million copies. In it, he encourages leaders to share why they're doing something. When we all understand the bigger picture of why we're doing something, we're motivated to do our part—and to do our best.

The same can be said for relationships. You need to remember why you are in your relationship. When you recall how much you love your partner, you'll remember that it's important to work hard to resolve conflict, overcome obstacles, compromise, and make sacrifices.

You wouldn't do all those things for just anyone. The deep love you have for your partner can motivate you to find ways to make your relationship work. It can also help you keep your eyes on the bigger picture. Perhaps you feel annoyed by what your partner is doing right this second, but it's just a small piece to a giant puzzle that makes up your love story.

Life is hard. But when you know that you have someone who is willing to stick it out with you—and you're happy to stick it out with them—life gets better.

Remembering why you fell in love stirs up nostalgia. And there's research that shows relationship nostalgia is associated with better relationship satisfaction. So recalling why you fell in love might help you feel better about the longevity of your relationship.

You have a rich history as a couple. The emotions, memories, and life experiences you have with your partner are unique to your relationship—you'll never have that experience with someone else. Keeping in mind how special that is and how amazing it is that the two of you crossed paths and joined forces can unite you as you move forward to face whatever challenges life throws at you.

Troubleshooting and Common Traps

Don't demand public declarations of love

Sometimes people think a social media announcement of how much you love your partner is an indicator of the amount of love you share. That's not the case. In fact, some research shows the more you brag about your relationship publicly, the less likely you are to have a happy relationship privately. While there's nothing unhealthy about sharing positive things about your relationship if you're both on board, just make sure you aren't looking for validation from other people that you look happy.

Don't share more than your partner wants you to make public. If you're with someone who doesn't want the whole world to know how you met, you don't have to go into detail when someone asks. Remember, the health of your relationship doesn't depend on how much you brag to other people about your relationship—it depends on how much the two of you privately talk about it.

Don't use old memories as a weapon

Bringing up the past as a way to insult your partner can seriously damage the relationship. Sarcastic comments like, "You used to want to change the world. Now you can't change the sheets," are hurtful and counterproductive.

It's unfair to say things like, "I fell in love with you because you were passionate about so many amazing things. Now you're boring and all you want to do is work and stay home." It's OK for your partner to grow and change (something we'll discuss in the next chapter) but just because their behavior changes doesn't mean the essence of who they are has changed.

Conversation Starters

Take a minute to review the following questions. If your partner is interested in building mental strength and they're open to answering, use these questions to get a conversation started.

- Do you know why I fell in love with you in the first place?
- What do I do that reminds you why I love you?
- What made you fall in love with me?
- What are your favorite ways to show me how much you love me?
- What are some times when you've felt most loved by me?

Interview with Lori Gottlieb

The stories we tell ourselves about our relationships greatly affect our everyday behavior. And fortunately, we have the power to change the way we see that narrative. Someone who understands this well is Lori Gottlieb. She's a psychotherapist and New York Times bestselling author of *Maybe You Should Talk to Someone*. Her book has sold over one million copies and is currently being adapted as a TV series. In addition to her L.A.-based practices, she's the cohost of a popular podcast called *Dear Therapists*. She also writes the *Atlantic*'s "Dear Therapist" advice column. I admire her work and wanted her to weigh in on how couples can keep their relationships healthy.

Since you started working as a therapist fifteen years ago, have the relationship problems that you're seeing changed at all, or are you still seeing pretty much the same problems now as you were then?

I would say fundamentally they're the same. I would say that the ways in which they present themselves are a little bit different. Just with technology, things have changed.

With technology, what kinds of changes are you seeing in the types of problems couples are having, whether it's social media or dating apps or texting each other instead of talking?

I think with married people, there's a lot of difference in terms of how much they want to be in contact during the day. When it was just calling someone, people kind of went off and did their days, and maybe they'd check in and be like, "Hey," but it wasn't constant texting all day long. And I think that people don't realize that they have different preferences around how much space they need, and with technology you don't get a lot of space. So they really have to talk about that and communicate about that.

I think other things that seem a little bit more obvious are things like the ways in which people are inappropriately in touch with other people on technology, and people in a couple might have different definitions of what is okay and what is not okay in terms of, "Oh, wow, you guys are in contact on Instagram?" or, "You guys are DMing about this stuff?" And that just didn't happen before. You didn't have access to so many different people whenever you wanted to have access to them, and so couples really need to talk about what does it mean to cross a line.

How about since the pandemic? Are you seeing changes in what couples are struggling with since then?

I think the pandemic did one of two things. The couples who were doing well became closer, because I think that they found that the ways in which they interacted were able to translate to that. So if they had a rupture, they could repair it. If they had difficulty, they could talk about it.

The people who were not doing well before the pandemic and could kind of distract themselves with other things—just the busyness of life—when they were faced with each other and they had nowhere else to go, they struggled, because they just didn't have those tools. They didn't have that precedent set already in their relationship.

What are the biggest misconceptions people have about what a healthy relationship is or should be?

Biggest misconceptions are we never disagree about anything. The other person is going, "If they really loved me, they would do X. The reason that I am not able to show up for you is because I need you to take the first step. I want the other person to . . . If you change, I will change," as opposed to not realizing that when you change, you influence the other person to change. So other misconceptions people have: that you know each other as well as you think you do, that you can read each other's minds, that you should just know. "You really don't know that I prefer this to this?" or "You really don't know that I wanted you to fold the laundry? You should just know what I want." Those kinds of things.

What are the most important things you think a couple should do to keep the relationship healthy?

I think that they should make sure that they aren't just depending on their marriage for their social support, that they have a circle of friends, that they have other people that they go out and have fun with. Then when they come together, they talk about their differences instead of avoiding them. Also, they're not afraid to bring up things that might feel like hard conversations or hard topics.

Any tips for couples who feel like they've grown apart?

I would say if you were connected at one point, what are the kinds of things that felt connecting, and what's preventing you from doing those now? And what is a version of those that you could still do?

In my work with couples, I'll say, "What I want you to do is, I want you to just, after this session, when we hang up here, I want you to go and I want you to dance for ten minutes together. There's no point, there's no anything. You're just going to dance together for ten minutes, and just dance in the same room, whatever that looks like." And people are like, "Wow, we never do that." Or like, "I'm a bad dancer. I don't want to do that," and "That's embarrassing." And then they do it and they're like, "We never do things like that." And all it is, is ten minutes.

So, whatever that version of dancing is for a couple, they usually figure it out. Sometimes it remains dancing, but other times it's like, "Let's just walk outside for ten minutes," or "Let's make cookies for ten minutes," or whatever it is. But just what are the things where you're not talking about big issues, but you're just having fun? I think that people forget to have fun. They forget what fun looks like.

So I think people need to put more fun into their relationships. That can be quick. It's not like, "We have to do date night," or "We have to do this big adventure. We have to go on a trip together. We have to take a weekend away." It's just in your daily lives; find five, ten minutes a day to have fun together.

CHAPTER 10

They Don't Expect the Relationship to Meet All Their Needs

Thirty-nine percent of people say their partner expects
more emotional support than they can give.
—Couples by the Numbers Survey

Cara called my therapy office asking for an appointment as soon as possible. She had struggled with anxiety and depression for a while, and was now eager to address it. She was in her mid-thirties, had a good job, and had been married for three years.

During her first appointment, she told me that her husband, Ben, didn't understand what she was going through, and she felt lonelier than ever. She described her relationship with Ben as good overall, but he seemed indifferent to her mental health issues.

Cara's medical facility job kept her so busy that she said she didn't have time to feel depressed or anxious at work. Weekends were a different story. She often spent Saturdays and Sundays home by herself and with little do, she had too much time to think.

Ben spent most of his weekends at car shows. He had inherited an antique car when his grandfather passed away and he enjoyed showing the car off any chance that he got.

Cara could think of nothing more boring than sitting at a car show all day while people talked about engines. At first, she went to the shows with Ben just so they could spend time together. But they argued because Cara wanted to leave as soon as the show was over. Ben wanted to stick around and talk to the other car owners. One time, Ben insisted they go to dinner with the other car owners after the show. They all drove their cars to a local restaurant and Cara spent the whole evening listening to people talk about carburetors. After that, she decided not to go to any more car shows.

She said, "It's like he doesn't realize that my anxiety and depression get worse when I sit at home by myself on the weekends. And he also doesn't seem to care that boring old car shows make my mental health even worse!"

Cara thought Ben should stop going to car shows and stay home with her on the weekends so she could feel better. She had already tried to convince him to do so, but it didn't work.

I asked her how she thought therapy could be helpful and she said, "I thought maybe we could bring Ben into a session and you could talk him into staying home on the weekends. If he knew more about how he's affecting me, maybe he'd change his mind about car shows."

I didn't agree to talk to Ben. This is a common request therapists often get. People ask us to write letters to their bosses or to call a family member to tell them to change their behavior. But that's not my role as a therapist. If she was having trouble communicating her needs, we could certainly do that in a session. But that's not what she wanted. She wanted me to tell him he needed to change his behavior.

So I let her know that I wasn't going to do that. I could, however, help her find ways to manage her mental health. She agreed to start therapy because her ultimate goal was to feel better.

Cara thought Ben should be meeting all of her emotional needs. As you'll see later in this chapter, however, she eventually learned to adjust her expectations and meet some of her own needs. But, before we get back to their story, take a minute to consider whether you expect your partner to meet all your emotional needs.

Quiz

Take a minute to see how many of the following statements sound like you.

- ❑ I rely on my partner to feel good about myself.
- ❑ I get angry when my partner isn't meeting my emotional needs.
- ❑ I don't tell my partner what my emotional needs are.
- ❑ I think there's a deeper meaning when my partner doesn't meet my needs (such as they really don't love me).
- ❑ I blame my partner when I feel lonely.
- ❑ When I'm upset, I think it is my partner's job to help me feel better.
- ❑ I expect my partner to avoid doing things that cause me to feel angry or sad.
- ❑ It's my partner's job to keep me happy.

Now, take a minute to think about how your partner might respond to those statements. If many of those sound like you or your partner, you're not alone. Fortunately, there are steps you can take to find a healthy balance between meeting your own needs and allowing your partner to meet some of those needs for you.

Starting Point

Cara thought the cure for the loneliness, anxiety, and depression she felt on the weekends was to ask Ben to give up something that he loved doing. If he stayed home, she'd feel better. She wasn't thinking about how staying home might have a negative impact on Ben's mental well-being.

Cara assumed that once she was married, her partner would cure her problems. She had bought into the *Jerry McGuire* notion that your partner should complete you.

Everyone has emotional needs. Those needs vary from person to person. And your emotional needs may vary throughout your life. You may need more empathy at some points and more autonomy at others.

It's tough to know your emotional needs, let alone your partner's needs. Research conducted by Willard Harley, the author of *His Needs, Her Needs: Building an Affair-Proof Marriage,* found that several needs listed as most important by one partner were usually the least important for the other partner. If one person has a strong need for companionship and their partner has a high need for space, each of them may feel disappointed by their partner's actions.

Expecting our partner to know what we need and expecting them to fulfill all those needs is an impossible order. Take a minute to consider the following questions:

- ○ Do you know what emotional needs are most important to you?
- ○ Do you expect your partner to meet too many of your needs?
- ○ Do you know what emotional needs are most important to your partner?
- ○ Do you think your partner expects you to meet too many of their needs?

If you aren't sure what your needs are, don't worry. We'll review those a little later in the chapter.

Why We Expect Our Relationship to Meet All Our Needs

Cara felt Ben met her needs at first. But, she didn't really know what her needs were until he developed a passion that she didn't enjoy.

She tried to talk Ben out of going to some of the car shows but her attempts were mostly passive-aggressive. She'd say things like, "Oh, that show is a long drive away and you probably don't want to take your car through the winding roads in the country to go all the way there."

If he still chose to go, even after she pointed out all the reasons why he shouldn't, she felt betrayed. She convinced herself that there were only two possible scenarios about why he would do such a thing: he either didn't care about her or he didn't understand being alone was distressing to her.

Like Cara, you might assume that a healthy relationship fixes everything or that it's your partner's job to help you cope with any uncomfortable feelings you might have. But the truth is, a relationship won't prevent you from feeling anxiety, sadness, disappointment, and embarrassment. In fact, there will probably be plenty of times when you think your partner is the cause of those emotions.

Books, movies, TV shows, and social media posts will try to convince you that being with the right person fixes everything. Hollywood romances show you that love conquers all and when you're in a committed relationship, the two of you will somehow come together to meet one another's financial needs, emotional voids, social demands, and self-esteem deficits. Believing that your partner should meet all your needs might prevent you from trying to meet any of your own needs—and you might blame your partner for not being enough for you.

Mental Strength Exercises

During Cara's second therapy appointment, we discussed her thoughts about Ben's responsibilities versus her responsibilities. She believed couples should always spend their spare time together. When Ben didn't stay home, she felt abandoned. That caused her to feel anxious about their relationship.

I asked her when in her life had she felt a strong sense of abandonment. She thought for a minute and then began sobbing. I handed her the box of tissues and she said, "My parents divorced when I was four. My dad was supposed to take me on the weekends. But sometimes, he didn't show up. I'd sit by the window and wait for him for a long time until my mom would say, 'I guess he's not coming again.' Then, I'd spend the weekend wondering if he was ever going to come pick me up and I worried that he didn't love me."

It was no wonder that Cara felt abandoned by Ben on the weekends. It reminded her of how she felt as a little girl.

We spent the next few weeks talking about what it was like to have a father whom she couldn't depend on. His commitment to her depended heavily on who he was dating or what he was doing for work. She said even now, not much had changed.

She still had a relationship with her father, but it wasn't a good one. He was remarried and his current wife had young children who lived at home. Cara felt jealous that her stepsiblings got to grow up in the same house as her father—something she had wished she had been able to do. She still talked to her father and saw him occasionally but by now, she knew not to trust anything he said. He might show up, call back, or actually be home when he said he was going to be there, but she also knew there was a fair chance he'd have an excuse to cancel at the last second. Or worse yet, he just might forget they'd planned something together.

We talked about how Ben wasn't her father. He was dependable. He was trustworthy and a person of his word. Cara said if Ben said he was going to do something, he did it. And she appreciated that. Deep down she knew he wasn't abandoning her when he left for a car show—but she said the sadness and anxiety she experienced sometimes caused her to think otherwise.

We discussed her options. She could certainly ask Ben again to stay home with her every weekend. She could also choose to go with Ben to car shows. Or she could find other things to do on the weekends.

Before she entertained those ideas, we talked about Ben's emotional needs. Cara thought it was important for Ben to do things he loved. She wanted him to be happy. She also thought it was important for Ben to be able to show off his grandfather's car. He'd been close to his grandfather and going to shows and talking about his memories of his grandfather was likely helping him heal. The car shows also gave him a chance to talk to his other family members about his grandfather's car—something the whole family loved. So maybe bringing his family together also met some of his needs.

Supporting Ben's desire to go to car shows was a great way she could meet his needs. Of course, that didn't mean she couldn't talk about her needs too.

After several more therapy sessions, Cara decided to talk to Ben. When she showed up for her appointment after their discussion, she said she told Ben how being home alone on the weekends reminded her of her childhood. She offered this as an explanation, not to guilt him into staying home. She acknowledged that he loved car shows and that they were probably good for him and said she wanted to work on a plan to meet both of their emotional needs.

She said Ben was surprised to hear what she had to say. He had just assumed she thought car shows were boring and he didn't think much more about it. It led to a discussion about their options. Ben said he didn't plan to go to car shows forever. For now, it was important to him but he acknowledged he was already getting a little tired of them.

Cara explained she felt inspired to find things she could do on her own when he was out of town, like explore some hobbies or visit friends.

I asked Cara how she felt about their conversation and she said, "I'm relieved that Ben was open to having a conversation. I am glad he showed some concern and I'm also happy that I feel empowered to improve my mental health by doing some things on my own."

Before we ended therapy, we discussed that they were likely to experience some more bumps in the road when it came to unmet emotional needs as time went on. But, now that Cara said she better understood emotional needs and healthy expectations, she knew she and Ben could have healthy conversations whenever differences arose.

Identify Your Needs and Your Partner's Needs

Author and researcher Willard Harley developed a list of the top ten basic emotional needs. Read the list and see which five needs are most important to you. Then, try to identify which needs you think are your partner's top five.

Then, if your partner is willing, ask them to identify their top five needs and what they think are your top five needs. Compare your lists and discuss any differences you see.

1. **Admiration.** Admiration involves compliments or signs of appreciation. Being affirmed by your partner may help you feel respected and valued.
2. **Affection.** Affection can involve anything from a card that says "I love you" to holding hands and giving a gift. Signs of affection help couples bond.
3. **Intimate conversation.** Talking about your hopes, dreams, and fears can make conversations intimate. These conversations require vulnerability and respect.
4. **Domestic support.** Domestic support refers to all the activities that are needed to maintain a household, like cooking, cleaning, raising children, and managing day-to-day affairs.

5. **Family commitment.** Couples who have children may experience a need for family commitment—essentially making the family a top priority to provide quality time and meet the needs of other family members.

6. **Financial support.** Some people gain a sense of security from knowing their partner can assist them financially. Even in families where both individuals have income, one partner may feel safe knowing that their partner could assist them if they became unemployed or unable to work.

7. **Honesty and openness.** A high level of honesty and openness is what helps some people feel secure. They may gain trust by sharing their innermost thoughts and feelings.

8. **Physical attractiveness.** While appearance changes over time, remaining physically attracted to one another is a high priority for some individuals.

9. **Recreational companionship.** Recreational companionship involves doing recreational activities together as a couple—such as shopping, watching football, going to the movies, or entertaining friends.

10. **Sexual fulfillment.** There's an emotional need for sex and in monogamous relationships, you'll depend on your partner to meet this need. This isn't the same as the need for affection as you can still hug your friends or kiss your pet. Sexual fulfillment is about satisfying your need for romantic passion.

It might be hard to identify your top five. All those things might seem really important to you. Or, when you talk about your list with your partner, you might discover that your partner wasn't aware of your needs (maybe you weren't aware either) or you didn't recognize your partner's needs. Now that you know, you can start a conversation about how to support one another.

Ask Yourself, "When Did I First Feel This Way?"

Once Cara linked the intense feelings she experienced when Ben left for car shows with the times she felt abandoned by her father as a child, she could make more sense of her situation. She realized that while her feelings were intense, it wasn't Ben's fault she felt so bad.

> The reason you have such a strong reaction to your partner's behavior might have nothing to do with your partner.

Whenever you're feeling an intense emotion, ask yourself about the first time you ever felt that way. The reason you have such a strong reaction to your partner's behavior might have nothing to do with your partner.

The way they talk to you might cause you to "feel small," like you did when your mother used to shame you. Or the way they ignore you when you're talking might remind you of how the kids used to ignore you in the cafeteria when you tried to tell a story. Or when your partner gets mad and walks away from a conversation, it may stir up the same feeling you used to get when your mom stormed out of the house when she was angry with your dad.

Tying your emotional response to something from your past can help you figure out how to heal an old emotional wound. It may also help you take more responsibility for meeting your unmet emotional needs.

Ask for What You Need

Your emotional needs will shift over time. As your family expands, your role changes, or you encounter new circumstances, your emotional needs priority list will shuffle.

You might want more financial stability after you have children. Or you may want more recreational companionship after you retire.

Your appreciation for your partner's behavior may shift as well. You might have loved how spontaneous your partner was when you first got together. But now that you have more responsibility, you might view those same "spontaneous" behaviors as impulsive or reckless. This might be a sign that your needs have shifted—you may need more stability now. But just because your needs have changed doesn't mean your partner's behavior will automatically shift.

Don't make your partner guess what emotional needs you have at various seasons in your life. Tell them what you need and take responsibility for meeting some of your own needs. Check in with your partner from time to time to see if their needs are being met and to discuss how your needs may have shifted.

Who's Motivated?

Take a minute to think about who thinks there's a problem and who is motivated to create change. Then, you can decide how to approach your situation best.

1. You depend on your partner to meet too many of your needs.

You need some non-negotiables in a relationship. And hopefully, you knew what those non-negotiables were before you got into a serious relationship—like you aren't going to tolerate someone swearing at you or you aren't going to put up with someone who lies to you.

But sometimes we confuse those big non-negotiables with smaller things. Let's say your partner forgot to honor the anniversary of your first date. You might assign meaning to that behavior by concluding that forgetting your anniversary means they don't care about you. Thinking that way may cause you to experience a lot of hurt and it could affect your behavior—perhaps you act cold toward them because they hurt your feelings.

An alternative option is to remind yourself that the fact that they forgot the anniversary doesn't necessarily mean they don't care about you. There are many other alternative explanations—dates may not be important to them, they may not know what today's date is, they may not have ever noted the date on the calendar when you first met, or it may have simply slipped their mind.

When your partner doesn't meet all of your emotional needs, it doesn't mean they don't care. It means they're working on meeting their own needs too—which is essential for a healthy relationship. You can contribute to the relationship by taking responsibility to meet some of your own needs.

2. You think your partner depends on you too much to meet their needs.

If you think your partner depends on you too much to meet their needs, stop and ask yourself whether you need to change your behavior or your partner should adjust their expectations.

Consider whether your inability to meet their current needs is temporary or permanent. If you're focused on something challenging right now—like caring for an elderly parent—you may not be able to meet their emotional needs. Go ahead and make that clear. Say something like, "Right now, I'm not able to do that."

Also, think about whether your needs are opposing forces. If you need freedom and they need more contact, discuss your options. There may be times when you can find a healthy compromise and other times when it's impossible to meet both of your needs simultaneously.

Challenge yourself to support your partner if you can but also give yourself permission to set healthy boundaries to preserve your inner peace. You may need to talk about the boundaries you think are essential to getting your own needs met.

3. Your partner thinks you depend on them too much to get your needs met.

If your partner tells you that you're too "needy," you might inadvertently cling to them a little tighter as they try to pull away. And while hearing that you're too needy is likely to hurt your feelings, don't lash out.

If your partner is brave enough to say that they can't do everything you ask, thank them for being up front. It can be tough to admit to someone you care about that you can't give them everything they need.

No matter how you feel, don't argue or insist that you're not asking too much or that your partner isn't giving enough. Instead, get clear on what they specifically think they can't give to you. For example, are they unable to satisfy your need for intimate conversation right now because they're so stressed about work or extended family issues? Or might they be struggling with a mental health issue that makes it difficult for them to earn money, and therefore that disrupts your financial security?

Once you know what needs they can't meet at the moment, you can find some alternatives for yourself. Discuss what boundaries they want to set and what strategies you want to try.

4. You both agree that you depend on one another too much.

If you and your partner guess what one another wants and you abandon yourselves for the other person, it's important to address it. Otherwise, you'll both end up feeling disappointed and burned out and neither of you will be happy.

One person might forgo doctor's appointments because they're meeting their partner's need for financial security. Meanwhile, the other individual might forgo their need for sexual fulfillment because they're trying to fulfill all their other family responsibilities.

There's a lot of wisdom behind the old saying, "Don't set yourself on fire to keep someone else warm." That's true even when it comes to your partner. Speak up and share your needs. But also share what you're doing to get your own needs met.

How Meeting Some of Your Own Needs Makes You Stronger

Once Cara connected the dots between her current emotional responses and the emotions she experienced during childhood, she was able to begin healing some old emotional wounds. She also realized that it wasn't Ben's responsibility to rescue her. She communicated her experiences with Ben and they talked about how to ensure she was getting what she needed—what he could do as well as what she could do.

Cara empowered herself to meet some of her own needs while also talking to Ben about what she needed from the relationship. She discovered that she still liked knitting—something her grandmother had taught her when she was young. And she enjoyed knitting scarves to give to people. When she was done knitting a scarf, it gave her a reason to visit a friend or a family member to present it as a gift. So she was no longer feeling sad and anxious on the weekends. She had something to do that gave her meaning and purpose that didn't involve Ben.

No couple is a perfect fit in terms of emotional needs.

No couple is a perfect fit in terms of emotional needs. In fact, it's the differences in emotional needs that often attract partners to one another.

Feeling a little uncomfortable because your needs aren't being met isn't a bad thing. You can learn a lot from discomfort—and you might learn that you have skills, resources, and strategies you had forgotten existed.

Being part of any good team involves some give-and-take. But that give-and-take has to occur on both sides. If you insist your partner meet all your needs, there's a good chance their needs won't get met. When both of you can identify what needs aren't being met and develop a clear plan for meeting those needs, you'll become stronger individuals who can also be stronger together.

Troubleshooting and Common Traps

Justifying your bad behavior

Some people try to justify bad behavior by blaming their partner for not meeting their needs. They may say they cheated because they weren't getting enough attention. Or they might claim they stopped giving their partner attention because they needed more freedom. If your partner can't meet your needs, it's your responsibility to talk about it and take action to meet your own needs—without damaging the relationship.

Trying to meet all your partner's needs

If you put a lot of pressure on yourself to meet your partner's needs, pause and take a look at what is going on underneath that desire. Do you fear that you might be inadequate if your partner has to meet some of their needs? Do you have a fear they may abandon you if you don't meet all their needs all the time?

Consider whether that pressure comes from your partner or from within. If you can't give yourself permission to meet your own needs and allow your partner to meet some of their own needs, you may want to talk to a therapist.

Conversation Starters

Take a minute and review the following questions. If your partner is interested in learning about mental strength, use these questions to start a conversation about your emotional needs.

- What are some examples of emotional needs that are important to you but less important to me?
- What are some examples of emotional needs that you think are more important to me and less important to you?
- What are some things we do well when it comes to meeting one another's emotional needs?
- What are some things we do to meet our own emotional needs that seems to work well?

Interview with Shane Birkel

While most couples don't walk into therapy saying, "We're here to talk about our emotional needs," that's often the reason they seek help. I reached out to Shane Birkel to learn how he treats couples who are struggling with the issue surrounding their emotional needs. Shane is a licensed marriage and family therapist with a private practice in New Hampshire. He's the host of a wonderful podcast called *The Couples Therapist Couch*. Since he's been a couples counselor for twelve years, he has some helpful insight into the emotional needs of couples.

What are the most common issues couples want to address in your therapy office?

It is common for people to say that their biggest issue is that they can't communicate. I think communication is what we see on the surface, but most people have a sense that there is something deeper going on as well.

As a couples therapist, I can teach people communication skills, but in order to truly be able to make progress, people have to learn how to work with the parts of themselves that don't want to use those skills.

There are two common issues that come up for a lot of people. Most people fall into one of these two categories. The first issue is when people feel like their partner is distant, disconnected, and not present. They try to communicate and feel like it just pushes their partner further away.

The second is when someone feels like no matter how much they do or how hard they try, their partner is never satisfied. They might feel overwhelmed by their partner's emotional needs.

If these two types of people form a relationship together (which they often do) it creates a dance where the more one partner pursues, tries to connect, tries to work on things, the more the other partner feels flooded and needs space and distances themselves. The more they distance themselves, the more the other partner feels anxious and continues to pursue. This can create a problematic cycle.

People can learn the communication skills, but if they aren't dealing with what's driving the fundamental needs and beliefs underneath the surface, they will continue to struggle. These issues are usually connected to experiences and themes from our childhood.

What are some of the biggest misconceptions people seem to have about how relationships *should* be?

Society and the media use terms like "soul mate" and "you complete me" and "true love" as though there is someone out there who you are destined for who is going to make you feel the love that you always wanted. This is a misconception that causes people to have the false belief that relationships should feel easy and be perfect all the time.

One of the most helpful things for people to realize is that their relationship won't feel perfect or easy all the time and that's OK. Relationships take a lot of work. When people understand this, they feel less pressure when they go through normal stressors with their partner.

People develop their beliefs about what relationships "should" be based on what they grow up with. An example of this is if a person grows up in a family where no one talks about emotions, they might take on the belief that emotions are a problem that need to be fixed. If they then find themselves in a relationship with someone who is emotionally expressive, they might have a hard time with that and define it as a problem. This might make their partner feel a lack of connection and acceptance for their normal, healthy emotions.

The most important thing people can do is to recognize that all of their beliefs about how a relationship "should" be come from things they learned in childhood either from their caregivers' modeling or from society. If someone sees things differently the best thing we can do is move into curiosity instead of judgment or criticism.

Can you think of an example from your therapy office where someone relied too much on their partner to meet all their emotional needs? What happened with them?

One of the most common issues I see is people depending too much on their partner to fulfill their emotional needs. This creates a feeling of codependence in the relationship. When we are children we need our parents to take care of our emotional needs. When this doesn't happen in a healthy way during our childhood, we grow up with a lack of maturity, still wanting someone to take care of us in the way we deserve.

When people are valued sufficiently as children they are able to develop a healthy self-esteem that comes from within. Most people have things they experience that make them question this, including the messages they get from their parents or society. Because of that, people have a hard time with self-esteem and question their own value in the world.

Instead of inherently having the belief that I am enough and I matter, people think I am enough and I matter because I can perform in the world (performance-based esteem) or because other people think I do (other-based esteem). When our partner shows us love we develop the belief that we are lovable. If we become dependent on that to value ourselves, it can be dangerous. If our partner is having a bad day or not doing the things we think they "should" if they really loved us, it can start feeling toxic and co-dependent.

If I am a healthy, mature adult in my relationship, I can move into compassion for my partner if they aren't having a good day, if I'm not getting what I want from them, or even if I feel hurt. My sense of value comes from within so I don't need them to do anything to feel like I am enough.

How do you help people find that balance between meeting their own emotional needs but also knowing their partner can meet some of their needs?

I think for humans there is a spectrum that each of us falls on. On one side of the spectrum is emotional neediness, on the other side of the spectrum is emotional avoidance. In the middle is emotional health.

Most of us fall toward one side or the other. Neither one is better or worse. They both have strengths and weaknesses. That being said, depending on which side someone falls will determine what it is they need to work on. There are different fears and limiting beliefs connected to each.

If you are someone who falls on the side of emotional neediness the work might be about challenging the belief that I need someone else to love me in order to feel worthy. I am enough and I matter despite what is going on with my partner.

If you are someone who falls on the side of emotional avoidance it might be about the fear that I am not worthy enough to say what I need. People should just take care of their own needs. The work might be about believing that it's OK to ask for help with your partner and to say what you want in your relationship.

CHAPTER 11

They Don't Neglect Their Partnership

Fifty percent of individuals say they feel
neglected by their partner sometimes.
—Couples by the Numbers Survey

Gary called my office asking for a couples therapy appointment. He said, "I just discovered my partner, Alex, is having an inappropriate relationship. Alex and I would like to start therapy to see if we can salvage our marriage."

When they showed up to their first appointment, they sat on the couch next to each other. When I asked them what they hoped to gain from therapy, Gary said, "Well, Alex was having an emotional affair. We want to know what to do now because we want our relationship to work."

Alex added, "I made some mistakes but I want Gary to acknowledge that he made some mistakes too. That's the only way we can really fix things."

They shared a bit about their story—they'd been together for about five years. Overall, they reported having a good relationship. But during the pandemic, when they were both home almost all the time, they argued more and got on one another's nerves. During that time, Alex started spending more time locked away in the home office.

After almost a year of working from home, Gary started going back into his company office. He started traveling for business trips again too, while Alex continued working from home.

Gary said, "Alex worked a lot of hours so I never questioned why he was working from his home office late into the evenings. I heard him on Zoom calls and it never occurred to me that he wasn't talking about business. But I discovered that he and his coworker Brian were having inappropriate conversations."

Alex acknowledged his friendship with his coworker had turned into an emotional affair. He said, "I just feel comfortable talking to Brian about everything. We discuss things that I can't talk to Gary about."

But Gary was quick to say, "Alex, it's not like you guys were just talking about politics. You were saying things like, 'Let's run away together,' as if you were fourth-graders planning to run away from home because your parents were too strict."

Alex acknowledged that he said things like that. But he added, "I only did that because I was so lonely, Gary. You're rarely around and when you do come home, you don't want to talk."

Despite the tough conversation, it was a good first therapy session. They both communicated how they felt and they were able to do so respectfully. But therapy was only going to be helpful if they were both invested in doing some work to fix their relationship. It was clear they had neglected their partnership for quite some time. As a result, they had some serious repair work to do.

They agreed they wanted to have a loving relationship. And they both said they were invested in getting the most out of therapy. I'll explain what happened with Gary and Alex later in the chapter. But before we get there, think about your own relationship and whether you or your partner neglects it sometimes.

Quiz

Take a minute to review the following statements and see how many of them seem to describe your relationship.

- ❑ We have busy lives and we don't make our relationship a priority.
- ❑ We have different interests so it's tough to find common ground or things we can work on together.
- ❑ We have different values so rather than try to combine our ideas, it's often easier to just work on separate plans.
- ❑ When we're physically together, we don't really try to connect with one another.
- ❑ We don't do things to grow together as a couple.
- ❑ We don't do much to nurture our friendship.
- ❑ We don't feel bonded with one another.
- ❑ We don't invest much time in genuinely connecting.
- ❑ We sometimes neglect one another's needs.

The more those statements sound true, the more likely you are to be neglecting your partnership. Fortunately, there are things you can do to devote more time and energy to one another and growing your relationship.

Starting Point

During their second session, Gary and Alex agreed they both neglected the relationship. When Gary was away from the home, he rarely called or texted Alex. And when they were both home, neither put much effort into connecting. Alex neglected the relationship by not talking to Gary about how he was feeling. Instead, he turned to someone outside the relationship to meet his needs for an intimate connection.

Even if you can't completely relate to Gary and Alex's situation, you might recognize times when you've neglected your partner, or have felt like your partner has neglected you.

There may even be good reasons for neglecting your partnership at times. Perhaps you and your partner agreed that you would put everything you had into getting out of debt this year, even if it meant you would both be working so much you wouldn't see each other as often. Or maybe you went back to school, and you needed to put so much effort into your classes that you didn't have much left over for your relationship. In cases like that— when you developed a plan together—it's often challenging but doable.

But when one or both partners neglect the relationship without the conscious decision to prioritize other things, the relationship suffers.

As we discussed in the last chapter, it's not healthy to try and meet all your partner's emotional needs. But at the same time, it's essential to devote time and energy to meeting some of their needs so you can nurture the relationship.

Take a minute to answer the following questions:

○ Do you neglect your relationship?
○ Does your partner neglect the relationship?
○ Do you both neglect the relationship?

If you neglect your partnership or you feel like your partner neglects your relationship, you're not alone. Fortunately, no matter how much you've neglected your relationship, there are things that you can do to start nurturing and growing your partnership again.

Why We Neglect Our Partnership

For Gary and Alex, nurturing the relationship felt inconvenient. Between Gary's hectic work schedule and Alex's need for companionship, they needed to put in a concerted effort to connect and build their relationship.

During that second therapy session, Gary said that until he discovered Alex's close relationship with a coworker, he didn't realize how bad things had gotten. He said, "We both took the easy route. I stayed focused on work and Alex turned his focus to someone that gave him a lot of attention."

In today's world, nurturing our relationships takes extra effort. Most people find their work lives bleeding over into what was historically considered "family time." On top of that, we've got endless passive entertainment opportunities at our fingertips. It takes less work to watch TV than hold a deep conversation. Not to mention, dozens of things vie for your attention if you have a smartphone nearby. Text messages, apps, emails, and social media alerts call your attention to your phone—not your partner.

> Text messages, apps, emails, and social media alerts call your attention to your phone—not your partner.

To better understand why you may neglect your relationship, review the following statements and see how many sound like you.

- ○ I put other people first because I think my partner will understand.
- ○ I have a lot of pressing things that demand my attention.
- ○ It's easier to have our own separate roles rather than work together.
- ○ I'm scared to combine too much of our lives just in case things don't work out.
- ○ Other people are sometimes a bigger priority in my life.
- ○ Work takes up a lot of my time and energy and I don't have much time left over for my partner.
- ○ I have difficulty saying no to other people or opportunities, even when it takes away from my relationship.

○ We have unresolved past issues that prevent me from wanting to put much effort into the relationship now.

○ I have a fear of being too committed to my partner.

The more items you checked, the easier it will be to put your energy elsewhere rather than build a stronger relationship.

Mental Strength Exercises

After a few therapy sessions, our focus turned to Alex. He acknowledged his late-night conversations and text messages were inappropriate. Like Gary, he referred to those conversations as "an emotional affair." He said he knew it was OK to have close friends, but he and Gary had decided a long time ago that secret conversations which would cause the other partner to feel uncomfortable were off-limits.

Alex knew he had damaged the relationship. He had broken Gary's trust. He used to say he had to be on late-night work meetings but he was really just retreating to the home office to hold secret conversations. Gary felt betrayed, and even though he wanted to trust Alex again, rebuilding that trust would take time.

We spent one session just focusing on boundaries. Gary wanted to make sure that Alex didn't have any more contact with Brian—and Alex agreed that he could end any one-on-one contact with Brian as they didn't need to have private meetings for work. To prevent any confusion, Gary said, "If you're saying things to someone that you wouldn't want me to overhear, it's not a conversation you should be having." Alex said he understood.

While it wasn't Gary's fault that Alex was having an emotional affair, he acknowledged the part he played in the deterioration of their relationship. For example, Alex frequently called him when he was away on business trips. Gary rarely answered the phone. If he did, he often cut their conversations short. He said, "I used to get annoyed that he interrupted my trip." But now he realized how hurtful that was to Alex, who was sitting at home feeling lonely or struggling with a problem.

Part of their treatment involved discussing what they could each contribute to the partnership and how they could nurture their relationship over time—even when they were apart often or when it wasn't convenient to connect with one another.

They decided that Saturdays would be their day together and that no matter what, spending the day together would become their top priority. They would take turns deciding what to do together each week and they would try to encourage one another to try new things so their experiences could help them grow.

We also discussed how they could foster their emotional intimacy. They agreed to connect every day, even when Gary was away from home on business, with at least one phone call in the evenings. And when they were both home, they wouldn't work after 7 P.M. Instead, they could eat dinner together, watch TV, or just enjoy one another's company.

They put that game plan into place right away. Within a few weeks, they reported that they were enjoying each other's company more. They were talking more and having deeper conversations. They both said they felt confident that they would turn to each other for support now—not turn away.

Affirm Your Commitment Often

Just because you made a verbal agreement or even a legal agreement to be partners at some point, doesn't mean you're still committed now. A healthy relationship requires an ongoing commitment that you'll invest time and energy to keep your relationship healthy. Beyond that, a healthy relationship requires a willingness to do hard things, hold tough conversations, and negotiate disagreements—even on the days when you don't feel like it.

Different relationships have different needs and expectations.

There's no predetermined amount of time and energy you should give your partner. Different relationships have different needs and expectations. In some relationships, there's an understanding that each partner will spend the majority of their time doing other things—spending time with friends, engaging in hobbies, working, and managing household responsibilities independently. This works when couples agree to that level of commitment.

Other couples might want to spend the majority of their time together. And when they're not together, they might be addressing issues that almost always help the family. That works when both partners agree to this arrangement.

Commitment isn't just about time spent together, either. It's a commitment to one another's happiness and well-being. It involves a willingness to step up and help out, even when it's inconvenient or you don't feel like it.

Affirm your commitment to your partner often by saying things like:

- "I am glad I get to spend my life with you."
- "I know times are tough right now but I'm committed to finding a way to work through this."
- "If I could do things over again, I'd still choose you."

In addition to verbalizing your commitment, show your commitment through your actions. One of my former therapy clients used to take her wedding ring off every night when she went to sleep. It wasn't because it wasn't comfortable. It was because she wanted to reaffirm her commitment to her partner each morning when she chose to put her ring on her finger. It was her way of showing her partner she was choosing to be committed every single day.

Use "We Talk"

The language you use might reveal how you feel about your relationship and whether you truly see yourself as a cohesive unit. But language is a two-way street. Changing your language might change how you feel.

When you talk about important things in your life, do you use singular pronouns to describe yourself or do you use plural ones that include your partner?

For example, are you more likely to say, "I'm working hard to save for retirement," or "We're working hard to save for retirement"? Here's another example. Would you say, "I've been busy lately," or "We've been busy lately"?

Research shows couples who use "we talk" are more likely to experience positive emotions about their relationship. The authors of the study found that greater "we talk" predicted less marital decline over time and it benefited both the partner using it as well as the partner who is listening.

If you tend to only refer to yourself, don't get too caught up in thinking it's clearly a sign of a deep-rooted issue. Change your language to include your partner when you're talking about the things that affect both of you—like time, money, and future goals. Doing so might not deepen just your investment in the relationship, it might also improve your partner's investment too.

Develop and Maintain Relationship Rituals

Whether you get your partner their cup of coffee every morning or you go to brunch every Sunday, relationship rituals might matter more than you think. They may also just seem like habits or even, perhaps, part of a boring old routine. But those rituals you and your partner engage in might be healthy for the longevity of your partnership.

Studies have found that when both partners agree that something is a ritual (and not just something you do every day out of convenience), it strengthens commitment. Rituals don't contribute to the staleness or boredom in a relationship. Instead, researchers found that they were linked to more positive emotions and greater relationship satisfaction over time.

If you don't have a ritual that you both enjoy, create one. Here are some simple ritual ideas:

- Share the best part of your day when you eat dinner together
- Get ready for bed at the same time and talk
- Go to dinner at the same restaurant whenever you pick one another up from the airport
- Play a game together on Sunday evenings
- Eat a certain meal on a specific day of the week (like Taco Tuesdays)
- Leave notes in each other's suitcase when you're going away on a trip without one another
- Send a lunchtime positive text message

Just remember, it doesn't really matter what the ritual is. What matters is that it's something you both buy into, enjoy, or find funny together. Engaging in your ritual together over the years means you share something special that keeps you connected across time, even as the things around you change.

Who's Motivated?

Take a minute to think about who thinks there's a problem and who is motivated to create change. Then you can decide how to approach your situation best.

1. You neglect your relationship.

If you struggle to fully commit to your partner, examine why. Ask yourself what would happen if you became fully committed? You might find there are some underlying fears. Sometimes, people are afraid to completely commit because they don't want to get hurt. Even when they're married or they've been in a relationship for a long time, they hold back emotionally because they don't want the other person to hurt them. Ironically, by keeping their partner at an emotional distance, they often feel hurt.

You also might find that other things get in the way of nurturing your relationship. Working long hours, engaging in a passion or hobby, spending time with friends, or maybe even parenting duties get in the way of nurturing your relationship.

But take a step and consider what it's costing you to not nurture your relationship. Are you at risk of growing apart? Are you missing some of the best years of your lives together? Are you creating more emotional pain for yourself? If you're having a hard time figuring it out or you aren't sure how to create change, you may want to talk to a therapist.

2. You think your partner neglects the relationship.

If you feel like your partner isn't giving enough to your relationship, talk to your partner about your expectations. Sometimes, a simple difference in beliefs about how much time you should spend together or how much effort you should put into serious conversations can be an issue.

In addition to different ideas about how much time to spend together, you might also have very different ideas about how you should spend your time. If your partner loves to watch sports and you prefer to hike mountains, you might go in opposite directions on the weekends. Or maybe you love quiet evenings at home and your partner prefers to go out with friends. You might need to get creative to find things that you're both willing to try.

Your partner might welcome having coffee together in the morning if you woke up earlier. Or they may appreciate having time together in the evenings—time that you're usually on the phone or watching TV. Be flexible regarding the activities you try and the time of day or week that you try them.

Invite your partner to do things with you. Share your feelings by saying things like, "I would love it if you would join me." A willingness to be vulnerable can help your partner see that you welcome their company.

3. Your partner thinks you neglect the relationship.

There may be times when your partner needs more attention than you can give. But if your partner believes you're neglecting the relationship, listen to them.

Ask them to get specific if you can. You might find they're not interested in a lot more of your time or a lot more of your energy. Instead, there may be some little things that would make a big difference to the relationship.

They might want you to go with them to see their parents one Sunday a month. Or maybe they want you to put your phone on silent when you're eating dinner or out on the town. If they give you vague answers, like "you don't try," ask them to point out times when they see this happening right in the moment. That can help you get a better sense of their concerns.

Keep in mind that you might have very different ideas about what nurturing your partnership should look like. You might think that by working a lot of overtime, you're showing that you prioritize caring for your family. Your partner might see that same behavior as evidence that you're neglecting your duties as a partner. Talking about your feelings and your viewpoints can go a long way toward helping you figure out a plan together.

4. You both neglect the relationship.

During the pandemic, many couples spent more time together than ever before. But just because they were physically in the same space didn't mean they felt as though they were nurturing the relationship. In fact, many couples felt like being around each other all the time meant they weren't really taking time to be together.

But pandemic aside, if you and your partner agree you both neglect the relationship, shift your priorities. Whether work, extended family, parenting duties, or other obligations come first, you can look for ways to move the relationship up a little higher on the priority list.

If you're in a short-term situation that is causing you to put your focus elsewhere—like you're caring for a sick family member—acknowledge what's happening. Just talking about what's happening can help you get through it better. Take the time and energy you do have together and focus on making the best quality time possible until you can give more.

Troubleshooting and Common Traps

Thinking You'll Have Time to Spend Together Later

It's easy to think you'll have time to spend with your partner once life slows down or once you have reached a certain milestone. But sometimes life doesn't slow down (at least not in the way you want). And the last thing you want to do is make it to retirement only to discover that you prioritized work over your relationship for so many years that you now struggle to enjoy your time together. Make time for your relationship in every season of your life. There's no guarantee that you'll be able to spend time together in the future.

Assuming Your Partner Will Understand

It's easy to assume that your partner will simply understand why you can't prioritize the relationship right now. After all, your partner is the person who knows you best, so of course they will understand why you have to spend so much time at work or why you have to help out other people so much. But just because your partner is kind doesn't mean they should go lower on your priority list than the other things in your life. So don't assume your partner will understand. Have conversations with them about what's happening and how they feel.

How Tending to Your Relationship Makes You Stronger

When Alex and Gary started tending to their relationship, they rekindled their intimacy and connection. By the time they ended therapy, they both reported feeling more secure and more satisfied in their partnership. And the better they felt, the easier it was to stay motivated to keep working on growing even closer.

During their last session, we discussed warning signs to look for that would indicate they weren't nurturing their partnership. They created a list of red flags that would let them know something was wrong—like if Alex started working more in the evenings again or if Gary stopped connecting while he was away on business.

Then we discussed a plan for how they could address those issues right away. If they worked on reconnecting when they saw such red flags, they could do so without damaging the relationship. If, however, they ignored the warning signs again and allowed things to get worse, it was going to be more difficult to build a trusting relationship. But they both ended therapy feeling more confident in their relationship than they ever had before because they had the skills, tools, and knowledge that would allow them to keep fostering a healthy connection.

Sustaining a relationship takes work. When you're committed to nurturing the relationship in a healthy way, you're able to tolerate the natural give-and-take that comes with a partnership. Some days you'll do more. Other days, your partner will do more. But you won't feel the need to keep score—instead, you'll both be invested in growing the best partnership you can.

Conversation Starters

Take a few minutes to review the following questions. If your partner is open to having a conversation, ask them these questions to start a conversation about how you might nurture your relationship.

- What are some things you think we do well together to nurture our relationship?
- What are some times when you've put extra effort into caring for our relationship?
- What are some examples of times when you felt like I put a lot of energy into caring for our relationship?
- What are some times when it's been tough to care for our relationship but we did it anyway?
- How do you think we've managed to do that?

Interview with Ty Tashiro

Good relationships are part art, part science. To learn more about the science part, I reached out to Ty Tashiro. Dr. Tashiro is a social scientist who received his PhD from the University of Minnesota.

He's taught classes at both the University of Maryland and the University of Colorado. Dr. Tashiro has written several outstanding books, including *Awkward: The Science of Why We're Socially Awkward and Why That's Awesome* and *The Science of Happily Ever After*. I thought he'd be a great person to offer a research-based perspective on how couples can keep their relationship strong.

When you were writing *The Science of Happily Ever After*, was there something really surprising that you uncovered about relationships?

So I think that was one thing that jumped out at me as I went through the different findings. There's really these robust predictors of long-term relationship satisfaction, and it overlapped with some of the qualitative wisdom I heard from people I spoke to or older couples I had met who had had a happily ever after, who had been satisfied and stable for decades on end. A lot of times the stuff they told me about the secrets to their success were similar to some of the scientific findings I uncovered for the book.

And what are some of those secrets to a happy, long relationship?

Some of the secrets I heard from older adults who had had successful relationships centered around this idea that marriage is not what you think it is when you're young. So a lot of times these older adults would say, "Hey, when you're young, you're just focused on the excitement. You're focused on how pretty or hot the partner might be." And they're like, "That's not at all what matters in the long run." And thirty, forty, fifty years later, they're like, "What really matters is that you've chosen a partner who is strongly committed to this enterprise that both of you have undertaken and you've chosen a partner who's willing to work hard and have a sense of grace about these imperfections that are inevitably going to occur in a relationship."

In your book, you talk a lot about picking the right person in the first place. What can someone do if they're already in a committed relationship but they're second guessing whether they chose the right person? What if they're thinking the grass would have been greener if they'd chosen someone else?

I think everyone's a little susceptible to some of that grass is greener. One thing I might tell folks is if the thought crosses your mind, it's okay. It happens to most everyone. But what's really important is how you deal with it.

So there's this economic model that's been applied to study relationship commitment, and it's called social exchange theory. And in social exchange theory, there are three variables:

1. What do you want from a relationship or a partner?

2. What do you perceive you're getting from the relationship or the partner?

3. And what are your attractive alternative options?

And what's been interesting over the years is they found that the strongest of those variables is your perception of your attractive alternative options.

People who are committed to their relationship do a good job of managing their perceptions of attractive alternative options. People who have shaky commitment or are likely to exit a relationship don't do a very good job of managing their attractive alternative options. So I actually think it's beneficial for folks to be really honest with themselves about their impulses to let their mind wander a little bit or to think the grass is greener.

They did these really clever eye tracking studies and what they found was when they showed pictures on the computer screen of attractive people who could be attractive alternative options, they found that people who were highly satisfied in a relationship actually reflexively looked away from the more attractive pictures.

Whereas people who were ambivalent or less satisfied did what someone might naturally do, which is stare at the attractive pictures longer than the pictures that were less attractive. It seems like people might actually even train themselves to try to just avoid the temptation in the first place.

Do you have tips or strategies that can help people stay committed over the long haul?

Successful couples who have enduring relationships oftentimes qualitatively report that they wake up every day and they actually renew their commitment as part of their morning routine. It's this ongoing thing. It's not just at the altar where they make this global commitment, but instead they, at least on a weekly or daily basis, are consciously thinking to themselves, "Hey, let's be the best partner I can be for my wife or for my husband today."

What can couples do when they feel themselves growing apart?

Be very intentional about saying, "Hey, let's be playful together and let's always be learning together, and let's do stuff that's pretty uncomfortable together and that's going to bind us together over time and instill that novelty that continues to be important to partners as a relationship goes on." We don't want things to get boring or stale and so you have to actively get ahead of that.

A strong couple will come back from that and say, "Oh, it was fantastic. We were totally pushed out of our comfort zone. We had to learn new things as far as language and customs, but we saw all of these things. It totally blew our mind." And the subtext to that is, "And now we share this new learning and this new experience together, and that's actually made us stronger."

CHAPTER 12

They Don't Take Each Other for Granted

Fifty-three percent of people say their partner
takes them for granted sometimes.
—Couples by the Numbers Survey

The receptionist asked to speak with me in between therapy appointments. She said she'd gotten an urgent call from a man who wanted to be seen right away. His name was Shane and he said his wife had just left him, and he was distraught. He was hoping therapy could help him make some changes so they could get back together. My schedule was booked and it could take a few weeks to get him in. She placed his name on the cancellation list—meaning he'd be offered any appointment times that became available if someone else canceled. When someone canceled the following week, Shane jumped at the opportunity. Shane showed up over an hour early that day and when I called his name in the waiting room, he stood up and said, "I can't wait to talk to you."

As soon as we shut the door to my office, he said, "My wife took the kids a few weeks ago and went to her parents' house. She said I took her for granted and I now realize she's right. I'm hopeful you can help me make things right."

Shane had been married to Katherine for twelve years. He said they got along pretty well so he was under the impression things were good.

When she announced she was taking the kids and going to stay with her parents, he felt blindsided.

When I asked Shane what Katherine's reasons for leaving were, he said, "I didn't appreciate her enough. I made everything about me, I guess. I thought the only reason people split up was because they fight, though. We never really argued."

But as we talked more, it was clear there were some signs that Katherine hadn't been happy for a while—but Shane missed those signs. Katherine had suggested couples counseling a few years ago. Shane refused. He had told her couples counseling was only for people about to get divorced. He thought bringing up their "petty problems" to a therapist would blow things out of proportion.

When I asked why she wanted to attend counseling in the past, he said, "Well, she always said things like I treat her like the housekeeper, or she feels like a single parent. I thought she was just being overly dramatic."

Shane worked long hours. Katherine had a part-time job. Their older child went to school and the younger one was in preschool part-time. Katherine took care of their household responsibilities including cooking, cleaning, and managing their finances and Shane acknowledged that she handled 99 percent of the parenting duties.

He said, "I'm tired when I get home from work and I don't know what 'rules' I need to follow to help put the kids to bed or anything. Katherine seemed to have all that stuff figured out. I don't have extra energy to worry about whether the kids had their baths or to think about what we're going to eat for dinner tomorrow. I thought Katherine had all those handled."

Shane had hope that he and Katherine could still make their relationship work, and he told me he was willing to do whatever it took to make that happen. But we couldn't really know what he needed to work on until he got some more clarity from Katherine.

It's common for people to come to therapy saying vague things like, "My partner wants me to get therapy so we can communicate better," but if they don't think they have a communication problem, it's impossible to help them know how to improve. So while Shane had general ideas about Katherine's concerns, we needed specifics.

So Shane's first therapy assignment was to ask Katherine what changes she would want to see before she and the children returned home—if, in fact, returning home was her goal as well. He would try to get clarity about what he could do to improve the relationship.

Shane was looking forward to telling her he had started therapy as he thought she would be pleased to know he was making an effort. I encouraged him to really listen to whatever she said without discounting her concerns. Then, we could consider the information she gave him as he established his treatment goals.

I'll share more about how their story unfolded later in the chapter. But before you hear about them, take a minute to think about whether you or your partner take one another for granted sometimes.

Quiz

Review the following statements and see how many of them sound familiar.

- ❏ I don't thank my partner very often.
- ❏ I spend more time complaining about the stuff my partner doesn't do, rather than appreciating them for the things they do.
- ❏ I am quick to notice things that aren't done "right" as opposed to things my partner does well.
- ❏ My expectations of what my partner does for me may be too high.
- ❏ I rarely show gratitude toward my partner.
- ❏ I rarely give my partner gifts or a token of appreciation.
- ❏ I assume my partner knows I appreciate them even if I don't say it.

Now review the statements again and consider how your partner might respond to them. The more of these statements that ring true, the more likely you or your partner are to take one another for granted. Fortunately, there are plenty of things you can do to become more appreciative of one another.

Starting Point

Shane returned to therapy the following week after talking to Katherine. He said, "She doesn't feel appreciated enough. And she thinks I take all the stuff she does for granted. I acted like my job was the only 'real job' and the work she did was trivial. I need to show her that I value all the things she brings to the table."

Shane said he'd done a lot of reflecting over the past week and he now realized some of his mistakes. He said, "I used to get annoyed if the kids were too loud when I came home from work and I'd get irritated when Katherine asked me questions about the bills when I came home. But I'd give anything to have those be my biggest problems now."

Shane said the house was quiet during the week without Katherine and the kids. Then, on the weekends, the kids stayed with him and he realized how much work it was to do everything without Katherine. He said, "The boys wear me out in just two days. To think Katherine was doing everything seven days a week, plus working part-time, blows my mind."

If you take for granted that your partner works hard or manages many of the household responsibilities, you can hurt your relationship. It's important to recognize the sacrifices they make and what they do to help you, your relationship, and your household.

Take a moment to consider how much appreciation you feel for your partner, and how much appreciation you show them. Also, think about how often you show or tell your partner how much you appreciate them.

Think about the answers to the following questions:

○ Do you appreciate the things your partner does for you?
○ Do you show your appreciation?
○ Does your partner appreciate the things you do?
○ Do they show their appreciation?

If you take your partner for granted or feel like your partner takes you for granted, you may want to take steps to show more appreciation. It can go a long way toward strengthening your relationship while also helping you grow stronger as a person.

Why We Take Each Other for Granted

Shane didn't want to just promise Katherine that things would be different. He wanted to uncover where he'd gone wrong in the first place and learn from his mistakes to create lasting change. We spent a session uncovering some of the reasons why he'd taken Katherine for granted. Shane drew three conclusions:

1. **He didn't recognize how much she was doing**. Katherine kept everything running so smoothly that Shane didn't realize how hard Katherine was working. "She is such a great mom it didn't occur to me that she needed that acknowledgment or that she could use a little extra help sometimes," he said. On the rare occasion when Katherine did ask for help, he brushed her off or minimized her concerns.

2. **He thought she knew he appreciated her even if he never told her.** Shane couldn't recall thanking Katherine. He thought

he sometimes complimented her on her cooking—but he couldn't really remember expressing true gratitude. When he did feel appreciative, he figured she just knew it and he didn't have to say it.

3. **He was self-absorbed**. Shane admitted that he was so focused on himself, he didn't think about Katherine's needs. He thought his role was to bring in the bulk of the income and her role was to do everything else. For much of their relationship, he thought this was a fair deal because he never really stepped back to examine how much she was doing or to ask her what she wanted from the relationship.

He'd never really taken the time to reflect on the situation and this was the first time he was really able to see that he'd missed out on a lot of opportunities to show appreciation for Katherine. With a better understanding, Shane felt equipped to address the situation moving forward.

There are many reasons we can take the good stuff our partner does for granted. Sometimes it's because we get used to the good things our partner does. When we grow accustomed to all the things they contribute, we typically expect them to keep it up.

At other times, we don't notice the good things they're doing because the lens we use to view the world is distorted. If you believe something about your partner—like they're lazy or they're selfish—you'll find evidence that reinforces those beliefs. And whenever you see possible evidence to the contrary, you'll filter it out. That's how our brains work with lots of things, not just relationships.

For example, when you're feeling frustrated with your partner or you're irritated with them, you'll likely magnify their mistakes and their shortcomings. And that can cause you to focus on the negative and not appreciate the positive.

Researchers Elizabeth Robinson and Gail Price published a highly referenced study in 1980 in the *Journal of Consulting and Clinical Psychology,* examining this issue. The study found that couples in unhappy marriages underestimate the number of positive things their partners do.

To conduct this research, Robinson and Price placed objective observers in the couples' homes. The observers recorded the positive behaviors they saw. The couples were also asked to note the positive behavior they observed from their partners. Then they compared their lists.

They found that partners in unhappy relationships underestimated positive behavior rates by 50 percent. That meant they didn't notice half of the good things their partners did. Their brains filtered out all those positive things.

You might take your partner for granted because you literally miss all the good things they're doing on a daily basis.

Mental Strength Exercises

After a couple of months of individual therapy, Shane invited Katherine to join a session. Katherine agreed, and during the appointment, she said she had seen big changes in Shane and was pleased with his progress. "I don't need him to praise me for putting my dishes in the sink like I'm a kid," she said. "But I do want to make sure he keeps noticing the hard work I put into making our household run smoothly."

Shane reached over and took her hand. She said, "You work really hard. And I do appreciate that but I don't tell you enough."

We established some gratitude rituals they could share. They agreed that they could establish a nightly habit of sharing what they appreciate about one another before they went to sleep. In the past, they both scrolled through their phones while lying in bed until they fell asleep—or sometimes, Katherine went to sleep first and Shane would go to bed later. Now, they would connect with one another before they went to sleep to share what they appreciated about each other and about life.

Katherine was still living with her parents. But they always called each other before they went to sleep so for now, they would express their gratitude over the phone.

Another thing we discussed is how Katherine could speak up and ask for help and Shane could respond to her requests in a healthy manner. Unlike a martyr, who refuses help, Katherine welcomed it but just couldn't get Shane to budge. Whenever she asked for help with the kids or help around the house, Shane would turn it into a joke and say things like, "Oh, I bet you can handle this all on your own!" She said his refusal to step in really hurt, so she just did things on her own and he never noticed.

Shane acknowledged that he used to minimize Katherine's distress and he now realized how hurtful that was. He agreed that he would pitch in when she asked for help but also said he didn't want to wait until she asked. Part of his new plan involved being more engaged in the household responsibilities so he would recognize what needed to be done.

Shane returned the following week and said their new strategy was working well. During their nightly calls they addressed "business" issues, like their financial situation and managing things with the kids. But he said their conversations felt different than they had in the past. He was now genuinely admiring Katherine for all the things she did. He just wished it hadn't taken her leaving for him to recognize how important she was to him.

Katherine joined Shane for a few more sessions and during one of them she said, "I'm embarrassed to admit that part of me moved out because I knew it would force Shane to take over things around the house if I just dropped everything in his lap. But I felt sort of desperate to get him to see what it was like for me. I don't want to punish him. I just want to make sure we're working together and appreciating one another's efforts—not ignoring our hard work."

Katherine felt badly that she had disrupted the kids' lives to prove her point to Shane. She and the kids moved back home shortly after that discussion in the office.

Observe, Assess, and Reassess

Observe your partner going about their usual activities, like cleaning the kitchen or sorting through the mail. Then, pay attention to the thoughts that pop into your head.

You might automatically make negative judgments, like, "He spends so much time scrubbing the same spot on the counter because he's a germaphobe," or "She thinks she has to look at every single line on the credit card bill like she's hoping to find a problem."

If you notice a lot of negative things, don't be too hard on yourself. It might signal your relationship is in a rough spot. Or, it may mean you're having a bad day and you're seeing everything through a negative lens.

Mental health issues can also affect how you see your partner. If you're battling depression, anxiety, or another issue, your brain might automatically focus on the negative.

Consider your negative assessments to be an opportunity. You can reassess each judgmental or critical thought you have about your partner and develop alternative observations. After all, there's more than one way to look at the same situation. Here are some ways you can respond to judgmental assessments with compassionate reassessments:

- ✗ **Assessment:** She's so slow when she's paying bills.
- ✔ **Reassessment:** She's careful when paying the bills to avoid any mistakes.

✗ **Assessment:** He never remembers to pick up the stuff at the store that I ask him to.

✔ **Reassessment:** He's had a busy day and it's tough to remember things sometimes.

✗ **Assessment:** She talks about the same things every day.

✔ **Reassessment:** She's passionate about the things she discusses and needs me to be a good listener.

Don't beat yourself up for having negative thoughts (you don't want to start judging yourself for being judgmental). But do reassess the thoughts that fuel negative feelings in your relationship. When you change how you're thinking, you can shift how you feel and how you behave. You might develop more loving feelings toward your partner and you also might extend some compassion toward them, instead of showing your irritation.

> **When you change how you're thinking, you can shift how you feel and how you behave.**

Express Your Appreciation

It's one thing to feel appreciation. But, it's another thing to show it. Showing your partner that you appreciate them can be instrumental in helping them feel loved.

The things you appreciate don't always have to revolve directly around you. Here are some examples of things you might say to your partner:

- I appreciate that you put so much effort into taking care of your health every day.
- Thank you for working so hard at your job so that we have plenty of money to pay the bills.

- I loved that you stopped to help that person today. I appreciate your kind heart so much.
- Thank you for answering my friend's questions about what they should look out for when buying their first home.
- I appreciate how much time you put into learning a new skill. It's inspiring.

You can express your appreciation without saying "thank you." You might write a quick note or send a text message. You could also give a gift. It doesn't have to be a huge present but instead, you might just surprise them with their favorite kind of coffee or make them their favorite snack to show you appreciate them.

Praise Your Partner in Front of Others

Sometimes, for one reason or another, it feels uncomfortable to sit around and thank each other for things. It might feel stale to thank them for the same things every day. Or, if your partner has low self-esteem, they might struggle to accept a compliment because it doesn't match up to the way they see themselves. If they argue when you say nice things, it's a sign that they may not feel good about themselves.

Instead of saying nice things directly to them, praise them to someone else when your partner is within earshot. While having dinner with friends, share something your partner did that was really kind. Saying, "It was a complete surprise that he was getting out of work early but he knew the event was important to me so he made it happen," can help your partner feel appreciated. Or, tell your mother that your partner is working really hard on the classes they started taking and you are proud of them for the work they're doing.

The intention isn't to make your friends jealous or to cause your family to think your relationship is perfect. But saying kind things about your partner to other people is a great habit to get into (sometimes we're quicker to complain than compliment them to others). And if you can do so in a way that your partner knows you talk them up to others, it can be especially affirming for them to know that you appreciate them enough to tell others.

Who's Motivated?

Take a minute to think about who thinks there's a problem and who is motivated to create change. Then, you can decide how to approach your situation best.

1. You take your partner for granted.

Identify whether the problem is that you don't feel grateful, you don't express your gratitude, or both.

If you don't feel gratitude, a great way to drum it up daily is to spend a few minutes picturing your partner doing kind things for you. You might recall the time they picked out a gift for you. Think about the fact that they spent time looking for a gift for you (rather than the gift itself) and that they spent time trying to pick out the best gift they could.

Or imagine them doing something for you that they didn't want to do—like clean out the garage so you could park inside or attend your company holiday party with you.

Make it a habit to express what you appreciate every day. You might say it over dinner. Or perhaps you send a text message at lunch or share your thoughts before you go to sleep. But make it a daily habit.

When you practice and share gratitude regularly, your brain will start looking for the good throughout the day. You'll likely notice more positive things about your partner without even trying which can shift the whole relationship dynamic.

2. Your partner takes you for granted.

If you feel taken for granted, showing your partner your appreciation can be a good place to start. They may reciprocate. Unfortunately, the reverse is also true. If your partner feels they are taken for granted, they might withdraw their appreciation. You don't want to get into a tug-of-war over who is more deserving of gratitude. So be generous with your partner even if you feel unappreciated.

While you might think you shouldn't have to ask for appreciation, telling your partner what you need is important. Express your needs as a request, not a complaint. So instead of saying, "You never show me any appreciation for all I do!" try saying something like, "Can you let me know what you appreciate about me sometimes? It really helps me to feel good when I know that you're taking notice."

If you need help with things, ask for it. Make sure you don't become resentful because you're sacrificing too much and not getting enough help.

3. Your partner thinks you take them for granted.

If your partner feels taken for granted, ask for specifics to better understand. Do they feel like you expect too much? Do you not show appreciation for what they do? Do you forget to thank them for little things?

Ask them what they need from you and work on trying to give it to them. You might ask if they want to take a minute each day just to say what you each appreciate about one another. It can be a great bedtime ritual for each of you to share—but ask your partner if that would fulfill their need. They may have some other specific ideas or requests and it's important to be flexible.

You also might consider whether you think you're showing appreciation but perhaps your partner doesn't think you're showing appreciation.

You might be offering small gifts or surprises thinking those are clear signs you are grateful but your partner might be hoping to hear those words that spell out your gratitude.

This is where the idea of *The 5 Love Languages* might come into play. The book, which was written by Gary Chapman, has sold over 20 million copies. Despite the fact that there's not a lot of research that backs up his claims about love languages, some therapists still use the idea in treatment as many couples say it has helped their relationship. Chapman says there are five ways people express or receive love—words of affirmation, acts of service, gifts, quality time, and physical touch.

You might look at your love language as compared to your partner's and see if perhaps you have a mismatch in how you express and feel love. You might be expressing your gratitude while they aren't receiving the message.

4. You both take one another for granted.

A short journaling exercise might go a long way toward helping you recognize how to experience and express more appreciation. Write down all the things you appreciate about your partner. Then, write down all the things you think your partner appreciates about you. Ask your partner to do the same and then compare notes.

Did you accurately identify what you each appreciate about each other? Hopefully, there's a long list of things you each appreciate about one another and maybe your lists weren't completely in sync—that's fine. The exercise may help you recognize if you don't talk enough about the things you appreciate. Perhaps your partner never knew you appreciate their work ethic or maybe you had no idea your partner appreciates your sense of humor. If you learn a lot from one another's lists, it might be a sign that one or both of you takes the relationship for granted (something everyone likely does sometimes).

Problem-solve together how you can make sure that you're each expressing your gratitude for one another. Whether you decide to create a daily ritual or you have a weekly dinner where you share all the things you appreciate, if you work together on developing a strategy you can ensure that both of you feel appreciated. Even a long hug and just saying, "Thank you for being my person," can go a long way toward reminding you why you love them and reminding them that they are loved.

How Appreciating Your Partner Makes You Stronger

Shane brought Katherine with him to his final therapy session and both of them said things were going better. Shane said, "The kids seem to be doing better too. It's like now that we're less stressed, they're behaving better and listening." Both Shane and Katherine felt confident moving forward that they would recognize warning signs if they were taking one another for granted, and they would be able to talk about their feelings so they could address it before things got out of hand again.

When we were finishing up the appointment, Shane said he wanted to raise kids who showed appreciation to other people. If he didn't show appreciation for the things Katherine did for the family, the boys probably wouldn't appreciate all she did for them either—and they might grow up not appreciating other people in their lives. He realized that showing appreciation was better not just for their relationship but for the entire family—and saying "thank you" was a powerful way to create positive change.

We all want to know that other people notice our efforts. And some acknowledgment helps us know when our efforts are valued. The benefits of gratitude go beyond just those warm and fuzzy feelings.

An unexpected benefit of gratitude might involve a better sex life. Researchers from the University of North Carolina at Greensboro discovered that people who felt appreciated became more responsive to their partner's sexual needs. Better sex isn't the only benefit—a closer romantic relationship also ensues.

According to John and Julie Gottman, relationship experts who studied more than forty thousand couples, saying "thank you" might be one of the most important things people can do for their relationship. Their research found that individuals who expressed and experienced gratitude had happier and healthier relationships than those who didn't say "thank you" very often.

> **Appreciating your partner has the power to keep a good relationship healthy.**

Appreciating your partner has the power to keep a good relationship healthy. But it also has the power to turn an unhealthy relationship around. When you start thinking more positively about your partner and your relationship, you'll feel better. And that will motivate you to put more effort into the relationship.

Troubleshooting and Common Traps

Sarcastic Thank-Yous

If you can't say "thank you" without being sarcastic, you're better off saying nothing at all. A snarky, "Gee, thanks for picking up your socks," or "Great job making it work today," damages the relationship further.

If you can't say anything without sounding condescending, do some internal work first. That means really thinking about the reasons you have to be grateful for your partner and what they mean to you. This can help you make an internal shift first, and then you may be able to make the compliments that come out of your mouth sincere.

Combining Compliments with Criticism

Resist the urge to point out your partners' flaws as you compliment them. A backhanded compliment won't motivate them to do better next time—but it will damage the relationship more than saying nothing at all.

If you say, "Thank you for actually going to the store today when I asked you to," you're not really showing gratitude. Stick to saying, "Thank you for going to the store today. I appreciate it."

Doing Things Just to Get Recognition

If you spend five hours creating a special meal that your partner scarfs down in ten minutes without acknowledging your hard work, you might think it's rude. But, what if they didn't ask for the special meal? Perhaps they don't even like that meal or maybe they have no idea how much work went into it. It's important to have conversations about what you're doing, what you want, and what your partner wants. If you spend too much time guessing what your partner wants, and then putting in tons of energy trying to please them, you'll likely be left feeling unappreciated.

Conversation Starters

Take some time to review the following questions. If your partner is interested in talking with you about mental strength, use the questions to start a conversation about showing one another appreciation.

- What are some examples of times when you've felt appreciated by me?
- What are some of the best ways I show appreciation for you?

- What are some times when you've shown me extra appreciation?
- What's an example of a time when we showed appreciation for one another even though it wasn't easy to do?
- How do you think we managed to show appreciation for one another during that time?

Interview with Andrew G. Marshall

When couples don't appreciate one another anymore, they sometimes feel as though they've fallen out of love. That's why I wanted to talk to marriage therapist Andrew G. Marshall. He has spent over thirty-five years helping couples create better relationships. He's the author of many books, including the international bestseller *I Love You but I'm Not IN Love With You* and he hosts *The Meaningful Life* podcast. I wanted to hear his thoughts on why people sometimes fall out of love.

I encounter so many couples who are busy—and investing time in their relationship often falls pretty low on the priority list. How do couples make their relationship more of a priority when they're busy with so many other things?

We think we have to take our partner on the *Orient Express,* or a cruise down the Nile. And not only do they cost a lot of money, but they take up an awful lot of time. A mini treat is bringing back a chocolate croissant, when you've gone out in the morning and brought it back. There's little treats that say, "I'm thinking about you."

It's sending an amusing meme that somebody sent to you. It's just a phone call to say, "I was thinking about you." So these little mini treats show you care, and there's always time to go on a mini date. A mini date is sort of like five, ten minutes. If you've got five, ten minutes to spare, what do you do?

Well, you've got ten minutes to spare, you go on your phone and see what's happening on Twitter.

Instead, you could think, "Well, actually, I could spend this ten minutes with my partner. I can actually go up to them, give them a nice big hug, and do something that I know they like, like kissing their neck, or something like that that." Thinking about that ten minutes, that spare ten minutes, how can I actually feed that into my relationship?

What are your thoughts on scheduling things? I hear some people say, "If you don't schedule it, it won't happen," but I hear other people say, "I don't want to schedule everything in my life. We need more spontaneity." Or even when it comes down to sex, do you schedule when you're actually going to have sex?

If you only have sex when both of you are in the mood, spontaneously at the same time, you'll have sex three times a year: Valentine's Day, when you're on holiday and you haven't got anything else to do, and once when you just were drunk.

You can't get by on spontaneous sex. You have to set aside the time, but that doesn't mean you have to have sex in that time. You can be sensual together. So Thursday night is going to be our night together. We're not going to put Netflix on. We're going to have a bath and wash each other's hair, and we'll see what develops. And we might even just do a massage exchange. We don't have to have sex . . . As far as I'm concerned, washing each other's hair, and having a massage exchange, that *is* sex.

What I always say is, if your husband or your wife was doing it with another person, and you'd be jealous about it, then it counts as sex. So, if your wife or husband was going around to somebody else's house, and they were going to wash each other's hair, I think you'd be bloody jealous.

Do you have any fun ideas for how couples can show appreciation for one another?

This is a variation of Queen for the Day. So, it's either Queen or King for a Day. And I got this from a friend who when they were on holiday, they would take it in turns. One day would be my day, and we'd do everything that I wanted. They knew each other very well, so they didn't do something that the other one hated, like going hang gliding or something like that.

So the whole day was their deep-down choice, and it was quite relaxing for the other person not to have to think about it. They also got to see what the other person really wanted, and they got to know them a little bit better, and they knew that the next day, it would be their turn to be Queen or King for the Day.

I would also say, "Look into each other's eyes more." That's also a very good thing to do. Most people don't look at the other person when they speak. I'm forever on my couch saying, "Could you turn and look at your partner, please? What do you see?" It's a huge moment of connection. But we are missing that, because we're speaking to each other from different rooms.

What can couples do if they feel like they've fallen out of love?

People fall out of love because they've switched off their emotions. So to live together, we say, "Oh, they're annoying, but I won't go there. Oh, that makes me angry."

But actually, what's the point of having a fight over the dishwasher? And we switch off our emotions to coexist. We think it's a nice thing to do. But, we can't choose which of our feelings we switch off. So we think we're just going to switch off our angry feelings, or our upset feelings. We'll keep all of the nice feelings, but it doesn't work like that. If you switch your feelings off, you switch all of them off. And that's how most people fall out of love. Not because they hate each other, because actually hate and love are bedfellows in a sense that they're both strong feelings.

So it's not doing more nice things together, it's actually having a really good argument that will bring the feelings up to the surface. As I say, the first ones will not be nice, but once you've begun to release some of the feelings, the rest of them can come up as well.

Why is it so important that people in a healthy relationship also focus on taking care of themselves?

Well, because when we're exhausted, we don't have very good resources. We tend to go back into old patterns. And the oldest pattern of all is blaming other people. So, "I'm unhappy because of all these terrible things you've done. And you won't listen to me, and you won't do this." And it's very easy to come up with 1,001 ways that your partner could change. How many ways could you change if you got on your list? Probably only one or two. "I could just give up." Or, "I could leave." But actually, there's thousands of things you could do differently.

And that is, and if you've had self-care, and you are in a good place, you actually begin to notice what you are upset about. It might not seem very rational, but I'm really upset about this. And you then begin to talk about that thing, and you raise it at the right time with the right amount of energy. You're not actually pulling forward seven hundred other things that you've been bottling up. So self-care is about knowing yourself, and if you know yourself, I think you can communicate much better. You're less exhausted, you're able to listen to your partner. And so, I think self-care is incredibly important for relationships.

CHAPTER 13

They Don't Stop Growing and Changing

Twenty-five percent of people fear their partner won't like them
as much if they make any big changes to themselves.
—Couples by the Numbers Survey

It's common for people to schedule a therapy appointment for their partners. Sometimes a practical barrier prevents a person from calling for themselves (like they can't make a private call from work easily). But the most common reason this happens is because the person calling wants the other person to change.

So it wasn't surprising when Brenda reached out to my office to schedule an appointment for her husband, James. She wanted James to get help. He wasn't concerned about himself but was willing to attend therapy. Brenda attended the first session with James and she tried to do most of the talking. They sat on the couch together and when I asked them what brought James to therapy that day, Brenda said, "James seems to be having a midlife crisis and I want him to get some help before he becomes 'that guy' who starts driving a red sports car and gets a girl-friend young enough to be his daughter."

James smiled and said, "Actually, I've just decided to make a career change. I don't think that's indicative of a 'crisis.'"

James had worked as an accountant for more than twenty years and while he liked his job, he wanted to pursue a new direction. His father had recently passed away after several years in declining health. As his health declined, so did his ability to care for himself. But his father didn't want to move to an assisted living facility. James and his siblings helped as much as they could but needed professional caregivers to fill in the gaps—which was really hard to find. The family was fortunate to have the money to hire someone to help but couldn't find reputable care that met their needs.

After James's father passed away, he wanted to open a caregiving business. "I want to make it easy for families to find someone they can trust to care for their loved one when they're not there," James said.

Brenda had reservations about this new venture. "We're way too old to take such a giant leap right now," she countered. "We were looking at retirement not too far into the future, not starting a business from the ground up. The death of James's father seems to have deeply affected his decision-making."

James agreed that the loss of his father did deeply affect him, but he didn't think that was a negative thing. "I learned a lot and I want to take what I learned and help other people," he said.

But Brenda was adamant that "being impulsive" was out of character for James and she was convinced he needed some help before he started making more rash decisions. Since Brenda was the one who thought there was a problem and James didn't think he had a problem, I suggested they both attend the next appointment.

You'll hear more about James and Brenda a little later in the chapter. But before we get there, take a few minutes and think about how you've changed over the years or how your partner has grown.

Quiz

Consider the following statements and see how many of them sound familiar.

- ❑ I often feel stuck in a rut.
- ❑ I haven't really grown as a person in recent years.
- ❑ Our relationship hasn't grown.
- ❑ My partner doesn't really grow and change.
- ❑ I'm bored with my life sometimes.
- ❑ I feel bored with my relationship.
- ❑ I think if I changed too many things about myself, my relationship wouldn't survive.
- ❑ I don't like it when my partner shifts their way of thinking or changes their habits.

Now think about how your partner might answer these same questions. If some of them sound familiar, don't worry. You can take steps to ensure your relationship allows you and your partner to grow and change.

Starting Point

Being married to an accountant with a consistent career made Brenda feel safe. The thought of James starting a new business caused a lot of anxiety.

James felt confident the new business could be successful. He was most excited that he'd be able to help people. He said he never really saw himself sitting around reading the paper and watching TV in his retirement, but he also never thought he'd find such a strong sense of purpose that would inspire him to keep going.

He thought Brenda's suggestion that he was having a midlife crisis was ridiculous but as an easy-going person, he agreed to therapy, hoping it might help calm her fears. Whenever she expressed her concerns about the business, he smiled and offered reassurance that he was confident in this idea.

But Brenda didn't feel reassured, so she kept reiterating the same points over and over. They couldn't move the conversation forward because she would just accuse him of having a midlife crisis. They were stuck in an unhealthy pattern of communication.

Like Brenda and James, you may have gotten stuck in an unhealthy pattern at one time or another. And you may have worried that doing anything different might even make things worse.

Routines can be good for relationships. A routine will assist you in managing your habits while also allowing you to look for opportunities and enjoy some spontaneity. A rut, on the other hand, can become so boring that it drains you of your zest for life.

A good routine allows room for change and growth. It's healthy for you to grow and change over time. Your partner should also be growing and changing. And your relationship should shift and change too.

Take a minute to consider the following questions:

○ Can you easily identify several ways you've grown as a person in the last few years?
○ Can you easily identify several ways in which your partner has grown in the last few years?
○ Can you identify how your relationship has grown over the past few years?

If you answered no to those questions you may be struggling to grow and change at a healthy pace. You and your partner don't need to adopt the same habits or believe in all the same things. You don't even necessarily have to understand or agree with the things your partner is doing. But that doesn't mean you can't support their efforts to grow and change.

Of course, you may have some nonnegotiables that you aren't interested in compromising. For example, if your partner does things that are against your religious beliefs or morals, you may decide you aren't interested in going along for the ride.

But hopefully, your opinions change, you learn new things, you do things differently, and you become better people as time goes on as you learn from one another.

Why We Avoid Growing and Changing

Overall, Brenda felt satisfied in her relationship with James. But she didn't feel secure about his new business idea. She feared big changes might ruin their financial future—as well as their relationship.

Initially she only expressed concern about their financial future, but during their second session she expressed some more insecurities. She said, "I am afraid we're going to argue about money and that our relationship will fall apart because James is going to have to put so much time into the business."

She feared the change would be like a chink in the armor—and would put everything they had worked so hard to create at risk. That's why she was confused and threatened by James's desire to change careers. While she understood he thought it would make him a little happier, she predicted it would make her a lot more miserable.

"Let's say he becomes ten percent happier but it puts our relationship at an eighty-five percent risk of divorce. That doesn't sound like a good idea to me!" she said.

But James didn't see it that way at all. As an accountant, he was used to quantifying problems, so I asked him for his risk calculation. "This business will likely give me fifty percent more life satisfaction," he said. "And when I'm a better person, I'll be a better partner and we'll have a better relationship. I predict it could make our relationship seventy-five percent better."

He went on to say, "I know she thinks this is a sign of a midlife crisis. But I don't see it that way at all. In fact, I think if I don't pursue something I feel so strongly about, I'll actually be at risk of having a midlife crisis down the road."

James thought taking a risk could make their lives much better. But Brenda wanted to keep things the same because she feared a change might make their lives worse.

In any relationship, one person will likely be more open to some changes than others. But for some people, there's a fear that changing something might make their partner love them less.

Take a moment to think about whether any of these fears might hold you back from creating change:

- Will my partner outgrow me?
- Will we make our relationship worse?
- If I change, will my partner still love me?
- Am I changing the things my partner loves about me?
- If my partner changes, will they try and change me too?

It's not always fear that makes people stop growing and changing—or from discouraging their partner from doing so. Sometimes life gets busy, and we put our head down to work on whatever is in front of us without focusing on the bigger picture. If we keep our heads down for too long, we can get stuck.

There may also be selfish motives for not wanting a partner to create positive change.

There may also be selfish motives for not wanting a partner to create positive change. I once worked with a woman who smoked—as did her partner. She was upset when her partner quit smoking. She said, "Now I'm going to be reminded that smoking is bad for me every time I light up a cigarette and my partner isn't. I don't want to feel guilty about smoking." She didn't want her partner's healthier habits to remind her of her unhealthy habit.

Jealousy can be another reason some people don't want their partner to grow and change. If one partner gets more attention, earns a higher income, or works on a big goal, the other person might feel left out.

In other unhealthy circumstances, people fear that their partners will leave them if they get better. One man I worked with said there were positive things about his wife's alcohol problems that he would miss if she got better. For example, after a night of heavy drinking, she was usually sick the next day. He'd take care of her and doing so made him feel needed and loved. He'd grown up in a home where he often had to help his mother, who had a substance abuse issue, so being a caretaker felt familiar. If his wife were to get better, he thought she wouldn't need him anymore.

Sometimes people don't change on purpose—their circumstances just change. A change in health, work schedule, or extended family situation might not be voluntary.

Some of those changes might be temporary—like caring for a parent who had surgery. Other changes—such as diet changes following a major health problem—might be permanent. In these cases, healthy couples adapt. Unhealthy couples are more likely to grow apart or reach their breaking point.

Mental Strength Exercises

In the third session with Brenda and James we discussed their unhealthy pattern. Brenda had dug in her heels and insisted James was having a midlife crisis, and James was moving forward full-speed ahead, which only reinforced Brenda's concerns that he wasn't thinking clearly.

We had a productive discussion about Brenda's fears—their financial situation would get worse, their dream to retire soon wouldn't work out, and their relationship would suffer. In that session, I asked James to listen to Brenda without minimizing her fears. With a little help, James was able to validate her concerns for the first time. He didn't agree he was having a midlife crisis and he didn't agree with her concerns, but he showed he cared about her feelings.

In the next session, they changed roles. Brenda listened while James talked about how important it was for him to make this career shift, how he wanted to have an impact on the community, and how it would help him feel as if he'd turned the painful experience of losing his dad into something meaningful. Brenda listened and reflected what she heard without inserting her worries or countering his points.

After they both had the space to talk and to listen, we focused on Brenda's emotional reaction to James's career shift. She felt anxious and those anxious feelings led to anxious thoughts like, "What if the new business doesn't work out? What if James starts reinventing all areas of his life—including his relationships—and he doesn't want to be with me anymore?"

Those fears were certainly possible. But there were thousands of other potential outcomes too. Perhaps the new business would be a huge success. And maybe James would be happier than ever and their relationship would get even better. But before considering alternative possibilities, she needed James to validate her feelings.

We also examined the meaning they assigned to one another's behavior. Brenda thought her discomfort should bring James's plan to a screeching halt. If he went ahead despite her feelings, she thought it meant he didn't care about her that much.

James, on the other hand, thought Brenda's opposition meant she didn't believe in him. If she worried that the new business venture would lead to financial ruin, she must think he's incompetent.

As they talked about their feelings, thoughts, and assumptions, they realized that they were working against each other rather than together.

Over the course of several appointments, they worked on finding ways to tackle the problem together. And they decided instead of this being "James's business" they'd make it their business. That didn't mean Brenda needed to do a lot of the day-to-day business activities, but instead, she was going to support James even though she was a little nervous about the new venture.

They identified strategies for preventing problems too—like how to make sure the new business didn't consume all of James's time and how to alleviate Brenda's concerns they wouldn't be able to afford to retire.

They also worked to break down their assumptions about one another. Just because James was making changes didn't mean he was being disloyal, and Brenda's apprehension of those changes didn't mean she thought James was incompetent. They just had different viewpoints. Once we discussed those viewpoints and the assumptions they each made about one another's behavior, they were able to challenge their own ways of thinking. They each became more open to one another's perspective, which made all the difference in their ability to move forward.

Recognize Your Emotional Reaction, Automatic Thoughts, and Assumptions

When your partner brings up change, pay attention to your emotional reaction, the thoughts you have about it, and the assumptions you make.

Here are some examples.

1. Your partner says they want to go back to college.

Emotional reaction: Frustration

Thoughts: They're going to waste a lot of money and not ever get a degree.

Assumptions: They're going to take a few classes and quit going. They don't care about wasting money that we could spend on something more important.

2. Your partner says they're going to stop eating meat.

Emotional reaction: Annoyance

Thoughts: They're going to lecture me now whenever I eat meat.

Assumptions: They're selfish. Our social life will now have to revolve around vegan restaurants and it'll interfere with the fun stuff we do.

3. Your partner says they want to start going back to church.

Emotional reaction: Anxiety

Thoughts: They're going to become a religious zealot.

Assumptions: They're going to want me to go to church too and they won't want to do anything fun because they're going to spend all their time volunteering for the church.

When your partner wants to make a change, pause and ask yourself how you're feeling. Try to put a name to your emotion or emotions. Then, identify your thoughts about that change. Finally, ask yourself what that thought means and you'll uncover your assumption. Once you do that, it's easier to back up and remind yourself that there are many possibilities other than the one thing you predict will happen.

> **We rarely tell our partner what our assumptions are.**

We rarely tell our partner what our assumptions are. Sometimes, we don't even recognize our assumptions. We just draw conclusions without examining the truth. If you slow down and really notice what's happening, you can choose to respond in a helpful way—rather than just make an assumption and then react.

Create Goals for Yourself

Over the years, I've heard many clients say things like, "I want to start going to the gym but my partner won't go with me so I don't go." But just because your partner won't do something with you doesn't mean you should allow that to hold you back.

Create goals for yourself. If you want to invite your partner to take part, go ahead. Sometimes, couples find it's easier to create change when they're motivating one another or holding each other accountable.

But the opposite can be true as well. Your partner might convince you to take time off from working on a goal or convince you that you don't need to put in too much effort.

Commit to taking care of yourself. It's not selfish to want to work on your well-being even if your partner doesn't want to. Becoming a better version of yourself can help you be a better person within your relationship.

Whether you want to learn a new language, train for a 10K, or start an art class for your community, doing new things and challenging yourself helps you grow.

> Becoming a better version of yourself can help you be a better person within your relationship.

Address the Domino Effect

There are lots of potential changes you or your partner might make:

- Adopt a new exercise habit
- Shift their sleep schedule

- Change in diet
- Develop a new hobby
- Change spiritual beliefs
- Shift friends
- Change careers
- Learn new skills

On the surface, you might think these changes you make might not affect your relationship. But there's often a domino effect.

Someone who decides to start working out in the morning may need to go to sleep earlier at night. Going to sleep earlier may mean that they no longer have an hour to watch a TV show with their partner. That time they spent watching TV together may have been the best quality time they had together all day. So the addition of morning exercise might indirectly impact the relationship.

Or someone who decides to take charge of their health by eating a better diet might decide to cook at home almost every day. For a couple who've loved takeout and dining out, this little change might greatly impact their relationship. What if their partner doesn't want to eat the same foods for dinner? Sharing a meal becomes more complicated—and that could impact how much quality time they have together. If they are used to dining out with friends, it could affect their social lives too. But it may also have a positive impact on their budget. And a partner who eats healthier may feel better and have more energy—which might mean they are happier too.

If you're making the change, it might be tempting to tell your partner, "But this won't affect you!" The truth is, it could have a big impact on them too. So acknowledge the domino effect—whether it's positive or negative. You may need to do some problem-solving to address those issues.

Who's Motivated?

Take a minute to think about who thinks there's a problem and who is motivated to create change. Then you can decide how to approach your situation best.

1. You struggle with change.

Whether you struggle with self-growth, you struggle to watch your partner change, or you have a hard time adapting as the world around you changes, change isn't always comfortable.

One thing that might help ease this discomfort is to focus on the positive outcomes rather than catastrophize the negatives. Write a list of all the reasons why a particular change might be good. Whether you're thinking about getting a new job, or your spouse wants to move, or you're both thinking about retirement, a list of all the positives might help balance out the thoughts that run through your head about the negatives.

Get support from your partner when you're having a hard time. Discuss any fears or concerns you have. And if you really struggle with change, consider talking to a mental health professional. The fear of change can become pervasive, especially when people have mental health issues like an anxiety disorder.

2. You think your partner struggles with change.

I've worked with many couples where one partner wants everything to stay the same. Maybe the partner wants to live in the town where they grew up, spend time with the same people they've always spent time with, and do the things they've always done.

There's nothing wrong with keeping a lot of things the same. But it can become a problem when that person doesn't make any changes at all—to the detriment of the relationship.

If your partner seems to struggle to do things differently now that you're a couple or they're struggling with a particular change, talk about your concerns. Say what you're afraid might happen if things don't change. Say something like, "I'm concerned if we don't start to do things differently, we're going to be stuck in a rut," or "I'm afraid if we don't move, we'll regret not taking the opportunity later on."

Don't try to force your partner to create changes within themselves. As we discussed in Chapter 6, nagging them about a habit you dislike or giving frequent "motivational speeches" isn't going to change their behavior.

3. Your partner thinks you struggle with change.

Perhaps you're married to someone who likes to move every six months. Or maybe you have a partner who never wants to do the same thing twice. It can be tough to deal with too much change.

But if your partner is concerned that you're resistant to change, pay attention. Listen and validate their emotions. And be open about any uneasiness you have.

You might decide that you have different levels of tolerance for change. That doesn't mean one of you is right and the other one is wrong. But recognizing this can create an opportunity to discuss your preferences.

Sometimes, partners enjoy different levels of risk in one area or two. Perhaps your partner loves shaking things up financially, but you prefer stability. Or maybe your partner loves social change—they like to spend time with new people but you prefer to stick with your core group of friends. Recognizing your needs and discussing your options can help you find creative solutions.

4. You both struggle with change.

If you and your partner struggle with change, challenge each other to do new things together. Instead of eating at your usual Saturday-night-dinner restaurant, mix things up. Go to a play, attend a sporting event, travel to a new town, or go on an adventure.

Keep some of your favorite rituals—like maybe you eat breakfast together every day or you go for walks on Sunday evenings together. But do spice things up with some new activities or fresh ideas.

You don't necessarily need to make huge changes to keep life exciting. Instead, you might set aside one date a month to do something that you've never done before. Just trying new things together can help you learn about one another and see that you can tolerate more discomfort than you think.

How Growing and Changing Makes You Stronger

About a year after I last saw James and Brenda in my therapy office, an article in the local newspaper featured their business. The article included a picture of the two of them smiling and described their positive impact on families who needed assistance with caregiving. There was a quote from someone who used their services who said knowing someone was available to care for his aging parents allowed him to keep working at his job during the day and he was grateful to them for starting this business.

I smiled as I read about how James had made his dream come true—and it was clear that Brenda had stuck by him. Their business was meeting a need in the community, just like James had hoped it would, and Brenda looked happy in the picture too.

You can always learn about other people, new experiences, different places, and world events. Doing so can help you gain a fresh perspective and gain some psychological flexibility—something that will help you become better able to adapt to change and solve problems better.

Growing and changing can be the key to keeping your relationship exciting. And that excitement might be what helps you stay together for the long haul.

People tend to think relationships end because there was too much conflict. But in reality, boredom is worse than conflict for relationships. Researchers have found that boredom is a huge predictor in marital dissatisfaction.

Changing things up might be the key to keeping the romance alive. Making changes to yourself could spark a little mystery that intrigues your partner again. Doing things differently as a couple might make things exciting—which may keep you excited to stay together.

Troubleshooting and Common Traps

Supporting Bad Ideas

Obviously, you don't have to support all your partner's ideas. If your partner came to you and said, "I am going to quit my job tomorrow because I found a course that says I can make a million dollars this week selling stuff online," you'd probably have something to say.

You can point out the potential drawbacks to your partner's plans. After all, that's one of the big benefits of having a teammate—another person to weigh in on what you're doing.

If your partner suddenly adopts a new religion and you fear it's a cult, what should you do? Or what if your partner says they're going to stop taking their medication that you think they need? Don't support bad ideas just because it's something different.

Confusing Silence with Support

Sometimes a partner will decide not to "complain" because they want to appear supportive of their partner's choices but secretly, they aren't on board. Addressing your emotions and problem-solving together isn't complaining. And not "complaining" isn't being supportive.

If your partner is creating change, talk about how those changes impact you and your relationship. Sometimes, a few little adjustments might go a long way toward helping you both thrive. Perhaps the most supportive thing you can do is talk to your partner about how you want to support their change while also wanting to support your relationship.

Conversation Starters

Take a minute to review the following questions. If your partner is on board, use these questions to start a conversation about change.

- What are some ways I've grown as a person since we've been together?
- How have you grown as a person since we've been together?
- What are some ways that we've grown together as a couple?
- What changes have we endured together (either because we had to or by choice)?
- What do you think helped us adapt to those changes?
- What are some things we've done to combat boredom in our relationship that you've appreciated?

Interview with Mariel Buqué

It's common for us to repeat the familial patterns we grew up with, which makes it hard to grow and change. Sometimes, even though we know those patterns are dysfunctional, it's tough to break free. That's why I reached out to Dr. Mariel Buqué, a

Columbia University–trained psychologist and sound bath meditation healer. Her clinical work focuses on healing the wounds associated with generational trauma. So I wanted to ask her about how people can change and stop repeating dysfunctional family patterns.

Why is it so difficult sometimes to recognize the dysfunction that we grow up in?

It's difficult to notice any dysfunctional patterns we carry, when it was considered the norm growing up. If the relationship dynamics that were modeled to you as a child were ones that had toxic traits or harmful qualities, then your young mind would have internalized those as conventional relationship dynamics, and not as dysfunctional. And this is especially so if those relationship patterns have been multigenerational and have lived in that person's lineage for a long time.

When children see these relational dynamics in their families of origin, they don't contest them. What children do instead is they mimic them and they eventually become the adults who unknowingly keep those harmful relationship cycles going.

A very common issue many people have around these dysfunctional patterns is lack of knowledge. They lack the understanding that their behavior qualifies as dysfunctional and so they continue to enter the same relationship dynamics time and again. They engage in what we call repetition compulsion, which is a traumatic reenactment of past painful circumstances, even if that repeated behavior is causing issues in the present. People will repeat what's familiar. They will do this when they lack the understanding that things could be different and that they have alternate ways to approach their relationships.

When people get into a romantic relationship, do they often realize that the way they grew up was more dysfunctional than they even knew?

Absolutely. Our adult relationships offer a mirror into our childhoods. They help us to see what attachment styles we have developed as a result of those primary attachments to our caregivers. They force us to see if we have unresolved childhood wounds that need tending to. They are a reflection of the past. What didn't get resolved then comes into the present and impacts every relationship we have.

We are hardwired for connection. We desire closeness. We seek emotional safety. So when you start having adult relationships and find it hard to connect to sequential partners, or find that a sense of safety is hard to maintain, you will start feeling distraught and eventually wonder about why you can't get out of the cycle of dysfunction. It's usually our romantic relationships that bring to light the patterns that have been there all along.

Do you find some people are protective of their families of origin and have trouble acknowledging intergenerational trauma?

People are incredibly protective of their families, especially if they have a close connection with members of their families or if they have cultural values that say that they must protect the honor or optics of the family. When this is the case, naming trauma responses can be especially difficult, because it can feel like a betrayal to your family of origin. People have trouble with understanding that they can call out trauma, heal that trauma, and still be loyal and honorable to the people they care about. The two experiences can coexist in a family.

Healing intergenerational trauma is honorable work. It means that you're devoted to creating better health for your family and lifting the generations of pain that they have had to carry. That's how we really protect our families: it's by healing them. When people start to recognize that, they feel motivated to heal, rather than keeping trauma in the shadows.

Knowing that your family was dysfunctional is one thing but deciding to do things differently is another. How can people start to create change even though it's going to feel uncomfortable?

People can start with settling their nervous system. Our nervous systems are usually in a chronic survival mode when we come from intergenerational patterns of family dysfunction. So approaching change has to start with the place where you feel most unsettled, which is your nervous system. Engaging in a daily process of relaxation and rest is a great place to start for anyone who is committing to a cycle-breaking journey. When people have more settled nervous systems, they're able to do deeper emotional work. The deeper the work, the deeper wounds you could heal. The deeper wounds you heal, the more generations that are impacted positively by your healing. So intergenerational healing has to start with the nervous system.

Sometimes I see people who are threatened by their partner's growth or transformation. Have you ever worked with someone whose partner didn't want them to change even if that individual was changing for the better? Can you share a little bit about them?

Yes, I see this so often in my work. People who undergo the process of healing from trauma typically have to undergo a complete change in identity. That is, because many of the personality characteristics that they have had for decades were really masked trauma responses. As a result, shedding trauma means they have to shed a part of who they are. If that part, the trauma part, was a source of bonding for them and their partners, then they will risk also losing the connection they once had.

One couple I worked with would frequently yell at each other. Both of their nervous systems were stuck in perpetual fight mode with one another. They were profoundly unhappy, but when they were presented with the tools to diminish the fighting, one person was resistant. At the heart of that resistance was a fear that he could lose the partner that he loved so dearly. He feared that without the fights, his partner would no longer be the same energetic person that he loved to connect with. However, that couldn't be further from the truth.

Their relationship still had a lot of energy and passion, especially when the daily verbal attacks lessened. And the fact that these were not happening with so much frequency actually helped them achieve an even deeper connection with one another. This is why for couples, I oftentimes invite the partner into the healing journey and establish bonds that aren't connected to the trauma. It's important for them to see that their union isn't founded on trauma, that it can survive the healing journey, and that they made a decision that benefits their union.

When an individual is in a long-term relationship and they're growing and transforming, how can they make sure that they don't grow apart from their partner?

The aim is always for a person to grow with their partner, rather than apart from them. And if that is a shared goal, then scheduled check-ins can help the couple to identify how they can continue to explore how they feel about each other's evolution. Healthy conversations about how they each have evolved as individuals and evolved together can help them to pay mindful attention to the changes that their healing is producing in them. This isn't something that we intuitively do in long-term relationships, but with a process like healing together, it can be the very thing that keeps a couple mindfully attuned, present, and connected.

CONCLUSION

Some researchers claim they can predict whether a couple is going to get divorced by assessing the way they talk to each other during a single conversation. But predicting whether a couple is going to divorce seems to be along the same line as the palm reader who tried to predict how many times my friend and I would get married—even if the person predicting it says they're a professional. As a therapist, I have no idea whether a couple will get divorced based on how they talk to each other during their first appointment—and I don't try to predict their future.

If there's anything I've learned as a therapist, it's that everyone is capable of positive change. I've seen couples who had spent years fighting with one another learn to communicate. And I've worked with plenty of individuals who started changing their relationships by changing themselves.

I also don't think "not getting divorced" is a good goal. Staying in a miserable relationship isn't a hallmark of mental strength. A better goal is to work on creating the best relationship possible so you can have a happy, healthy relationship. And there are times when people decide going their separate ways is ultimately the healthiest option.

To create that healthy relationship—and maintain it—one of the best things you can do is avoid the 13 common counterproductive habits that could keep you stuck. But, of course, knowing what those 13 habits that damage relationships are is only half the battle. Actually avoiding them is a different story.

If knowledge alone could change behavior, no one would smoke, drink, eat junk food, or stay up too late. So even though you know those

13 habits are bad for your relationship, you will likely still struggle with some of them sometimes.

Keep in mind that just because you don't do any of the 13 things mentally strong couples don't do right now, doesn't mean you won't struggle with them later on. From illnesses to financial problems, life won't always go smoothly. When life tosses you curveballs—as it inevitably will—it's easy to fall into those unhealthy habits.

And those things can either tear your relationship apart or bring you closer together, depending on how you respond.

Just remember, don't start pointing out your partner's violations (unless they ask you to support them in noticing when they're doing the 13 Things). Saying "That's the seventh thing mentally strong couples don't do, John!" in the middle of a disagreement isn't helpful. Stay focused on your own behavior and create positive change within yourself first—and you'll change the dynamics of the relationship.

Keep Working on Building Strength

Some research indicates couples in arranged marriages become happier over time while people who are in free love marriages report decreased marital satisfaction as time goes on. The research has been questioned by some experts who say it's tough to compare these two groups since they likely have different cultural backgrounds and different opinions on happiness and marital satisfaction. Although the idea seems surprising at first, when you look a little closer, the findings make sense.

Researchers who believe the findings are accurate say couples in arranged marriages have to work to find strategies to strengthen their relationship right from the beginning. They don't start out with all those same romantic feelings people in free love marriages have. So working together isn't going to feel as fun or exciting as it might to a couple with intense romantic feelings.

We also know the romantic feelings in free love marriages naturally shift over time. When that happens, some couples stop working on the relationship. As time passes, their connection and happiness with one another declines.

Essentially, the individuals in free love marriages might only be motivated to work on the relationship when they feel deeply in love. The couples in arranged marriages may accept that they need to work on the relationship even when they aren't feeling all those romantic feelings.

So the good news is, putting extra effort into your relationship can pay off. It takes ongoing work to stay connected to your partner. When you aren't feeling tons of romantic love for one another, you may be tempted to pull apart. But that's the time when you should work harder than ever to keep the love and passion alive.

As we discussed, there are reasons you and your partner got together in the first place. And remembering why you chose one another might motivate you to keep putting in the work and avoiding the unhealthy habits that can tear you apart.

Be Your Own Mental Strength Coach

I can't promise you that changing yourself will change the relationship, but I can tell you there's a good chance that when you become the best version of yourself, you'll change the dynamic of your relationship in some fashion. Building mental strength may inspire your partner to create positive change too.

Check in with yourself often to see how you're doing. Review the 13 Things Mentally Strong Couples Don't Do and take stock of how many of those things you struggle with. Start small and focus on one or two things that you want to change. Over time, you'll build momentum that can snowball into even bigger changes. And when you make mistakes—which you will—you can turn that into a learning opportunity where you can do better tomorrow.

Don't hesitate to ask for help if you need it. That help can come in many different forms. You might decide to get individual therapy for yourself (getting help for yourself can be instrumental in improving your relationship). Or if your partner is on board, you might consider couples counseling. You can even get couples therapy online if in-person meetings are a challenge.

But you don't always need to talk to a mental health professional. There may be a clergy member, support group, or trusted friend you can also talk to.

There are also many options for specific relationship issues. If your partner has a substance abuse issue, consider Community Reinforcement and Family Training (or CRAFT). It's a specific training for people who have a loved one with this issue. If your partner has a chronic health issue, you might join a support group so you can talk to other partners who understand your experience. There are many other relationship boot camps, retreats, and meetings that you can likely find online for a whole host of issues.

Asking for support takes mental strength. But you can build a lot more mental muscle when you have a whole team of people who are invested in helping you make good decisions about your relationship.

What to Expect as You Grow Stronger

As you grow stronger, you'll have better skills for managing your emotions, responding to unhelpful thoughts, and behaving productively. These changes can strengthen your relationship as you'll communicate more effectively, handle conflict successfully, and be better equipped to do hard things that can build a healthier relationship.

You'll also recognize when you need a course correction sooner. If you're heading down a dangerous path with your behavior, or your relationship is going down a road you don't like, pause and change course. That can prevent small problems from turning into big ones, and it can give you confidence in your ability to repair and improve your relationship.

Don't underestimate how powerful small changes can be. A slight shift in your mindset, a change in how you respond to your partner, or an adjustment to your behavior might make a big difference in your relationship.

You have an incredible opportunity to take your relationship to another level so you can experience the biggest, fullest life out there as you reach your greatest potential. When you truly become a team who works together, your sorrows will be halved and your joy will be doubled.

ACKNOWLEDGMENTS

It's been an honor to turn what started out as one article into a series of six books over the last nine years. I am grateful to HarperCollins for seeing the value in my message on mental strength. I'm especially grateful to Lisa Sharkey, who took a chance on a therapist from rural Maine who hadn't intended to become an author. Lisa has supported my work every step of the way.

I'm also grateful to my editor, Maddie Pillari, for her editorial assistance and the entire team at HarperCollins for all their work turning my ideas into books.

A big thank-you goes to my agent, Stacey Glick, who first reached out to me in 2013 after reading my viral article. At that time, I would have never imagined that article would become a book, let alone a whole series.

I'm grateful to Julie Leventhal at my speaker bureau, Wasserman Speakers. She manages my busy speaking schedule and helps get my message on mental strength in front of many different audiences.

Thank you to all the couples therapists who let me interview them for this book. They were all gracious to share their time and wisdom.

Thank you to my friends and family who support me when I'm in "book writing mode." I owe a special thank-you to Emily, who fact-checked the details of the palm reading story by ensuring her junior high diary lined up with the way I recalled the events. Despite everything else that has changed in the last thirty years, my friendship with her hasn't.

I'm grateful to Nick Valentin, my producer, who helps me spread my message on mental strength to the *Mentally Stronger* podcast audience. And he makes our episodes sound amazing even though we record on a boat that can be kind of noisy sometimes.

My career wouldn't be where it is without Steve. Not only does he read my roughest drafts but he's also an amazing teammate who helps me live a life beyond my wildest imagination.

The biggest thank-you goes to my readers, who make all of this possible. Because you've read, bought, shared, and told other people about my work, I still get to write books and talk about mental strength to people around the globe.

NOTES

CHAPTER 1: THEY DON'T IGNORE THEIR PROBLEMS

24 A 2019 study: Rauer, Amy, Sabey, Allen, Proulx, Christine, and Volling, Brenda. (2019). "What Are the Marital Problems of Happy Couples? A Multimethod, Two-Sample Investigation." Family Process. 59. 10.1111/famp.12483.

32 The silent treatment: Kawamoto, T., Onoda, K., Nakashima, K., Nittono, H., Yamaguchi, S., and Ura, M. (2012). "Is dorsal anterior cingulate cortex activation in response to social exclusion due to expectancy violation? An fMRI study." Frontiers in Evolutionary Neuroscience, 4, 11. https://doi.org/10.3389/fnevo.2012.00011.

CHAPTER 2: THEY DON'T KEEP SECRETS

42 Researchers estimate: Slepian, M. L., Chun, J. S., and Mason, M. F. (2017). "The experience of secrecy." Journal of Personality and Social Psychology, 113(1), 1–33. https://doi.org/10.1037/pspa0000085.

44 While secrets can damage relationships: Davis, C. G., and Tabri, N. (2023). "The secrets that you keep: Secrets and relationship quality." Personal Relationships, 1–16. https://doi.org/10.1111/pere.12472.

45 A 2023 study: Davis, C. G., & Tabri, N. (2023). The secrets that you keep: Secrets and relationship quality. Personal Relationships, 30(2), 620– 635. https://doi.org/10.1111/pere.12472.

48 lie to their therapists: Blanchard, Matt, and Farber, Barry A. (2016) Lying in psychotherapy: "Why and what clients don't tell their therapist about therapy and their relationship." Counselling Psychology Quarterly, 29:1, 90–112, DOI: 10.1080/09515070.2015.1085365.

53 A research study found: Brick, D. J., Wight, K. G., and Fitzsimmons, G. J. (2022). "Secret consumer behaviors in close relationships." Journal of Consumer Psychology. https://myscp.onlinelibrary.wiley.com/doi/10.1002/jcpy.1315.

CHAPTER 3: THEY DON'T HESITATE TO SET BOUNDARIES

70 "Romeo and Juliet effect": Sinclair, H. C., Hood, K. B., and Wright, B. L. (2014). "Revisiting the Romeo and Juliet effect" (Driscoll, Davis, and Lipetz, 1972):

"Reexamining the links between social network opinions and romantic relationship outcomes." Social Psychology, 45(3), 170–78. https://doi.org/10.1027/1864-9335/a000181.

70 While there is some: Felmlee, D. H. (2001). "No Couple Is an Island: A Social Network Perspective on Dyadic Stability." Social Forces, 79(4), 1259–87. http://www.jstor.org/stable/2675472.

CHAPTER 4: THEY DON'T BECOME MARTYRS

87 Evidence suggests: Seery, M. D., Leo, R. J., Lupien, S. P., Kondrak, C. L., and Almonte, J. L. (2013). "An Upside to Adversity?: Moderate Cumulative Lifetime Adversity Is Associated With Resilient Responses in the Face of Controlled Stressors." Psychological Science, 24(7), 1181–89. https://doi.org/10.1177/0956797612469210.

CHAPTER 5: THEY DON'T USE THEIR EMOTIONS AS WEAPONS

106 Researchers from the: Velotti, P., Balzarotti, S., Tagliabue, S., English, T., Zavattini, G. C., and Gross, J. J. (2016). "Emotional suppression in early marriage: Actor, partner, and similarity effects on marital quality." Journal of Social and Personal Relationships, 33(3), 277–302. https://doi.org/10.1177/0265407515574466.

CHAPTER 6: THEY DON'T TRY TO FIX EACH OTHER

141 Over time: Bacon, I., McKay, E., Reynolds, F. et al. "The Lived Experience of Codependency: an Interpretative Phenomenological Analysis." International Journal of Mental Health and Addiction 18, 754–71 (2020). https://doi.org/10.1007/s11469-018-9983-8.

CHAPTER 7: THEY DON'T COMMUNICATE WITH DISRESPECT

151 Relationship researcher John Gottman: Gottman, J. (2000). The Seven Principles for Making Marriage Work. Orion, 2000.

153 A 2014 study: South Richardson, D. (2014). "Everyday Aggression Takes Many Forms." Current Directions in Psychological Science, 23(3), 220–24. https://doi.org/10.1177/0963721414530143.

164 Studies show: McNelis, Melissa, and Segrin, Chris (2019): "Insecure Attachment Predicts History of Divorce, Marriage, and Current Relationship Status." Journal of Divorce & Remarriage, DOI: 10.1080/10502556.2018.1558856.

CHAPTER 8: THEY DON'T BLAME EACH OTHER FOR THEIR PROBLEMS

175 It takes a while: Ngo, L., Kelly, M., Coutlee, C. et al. "Two Distinct Moral Mechanisms for Ascribing and Denying Intentionality." Science Republic 5, 17390 (2015). https://doi.org/10.1038/srep17390.

181 a natural disaster can bring couples together: Williamson, H. C., Bradbury, T. N., & Karney, B. R. (2021). "Experiencing a Natural Disaster Temporarily Boosts Relationship Satisfaction in Newlywed Couples." Psychological Science, 32(11), 1709–19. https://doi.org/10.1177/09567976211015677.

CHAPTER 9: THEY DON'T FORGET WHY THEY FELL IN LOVE

197 your brain responds similarly: Zou, Z., Song, H., Zhang, Y., and Zhang, X. (2016). "Romantic Love vs. Drug Addiction May Inspire a New Treatment for Addiction." Frontiers in Psychology, 7, 1436. https://doi.org/10.3389/fpsyg.2016.01436.

200 There's research that shows: Langeslag, Sandra J. E., and Kruti, Surti. 2022. "Increasing Love Feelings, Marital Satisfaction, and Motivated Attention to the Spouse." Journal of Psychophysiology, February. doi:10.1027/0269-8803/a000294.

202 "couple defining songs": Harris, C. B., Baird, A., Harris, S. A., and Thompson, W. F. (2020). "'They're playing our song': Couple-defining songs in intimate relationships." Journal of Social and Personal Relationships, 37(1), 163–79. https://doi.org/10.1177/0265407519859440.

206 Simon Sinek highlights this: Sinek, S. Start with Why. Penguin Books, 2011.

206 relationship nostalgia: Mallory, A. B., Spencer, C. M., Kimmes, J. G., and Pollitt, A. M. (2018). "Remembering the Good Times: The Influence of Relationship Nostalgia on Relationship Satisfaction Across Time." Journal of Marital and Family Therapy, 44(4), 561–74. https://doi.org/10.1111/jmft.12311.

207 your relationship publicly: Emery, L. F., Muise, A., Dix, E. L., and Le, B. (2014). "Can You Tell That I'm in a Relationship? Attachment and Relationship Visibility on Facebook." Personality and Social Psychology Bulletin, 40(11), 1466–79. https://doi.org/10.1177/0146167214549944.

CHAPTER 10: THEY DON'T EXPECT THE RELATIONSHIP TO MEET ALL THEIR NEEDS

216 Research conducted by Willard Harley: Harley, Willard F. His Needs, Her Needs: Building an Affair-Proof Marriage, Fifteenth Anniversary Edition. Revell Publishing, 2001.

220 Author and researcher Willard Harley: Ibid.

CHAPTER 11: THEY DON'T NEGLECT THEIR PARTNERSHIP

241 couples who use "we talk": Ouellet-Courtois, C., Gravel, C., and Gouin, J.P. (2023). "A longitudinal study of 'we-talk' as a predictor of marital satisfaction." Personal Relationships, 30(1), 314– 31. https://doi.org/10.1111/pere.12463.

242 something is a ritual: Garcia-Rada, X., Sezer, O., and Norton, M.I. (2019). "Rituals and Nuptials: The Emotional and Relational Consequences of Relationship Rituals." Journal of the Association for Consumer Research, 4:2, 185-97 http://dx.doi.org/10.1086/702761.

CHAPTER 12: THEY DON'T TAKE EACH OTHER FOR GRANTED

257 published a highly: Robinson, Elizabeth A.; Price, M. Gail. "Pleasurable Behavior in Marital Interaction: An Observational Study." Journal of Consulting and Clinical Psychology, v. 48, no. 1, pp. 117–18, February 1980.

267 people who felt appreciated: Brady, A., Baker, L. R., Muise, A., and Impett, E. A. (2021). "Gratitude Increases the Motivation to Fulfill a Partner's Sexual Needs." Social Psychological and Personality Science, 12(2), 273–81. https://doi.org /10.1177/1948550619898971.

267 individuals who expressed and experienced gratitude: Gottman, J. The Seven Principles for Making Marriage Work. Orion, 2000.

CHAPTER 13: THEY DON'T STOP GROWING AND CHANGING

289 boredom is a huge predictor: Tsapelas, I., Aron, A., and Orbuch, T. (2009). "Marital Boredom Now Predicts Less Satisfaction 9 Years Later." Psychological Science, 20(5), 543–45. https://doi.org/10.1111/j.1467-9280.2009.02332.x.

CONCLUSION

296 Some researchers claim: Buehlman, K. T., Gottman, J. M., and Katz, L. F. (1992). "How a couple views their past predicts their future: Predicting divorce from an oral history interview." Journal of Family Psychology, 5(3-4), 295–18. https://doi .org/10.1037/0893-3200.5.3-4.295.

297 couples in arranged marriages: Epstein, R., Pandit, M., & Thakar, M. (2013). "How Love Emerges in Arranged Marriages: Two Cross-cultural Studies." Journal of Comparative Family Studies, 44(3), 341–60. http://www.jstor.org /stable/23644606.

ABOUT THE AUTHOR

AMY MORIN is a licensed clinical social worker and a psychotherapist. She's the award-winning host of the *Mentally Stronger* podcast. She's a former lecturer at Northeastern University. She gave one of the most popular TEDx Talks of all time and was named one of the Top 100 Leadership Speakers by *Inc.* magazine. Her books have sold more than one million copies and have been translated into more than forty languages. She lives on a sailboat in the Florida Keys.